My Brother,

My Brother, Ronald
by
Barbara Cartland

Preface by
SIR WINSTON CHURCHILL
Foreword by
SIR ARTHUR BRYANT

SHELDON PRESS
LONDON

First published in Great Britain in 1942 by
William Collins Sons & Company Limited

This edition first published in Great Britain in 1980 by
Sheldon Press, SPCK, Marylebone Road, London NW1 4DU

Printed in Great Britain by
Biddles Ltd, Guildford, Surrey

ISBN 0 85969 286 8

To Ronald's 'most perfect Mother'
and mine

RONALD CARTLAND

Obituary

From Rt. Hon. L. S. Amery, Secretary of State for India.

"The House of Commons and the country have lost in Ronald Cartland a spirit of high endeavour, generous outlook, and rare courage. Winning a difficult seat while still in his twenties, he immediately made his mark in Parliament by fearless and constructive criticism. In the crisis of recent years he was one of those younger Conservatives who were dismayed by the drift, both in policy and in preparation, which led to Munich, and took his line regardless of the consequences it might have upon his position as a junior member for the then Prime Minister's own city of Birmingham. During the months that followed he played an active part in the movement for universal service, even more concerned perhaps to fit himself for the personal service he wished to give when the time should come. Many members will recall his last prophetic speech, uttered just a month before the outbreak of war, when, pleading that Parliament should not be adjourned too long, he said: 'Within a month we may be going to fight and we may be going to die. . . . There are thousands of young men at this moment training in camps, and the least we can do here is to show that we have immense faith in this democratic institution.'

"The reports which have now reached this country of his death in action last May bear glowing witness to his shining courage and inspiring leadership in the field. He died, as did his father before him, in his country's cause, and was himself, we may believe, well content. For us the greatest loss is of the service which he might have rendered after the war. From his maiden speech—a remarkable piece of searching analysis of the patchwork attempt to deal in the depressed areas with the problem of unemployment—his plea, reiterated in speech after speech over the next three years, was for a policy which should look ahead and envisage the problem of the condition of the people as a whole, both in its economic and in its human aspect. 'What sort of a country do you want to make? How will you convert unemployment into leisure? How do you propose to maintain the level of your population?' These were the far-reaching, oft-repeated questions to which he got none but dusty answers then, but to which he might have contributed his own answer in after years: *si qua fata aspera rupisset.* His keen, handsome face, his gay and gallant spirit, will live long in the memory of his friends."

From Richard Law, M.P.

"It was too much to hope that Ronald Cartland should be spared, and all who enjoyed his friendship must, I think, have known—although we could not bring ourselves to admit it—that he had fallen. He was so evidently the kind of person, gay, gallant, vivid, and true, who was born to die in action. I remember so well his appearance in the House of Commons after the General Election of 1935. He used to sit on the second bench below the gangway on the Government side. It was a quarter of the House which was occupied, in the main, by the older, the sterner, and the less compromising sections of the Tory Party, and the contrast between Ronald, slender, elegant, and boyish, with his sleek black hair and his dancing black eyes, and the mass of the benches around him was both comical and alarming.

"He was so pleasant to look at, so polished and assured in his manner. He was an excellent speaker, but although there was knowledge and thought in his speeches and although he had the ear of the House in a degree remarkable for so young a man, there was very little of that diffidence which the House of Commons expects from those who seek its approval. But that was one of Ronald's most marked characteristics. He never did seek approval of anybody. He disdained altogether those arts by which the ambitious young politician (and Ronald was ambitious) can gain, if he wishes, the patronage of his elders and the approval of those whose approval means advancement. He was content to be himself. And in the end he won for himself an ever-widening circle of friends who will remember him for ever, not only with affection, but with respect as well. For Ronald Cartland had those qualities which compel respect—intelligence, conviction, wit, courage, and a deep religious sense.

"I am certain that Ronald Cartland, had he lived, would have been one of the architects of the new England. I am certain that his bright spirit lives now as I know that, in the hearts of his friends, his memory will never die."

From Paul Emrys-Evans, M.P., in the *Birmingham Post.*

"How much we have missed Ronald Cartland through the long months of fading hope his friends only fully realise now that he will not come back. His gay courage would have made the difficult places easier and his counsel in time of peril would have been bold yet wise. Ronald's character was solidly built and his sympathies were wide. There lay behind his charm and his attractive personality a certain austerity and deep religious convictions. His clear mind quickly grasped the essentials of the pre-war controversy. He early saw that the dictatorships were a threat not only to our own national interests but to the whole Christian way of life in the world. He knew that compromise was impossible. He fearlessly attacked those who cried ' Peace, peace,' when there was no peace, and warned his constituents that there was no easy way out of the growing dangers.

"Ronald prepared himself for war with the same thoroughness which he showed in all things. He was determined to make his full contribution up to the very end and his valiant spirit was worthy of the high cause in which he fell. We shall long feel his loss and it is a grievous one, but rather than complain, for he would not have complained, of the shortness of his days, let us rejoice in a life so fully lived and freely given."

From Capt. P. R. LEGH, in *The Times.*

"Cartland was a true Christian in the sense that he would insist that every subject has its spiritual aspect. Conversations with him about the spiritual nature of democracy—a favourite theme—will remain among my happier memories. Fervent was his faith, yet he was one of those exceptional Christians who are both ready and able to defend their beliefs in argument. I fancy the secret of his entrancing personality was in his pride, a superb pride, which itself sprang from unconscious awareness that he lived up to his own standards. Self-esteem mattered always more than success, always more than the opinion of his fellows. Ronald Cartland graced and adorned the House of Commons as much with the individuality of his character as with the independence of his views. He really was an honourable and gallant gentleman. He gave fully of himself, and had much to give."

The Prime Minister sent the following message to Captain Peto, the Conservative Candidate in the King's Norton Division of Birmingham by-election.

"King's Norton had in Ronald Cartland a young man of high promise who was loved by all who knew him for his great personal charm, and respected by friends and opponents alike for his courage and intellectual integrity. His death on the field of battle has left a sad gap in our ranks."

Countless letters of sympathy and appreciation showed that Ronald had left a mark and an impression during his short life—especially in the political world he loved so well. The few that are quoted here have been chosen not because they are the best—hundreds of others are equally valued—but because they show particularly his character, ability, and the influence he had on those with whom he came in contact.

From the Prime Minister, the Rt. Hon. Winston Churchill, M.P.

"Pray accept my deepest sympathy in the loss of so brilliant and splendid a son, whose exceptional abilities would have carried him far had he not proudly given his life for his country."

From the Rt. Hon. Anthony Eden, M.P., Secretary of State for Foreign Affairs.

"Ronald had everything before him. We were all so sure that he had a great part to play in the world after the war, for he had the true qualities of leadership, vision, courage and faith. Of all the younger men I knew, his was the fairest future. We who were his friends had the deepest affection for him. It could not be otherwise, and he has left a gap in all our lives that cannot be filled. He could least be spared. The last time that I saw Ronald was when he was home on leave. He was in such splendid spirits, and looked so well and happy, that I shall always remember him as he was then. He had made such a brilliant success of his military career, and I felt then how much this would help him to lead and govern us all when the war was over.

"We who are left have, thank Heaven, the inspiration of his dauntless courage and example. I, for one, shall never forget either, for I have never felt such confidence in the future of any young man, a future which his qualities must command."

From the Rt. Hon. Clement Atlee, M.P., Lord Privy Seal.

"He was, in my view, one of the coming men in the House, having personal charm, ability and courage. He would, I feel sure, have gone far, had he been spared. The country can ill afford his loss."

From the Rt. Hon. Brendan Bracken, M.P.

"He was a marvellous boy. Burke's description of Charles Townshend well fitted Ronnie—' He was the delight and ornament of this House and the charm of every private society which he honoured with his presence.' Ronnie played a great part in ending the squalid policy of appeasement—a policy which almost ruined England. He died fighting manfully for his country. And his generation will never forget him. There is lost to England, in everything save the example of his life and his noble death, one who would have greatly helped to create a new and better way of life for our people."

From the VISCOUNT WOLMER, M.P.

"I have just left the House of Commons after thirty years there and I have never seen a young M.P. of more sterling qualities than he. I first came across him in the fight some of us put up in the House for resolute and sane treatment of the depressed areas. I was at once immensely struck by his personality and our friendship rapidly ripened into an intimate one. I think his most outstanding quality in politics was his courage. Believe me, it is the rarest of all gifts among politicians, and I have never seen more splendid courage than his. Then his sincerity. Crystal clear was his political soul. He meant every word he said, and every one knew it. And he had other great gifts as well. He *at once* made his mark as a speaker, and his ability was clearly very great. England has suffered a *great* loss in his early death, and had he lived I do not doubt that he would have played a great part in politics and would have rendered great service to the State."

From the DUCHESS OF ATHOLL, M.P.

"I cannot say how I was encouraged and stimulated by some talks I had with him, and indeed by a letter he wrote me in the early months of this war. He had such clear sight, such courage and such energy—and such gifts of speech. I felt him the young man in the House who showed more promise than any other—and feel him a great loss to the country as well as to those who knew him well."

From the VISCOUNTESS ASTOR, M.P.

"I feel Ronald will never be away from God. He seemed so near him. In his uprighteousness, courage—love of country and all things good."

From J. P. L. THOMAS, M.P.

"I was always happiest when I was with him, and so, I know, were a great many of his friends. Talking to him was like climbing out of a valley on to his Malvern hills. Our doubts were blown away and he made us see and think so clearly. All we younger ones, and also the older ones like Anthony, owe so much to his courage and strength and loyalty. His influence will live on and guide us all."

From RICHARD LAW, M.P.

"It is impossible to write adequately of Ronald. I shall always think of him as one of the really great men that I have known . . . to him there was always a reality behind the appearance of this life. I think that Ronnie will be remembered by his friends when all else has been forgotten, if we have lost much we have gained so much more in knowing him."

From DUNCAN SANDYS, M.P.

"Ronald approached life in the spirit of a continuous crusade. Wherever he saw oppression, injustice, or incompetence, he attacked it. What is more, he enjoyed every moment of the fight, in which he neither gave nor expected quarter.

"To his friends his personality was stimulating and inspiring. He never seemed tired. He found pleasure and interest in all he did. His gaiety and love of life were infectious. He had a persistent premonition that he was going to be killed and spoke of it many times—always in the same easy carefree way, as though it really did not matter. He died as he lived—a 'Happy Warrior.'"

From RONALD TREE, M.P.

"I have always had a very high regard for his bravery—for the way in which he stood up for his principles and above all for his high-mindedness. I also counted a great deal on his judgment. His gaiety and high spirits were always a joy—and he went off to France with the same outlook—that he always had when there was a difficult fence in the House of Commons: with confidence—and serenity in the job ahead."

From EARL BEAUCHAMP.

"I shall always count myself extremely fortunate to have known him, and it was no surprise to me that he did so brilliantly in Parliament, accomplishing there in a few years much more than many do in a lifetime. At the same time—and this is rare with clever people—every one liked him who knew him. I think his whole outlook was an inspiration to us all for he was an example of what every one ought to be."

From the HON. CHARLES LYTTELTON.

"His keeness, his integrity and his vision would have brought him right into the forefront of his contemporaries:—he was a natural leader of men, and his power was enduring for it came from outside:—like Joan of Arc he had his voices, and trusted them implicitly."

From MAJOR T. B. PRITCHETT, Chairman of the King's Norton Unionist Association.

"He has left King's Norton far cleaner and more healthy than I ever knew it. On all sides he has made many friends—everywhere he has commanded respect because of his real ability, his great sense of duty to his country and his fellow citizens. His mark in our National life was only partly made. He had that wide and fruitful imagination, such determination and courage as would unquestionably have carried him to far greater responsibilities than the mere representation of the Division."

From MAJOR L. J. GIBBONS, Worcestershire Yeomanry.

"As one of his fellow officers I do want to say how terribly we have missed him since we have been back in England. His enthusiasm was always terrific and I never saw him tired or depressed. He had said so many times that he was determined never to surrender and from the little bits that one has been able to hear of his last action we know how gallantly he must have died."

From REV. R. E. UNWIN, Chaplain to the Forces.

"I knew him well in France, as Chaplain to his Regt., and he was such a live wire and help in fixing up services for his troops, and also in attending them himself. To us he was a flaming star and guide for the future—a strength which will always be present with us in our work for Goodness, Truth and Beauty."

From MAJOR WILLIAMS THOMAS, Worcestershire Yeomanry.

"We had fostered such hope of Ronnie—somehow he seemed immortal. It seemed impossible that God could rob the world, his friends and dear ones, of his charm, his brilliance and courage. We all loved him so—but he died so bravely, as he would have wished for his men and his country."

From ROM LANDAU.

"His death is a far greater loss to the country than people realise.

If there was any one among the young people with enough vision, courage and faith to lead the country out of war into the right sort of future—it was Ronald."

From PETER CHAPMAN WALKER to Barbara.

"I think very few of his friends can know as well as I do how happy and complete was your love and companionship for each other. I had seen that wonderful relationship so well from both sides and it has always seemed to me the finest example in my own experience of human love and understanding. Ronald was so splendidly direct and aware that he was in spirit ready to pass into that larger life in which you both believe. The sadness is not so much that he has died, but that we are so long without him."

From the SELLY OAK AND DISTRICT CONSERVATIVE AND LIBERAL UNIONIST CLUB, LTD.

"We had all learned to love him as a brother. He will always be remembered as a fearless fighter, true to his party, but with an unflinching zeal to his own convictions from which no one could turn him. Even his opponents have expressed their sorrow at his loss, and how he had always a deep interest in their welfare. He died as he had always lived, a hero in the eyes of those who knew him, fearless and upright with a love for the well-being of his country, and it may be some consolation to all of us to remember and emulate his life and his ideals."

From the YOUNG WOMEN'S CHRISTIAN ASSOCIATION OF GREAT BRITAIN.

"The whole impression left in the lives of Association members with whom he came in contact was that of a gifted radiant Personality—dedicated to the service of God and of his fellow-men."

From M. F. HODGE, Agent for the King's Norton Division.

"We who were so closely associated with your son learned to admire him for his purity of mind, honesty of purpose, and sterling qualities, and it seems unfathomable that one so gifted and endowed with such courage, independence of thought and foresight, should have been taken from us."

From TWO ELECTORS in King's Norton.

"Although we did not vote for your son in the 1935 election here—in fact we voted against him—we came to regard him as 'our M.P.' We wrote to him many times during the progressive debacle of the Government he was expected to support, for his disregard of the Party Whip when his convictions diverged from Government policy showed us that we had a man as our M.P. and not a mere cog in a machine."

From A STRANGER.

"For the last few years I have followed his career in the House and looked forward to the time when he would become one of our leading citizens. The sincerity of his speeches was like a breath of fresh air in the midst of so much cowardly compromise and party politics. His help in Parliament after the war would have been so valuable that the loss of it is a tragedy for England. Thousands of folk who never had the honour of knowing your son are feeling that they have lost something that meant a great deal to them by his death."

From LT. C. H. W. TROUGHTON, Prisoner of War.

"I saw a lot of him during the last days and he was absolutely magnificent. I don't know a more charming or braver person than Ronnie and I hate to think that no one got through to tell how absolutely splendid he was."

From *A Prophet at Home* by DOUGLAS REED, published in 1941.

"Here and there was a man whom nothing could silence, but his voice was but one in a wilderness. Such a man was the young Tory member, Ronald Cartland . . . of him it may truly and proudly be said 'That was an Englishman.' . . . He knew of and detested the derelict areas and called them by this name, and refused to call them by the name, Special Areas, which his fellow Tories had given them in the English fashion of playing shut-eye to all unpleasant things, of side-tracking the necessity to cure them by pretending that they do not exist. He wanted them to be abandoned and completely rebuilt. He hated the commercial ruination of England's countryside, and everything else that an Englishman should hate who feels himself an Englishman, and not just a member of this party or that class. For years he fought against the Whip's Hand and on the eve of the present war, when it came, he made a bitter attack on Mr. Chamberlain which was angrily reproved by the elderly Tory members who formed that Tory leader's especial bodyguard.

"'We are in the situation,' he told the House, 'that within a month we may be going to fight and we may be going to die.' He went, he fought, and he died.

"And so it has been in England since 1914. The best go, and as they go old men yap at them. Some do not return."

MR. ELLIS SMITH, Labour Member for Stoke, in the House of Commons, July 10th, 1941.

"Some of us long ago saw the danger of the growing expansion of German armaments, and our consciences stimulated us to work. Ronald Cartland was an example of what I mean, with his clear-sightedness, his great energy, his far-seeing qualities, his courage—and it took some courage in those days—drive, and dynamic personality, all those qualities that find avenues of service."

LIST OF ILLUSTRATIONS

1 Ronald Cartland, 1934, aged 28

2 Ronald's father, Capt. Bertram Cartland, APM, 1915

3 Ronald's mother, Mary Cartland, 1920

4 Ronald, Barbara and their Mother

5 Ronald in a horse push-cart with Barbara, 1908

6 Tony, Ronald and Barbara, Christmas 1930

7 Ronald speaking at the Eccles Works, Birmingham, 1935

8 The Unionist Candidates for the twelve Birmingham Parliamentary Divisions

9 Ronald with Anthony Eden at the Junior Imperial League rally, 1938

10 Ronald with Winston Churchill at the Austin Motor Works, 1938

11 Ronald, Raine, Ian, Barbara and Tony, Christmas 1938

12 Ronald with his nephew and godson Ian, August 1939

13 Ronald the day before he left for France, January 1940

FOREWORD

RONALD CARTLAND, had he not died for his country and his faith on the retreat to Dunkirk, would almost certainly have risen to high, perhaps supreme command in his party and would, had he remained a member of it, undoubtedly have shaped its idealism and beliefs. For, by nature and conviction, he unflinchingly followed not the middle road of expediency but the high road of honour.

He entered the House of Commons in 1935 at the age of 27 and supported himself there by his own efforts – no easy feat in those days for a penniless young man on the Conservative benches. Five years later both he and his only brother, like their father before them in the 1914–18 war, were killed in action.

In his speech at his adoption meeting in 1934, delivered before an audience of hard-boiled Birmingham Tories, with astonishing courage he outlined his political faith; one for which, and for the country that enshrined it, spurning consideration of health and political privilege, he was later to lay down his life.

"Our philosophy as Unionists," he told his future constituents, "rests on the belief that a man's life in this world is a preparation for the next; that the soul of man is more important than his body; and that, as far as is possible in the state of society in which he lives, a man should be allowed to work out his destiny in his own way . . .

"As individuals our duty is to harmonize our own personal search for God with the need for living in the world with other men, and doing what we can to help them. We believe in the divine purpose in life. We think that every man and every woman has something to add to the stream of a nation's life and that every nation has its particular part to play with the other nations of the world in the general advance of mankind.

"In this uncertain, dangerous, difficult world," he ended, "I am certain of only two things; my faith in God and my faith in the English people. There is an instinct in us – our greatest heritage – for what is right and for what is noble. In times of trouble and in times of happiness it has never failed us. We have so much to be thankful for, so much to do. God grant that you and I, and England, will never fail."

He never did. In this biography by his sister, Barbara Cartland, published during the war in which he fell one sees the shining faith of this lost leader. One who, I believe, would have lifted, as great statesmen like Gladstone and Disraeli did in the past, our political life as a nation on to less mundane heights than those to which we have grown accustomed.

"My philosophy as a Christian," he declared, "rests on the belief that a man's life in this world is a preparation for the next. The fundamentals of Christianity do not change. They are the rule by which one can measure the achievements or failures of the age . . . No government can change man's soul; the souls of men change governments . . . Only through freedom in his own soul will man find salvation."

The prime function of government, therefore, is to give him that freedom and protect and safeguard it for him.

As Ronald said:

"The heritage of the British people is their instinct . . . It is the natural growth of centuries; even now it can be temporarily misled; but by oppression and class warfare it might be permanently destroyed. It is the creation of a free people with a sense of their nationhood."

It is just this, as I see it, that Ronald Cartland died to preserve.

SIR ARTHUR BRYANT, C.H., C.B.E.

PREFACE

RONALD CARTLAND was a man of noble spirit, who followed his convictions without thought of personal advancement. At a time when our political life had become feckless and dull, he spoke fearlessly for Britain. His words and acts were instinct with the sense of our country's traditions and duty. His courage and bearing inspired those who met him or heard him.

Fortunately this country has not lacked men prepared to spend their lives in its service. Ronald Cartland was one of these. On May 30, 1940, when he was killed fighting with the rearguard of the British Expeditionary Force during its retreat to Dunkirk, the Army and the House of Commons suffered a grievous loss. Those who read this book will realise that this is true. They will also derive from it a renewed assurance that the way of life for which he fought will certainly prevail and persist because of the striving and sacrifices of such men as he.

WINSTON S. CHURCHILL

7th November, 1941.

INTRODUCTION

In presenting this record of my brother's life I have left it a diary, making no effort to catalogue speeches or actions under separate headings. It was how Ronald lived—each day filled with activity, each day one of vital importance to him. I have tried to let him tell his own story.

I may seem to have included many trivialities. But it is the little things on which character breeds and develops and which finally make up a personality. Great events are only the final testing of what has been forged by long, often dreary hours of overcoming petty difficulties and trivial occurrences.

Ronald, sensitive and perceptive, felt the little things of life deeply; his vision and his ideals always carried him beyond them towards an ultimate goal, but he never despised "the daily round, the common task." Believing that to-day must always justify the importance of to-morrow, he had no use for lack of preparation, either in work, in politics, or in life.

To him mere "window-dressing" was dishonest. Even as he prepared a speech for half a dozen people as carefully as one to be delivered in the House of Commons, so all his life the so-called trivialities of everyday existence were treated punctiliously. Finally, as he said at King's Norton in 1935:

"A man's life in this world is only a preparation for the next. We die and are buried. The English people go on. We neither expect or desire always to see in our lifetime the fruits of our labour."

CHAPTER ONE

1907-1916

"The Childhood shows the man."

MILTON

IN 1910 a small boy aged three sat at a minute table in a big toy cupboard scribbling on the backs of old Primrose League tickets. Every now and then he would rise solemnly and, coming to the front of the cupboard, would make a speech to the assembled throng in the nursery, consisting of Nanny and his elder sister who paid little attention to him. Clapping himself enthusiastically at the end of a short peroration he would return to "his desk" and continue to write.

Ronald Cartland was playing at "politics." In the world outside tyres of motor-cars were being slashed, carriage rugs stolen, bricks thrown through windows, speakers heckled and booed from their platforms, meetings broken up, while Members and Candidates for Parliament "went to the Country" for a General Election.

In the South Worcestershire Division Mr. Bolton Eyres Monsell was the Conservative Candidate. His meetings in Pershore and District were arranged and organised by Captain Bertram Cartland —Secretary of the Primrose League.

At Amerie Court, Pershore, a somewhat pretentious name for what had originally been a small farmhouse, there was tremendous activity; speakers arrived for a night, voluntary workers called for advice and literature, telegraph boys were continually at the door; there were piles of posters, boxes of celluloid badges, and dozens of rosettes piled in the hall and smoking-room, while every member of the household wore a ribbon emblem of "true blue."

Meals were required at strange hours, meals for two, three, or perhaps a dozen people, served in the low-ceilinged dining-room which had once been the farmhouse kitchen. The range, with its big ovens, still stood in the fireplace, for it had been too expensive to move it and was in strange contrast to the Chippendale chairs, to the big grandfather clock with its brass embellishments, to the bow-fronted mahogany sideboard on which were arranged silver tankards and antique salvers—relics of better and richer days. But the silver shone bravely against the red papered walls and the woman to whom it owed its sheen and the furniture its polish carried her head high.

Small boned, with a round baby face and brown eyes which sparkled as she talked, Mary Cartland was outstandingly pretty. But her chief attractions were a vivacity which was inexhaustible, a sympathy which drew to her all sorts and conditions of people, and a courage which never failed her and which was, in the passing years, to defy the almost unbelievable reverses of fate.

She had married from luxury into luxury. The fourth daughter of Colonel Sanford George Scobell, she had been brought up at the Down House, Redmarley, hunted in the Ledbury country, and been one of the most attractive and popular girls in the neighbourhood. She had married during the Boer War the only son of one of the richest men in Birmingham, swept off her feet by a courtship which began from the moment Bertram Cartland had set eyes on her at a ball and decided that she was the girl he was going to marry.

Bertram Cartland, tall, good-looking, and exceedingly smart, had been spoilt by an adoring mother, indulged by a rich father; how could he be anything but bewildered when, three years after he was married, the world as he knew it crashed about his ears? His father, James Cartland, a J.P. and a director of many public companies, had, in conjunction with Joseph Rowlands, started the Fishguard Railway, being the shortest route to Ireland. This was subsequently taken over by the G.W.R., but in 1903, immediately after it was completed, came an economic slump.

The banks called in their loans and James Cartland was asked to find over quarter of a million in cash. This meant that for about five years he would have to live on his director's fees which, incidentally, brought him in £6000 a year with income tax at only 11d. in the pound. His wife, however, a pretty, pampered woman who, coming from a distinguished Scottish family—the Falkners—disliked Birmingham and everybody in it, cried out in horror at the idea of existing in such "terrible poverty." James Cartland, worried and disillusioned, took the easiest way out, leaving his widow and only child practically penniless.

Bertram and Mary Cartland's home at Peopleton was sold, their hunters put under the hammer, their servants, grooms, and gardeners dismissed, and they moved to Pershore, leasing Amerie Court from Lord Coventry. One maid was all they could afford in their new home (who received the quite average wage of £10 a year) and a nurse for their baby daughter, Barbara. Bertram was stunned; he had no idea as to how to begin to adjust himself to the new situation. He who hunted five days a week in the winter and played polo in the summer must now try to budget for an income of £300 a year. There was only the courage, the good humour, and inexhaustible spirits of his wife to keep him from utter despair.

Mary Cartland had no intention of being crushed by the reverses of fate. She had friends—good friends—loving friends who were to love and admire her increasingly. They drove over to condole and came away speechless with admiration. They would find her working in the garden or in the three acres of fruit farm. She and her husband were, in the years to come, to make a definite income out of growing, sorting, packing and posting specially picked plums from the heavily laden trees.

They found her, too, determined to keep in touch with the social life she knew and enjoyed. She could ride a bicycle—she taught her husband. In the summer they would bicycle ten miles to a tennis tournament, win a prize in the mixed doubles, and bicycle home. In the winter if, as very often happened, the Master of the Croome Hunt had given them a mount they bicycled eight miles to the Kennels and bicycled home at the end of the day.

For Barbara, too, and later for Ronald, Mrs. Cartland "kept in touch." The village cab, creaky, slow, and smelling of must and mildew, would jolt twelve or fifteen miles to a children's party;—Barbara, with her persistently straight hair in rags until their destination was almost reached, Ronald in a long-trousered white sailor suit, both listening enthralled to the fairy stories which whiled away the long drive. Mary Cartland was determined that her children should have friends and she pinched and saved, making endless personal sacrifices that such expeditions should be possible.

There were, however, times of desperation when the bailiffs seemed inevitable, when illness or accidents ate up the money which should have paid the butcher, when storms or drought ruined the fruit crop. Mary Cartland had through all this two sources of strength which never failed her—her faith in God and the ever increasing adoration of her husband.

Bertram Cartland was so proud of his pretty wife, so bitterly ashamed that he could give her nothing but a life of toil and trouble. Yet what could he do? He was completely untrained for every sort of work, educated only to hold a commission in the Army (no officer could live on his pay), to ride, shoot, and spend money.

No one admitted his shortcomings more readily than he, and often in a wild desire to make up to his wife for all she had lost he would buy her some ridiculously expensive present, being unreasonably hurt that she must refuse it with tears in her eyes while the baker gave his ultimatum at the back door that he would deliver no more bread until his long-standing account was paid. There were moments when Mary Cartland did not know which way to turn, when bills confronted her on every side, when there was nothing left to pawn and the future seemed to hold only disgrace and destitution.

At such a moment Ronald was born, coming into the world unexpectedly early. Mary Cartland's father, Colonel Scobell, was an extraordinarily good-looking man, with fine classical features and white curly sidewhiskers. The son of a clergyman he was proud of his family which, originally resident in Cornwall, was of pure Saxon blood and could trace its descent in a direct line to before the arrival of William the Conquerer. Thomas de Scobehull (the name changed in the passing centuries) was Sheriff of Devon in 1032.

Colonel Scobell, himself, was of the old school of Victorians who boxed his children's ears, thought every one who disagreed with him a fool or a revolutionary, and who was liable to bursts of uncontrolled anger. To the outside world he appeared the personification of charm and dignity; in the home he was a petty tyrant. He had, perhaps, a slight provocation. He did not care for children and had been blessed with five daughters before the much desired son and heir arrived.

He lived well. Owner of a big estate where he hunted during the winter, he took a house in London every year for the season and could afford to indulge his and his wife's love of travelling. They encircled the world three times in the days of sailing ships, visited Japan and China, and crossed Russia the first year the Trans-Siberian railway was opened.

Mrs. Scobell, a clever, handsome woman, loved her husband, and never opposed his wishes. She was not by any means the weak Victorian woman of contemporary novels for she was witty, intelligent, and exceedingly well-read. Most people found her rather awe-inspiring, but to her husband she was completely subservient despite the fact that she was an heiress when she married. Bearing the ancient Huguenot name of Palairet, her mother had been a Hamilton from Philadelphia, an offspring of that branch of the Duke of Hamilton's family who journeyed from England with

William Penn to develop the country.

Mary Cartland was, perhaps, her father's favourite child, for she was the only one of the family who dared stand up to him and who was not cowed and crushed to a silent misery by his rages, but it was to her mother she turned in her desperation just before Ronald was born. Colonel Scobell, however, accompanied his wife when she drove over to Pershore for what should have been a quiet, amicable discussion but which became, when the bills were produced, a tumult of tears and recriminations. Ronald arrived precipitately on January 3rd, 1907, and with his coming brought comfort, peace, and a new happiness to his parents.

A son! It meant so much, it gave his father ambition and a new determination to succeed, it smoothed his grandfather's anger, and brought his mother a pride and a joy beyond all expression.

Life changed from the moment of Ronald's arrival. It was the turning point of Bertram Cartland's life. After his son was born he discovered his brain, he started to read, to study politics, and in 1908 when the Primrose League started in Pershore and district he was made Honorary Secretary. In a year he was appointed a Knight of the Grand Star, and three years later Provincial Secretary for five counties, with a salary.

In the General Election of 1910 he organised the campaign for the Conservative candidate—this was part of the work of the Primrose League for there were no provincial Conservative organisations in those days—and Mr. Eyres Monsell was so impressed by his efficiency that on becoming a Member of Parliament he asked Bertram Cartland to become his secretary. Each succeeding year was to show the latter absorbed, interested, and increasingly active, and Ronald from his babyhood heard political discussions, speeches, and arguments.

Mary Cartland, optimistic and full of hope, was her husband's inspiration, guide and spur. She helped him with every speech he made, criticised and approved everything he wrote. There was work in the fruit farm to be done during daylight, for that was still their main source of income, so it was at night that Bertram Cartland began his political work, writing at his desk in the smoking-room, his wife beside him, seldom going to bed before the early hours of the morning.

But it was not all work and no play. There were joyous times too—tennis parties, hunting days on borrowed mounts, Hunt Balls when people would come to stay and when, after getting the house and meals ready for her visitors, Mary Cartland would put on a dress copied by the village dressmaker from a Paris model, thread a ribbon through her brown hair, and go gaily off to be the prettiest and gayest person in the ballroom.

As times improved, once a year the family went to the sea—usually to Eastbourne—where Ronald was taught to swim and where once on a windy day his pram was blown over on the front. Barbara burst into floods of tears, the Nurse, white-faced and breathless, was helped by anxious passers-by, while the occupant of the pram smiled and chuckled at this unexpected break in the monotony of the morning walk.

Ronald, fat and contented, smiled his way all through his childhood, and it seemed as though he created happiness wherever he went. Was it any wonder that his mother believed him to be a direct answer to her prayers?

There were many domestic changes in the following years. A second son, Anthony, was born on January 4th, 1913—the day after Ronald's sixth birthday. With the arrival of a new baby, Barbara was sent to a boarding school to make room for a Governess. Amerie Court was so small that Barbara and the Governess must play box and cox for the spare bedroom, Miss Williams arriving the day she left and leaving the day she returned. Edith Williams, who was known to the children as "Juicy," was an excellent teacher as well as a delightful personality. Ronald was to bless her all his life for the grounding she gave him and for teaching him how to learn.

He developed quickly; he was a handsome little boy with beautiful manners and attracted, wherever he went, attention and friends. When he was four and a half he went hunting on a small Shetland pony given him by his godfather. The youngest member of the Croome Hunt he was blooded when he was five.

At seven years old Ronald was keen and alive, throwing himself wholeheartedly into everything he did. He still played at politics and every wet day the schoolroom chairs were arranged in rows and he would make a speech to "Juicy." Before he started he would present her with a piece of paper on which were written two questions. These she was to ask by way of "heckling" him. She must only ask those on the paper because he knew the answers to them!

The same year, November, 1914, he brought out a magazine written entirely by himself. It was called *The Amerie* and cost a halfpenny a month. The proceeds were, in his own words, "in aid, for pipes for the men at Fort Tregantle," the latter where his father was stationed before proceeding to France.

Page 1 contained "THE HEAD'S LETTER."

"My dear People. Do you understand that it is *War* time, and that everybody in England ought to give up something. Now think of *Poor* Belgium who has gone through such a lot, and we have not gone through anything, except someone who we loved very much has been killed. Yours faithfully Ronald Cartland HEAD OF BOOK."

On the last page a notice read, "The Head of the Magazine is Ronald Cartland he has no one to help him." This somewhat pathetic utterance doubtless explained why there were only two editions of *The Amerie*—the effort of writing them out by hand proved too arduous.

He was bright and interested at his lessons, as he was in everything that went on around him, but his impressions of what was the right thing to do sometimes had amusing consequences. The first time he travelled alone it was discovered afterwards that he had tipped the Station Master at Defford—an important personage—twopence!

In March, 1914, the Cartlands moved to London and took a flat in Queen's Gate. Trouble was brewing in Ireland. The Women's Conservative Association, headed by the Duchess of Abercorn, had promised to find accommodation for 10,000 women and children if Civil War broke out, and having founded the "Help the Ulster Women and Children Committee," wanted an organiser. Mr. Gerald Arbuthnot, Head Organiser for the Primrose League, offered to lend them Bertram Cartland. The latter went over to Ireland, arranged about the transport, and had vast camps in preparation in various parts of England.

By this time he had a reputation for exceptional organising ability. His wife was growing prouder of him every day, but unfortunately the move to London was to prove disastrous to her. Mary Cartland was about to have another child and the effort of packing up, of travelling, the traffic, the noise, and because she spared herself nothing, was too much for her. In July the baby arrived prematurely. It was a girl—still-born—and for the first time in her life Mary Cartland's vitality and energy were drained; she lay quiet and still, and the household crept around, apprehensive and afraid.

Clouds were gathering over Europe, events were growing daily more threatening, rumours of war began to be whispered by those in authority. Brigadier-General Francis Davies, an old Worcestershire friend, told Bertram Cartland to get his family out of London.

Barbara came back from school, but after two days at the flat Mary Cartland, weak, white, and shaky, packed up and they went home to Amerie Court, arriving on August 4th.

The special reserve of officers, in which Bertram Cartland held his commission, was called up the same day and on November 15th he sailed for France as A.P.M. on the staff of the 8th Division. He was in the battles of Neuve Chapelie and of Festubert, mentioned in Dispatches in June, 1915, and a month later specially recommended for promotion by the G.O.C. 8th Division.

CHAPTER TWO

1916-1919

"But God will keep us."

IN 1916 Ronald went to a preparatory school at Parkfield, Haywards Heath. There he was desperately homesick and desperately unhappy. He had already proved himself quick and intelligent at work but he was to some extent precocious. He never hesitated to express an opinion whatever the cost to himself; he had also a freedom of speech and a strength of will unusual for his age. It was inevitable that he should endure a certain amount of ragging, but unfortunately he also fell out with his Headmaster.

Mr. Bent was an old man who found individualists among his boys more trouble than they were worth. He disliked Ronald, thought him self-opinionated and conceited, and went out of his way to snub him on every possible occasion. He was also incensed by the fact that Ronald was extremely religious; he had no use for what he considered ostentation of that sort and made the Scripture lessons which he taught an almost continual attack on a small boy who remained undaunted by both criticism and sarcasm.

After the first term at Parkfield Ronald begged not to return; at the end of the holidays he cried all night, clinging to his mother, beseeching, praying, pleading with her not to make him go back. He had to go, but he was never happy there, and his feud with the Headmaster continued up to the time he left. His letter, written soon after his return, shows not only his acute distress and a touching faith in the efficacy of grown-up help but also an extraordinary thoughtfulness for his mother both mentally and financially.

Ronald knew that sacrifices were being made to pay for his education, and that every penny spent on him meant personal sacrifice on the part of his mother. On January 27th, 1917, three weeks after his tenth birthday, he wrote to her:

"PARKFIELD,
HAYWARDS HEATH.

"MY OWN DARLING,

"Thank you *Darling* so very much for the letter which you sent me. I am so *very very very* depressed and I cry *every* evening and nearly every morning. To-day (Sunday) *I have cried all the time and am crying at this very moment.* It is not the work or the Masters, as I try my very hardest to please the Masters also to work hard to please you. But darling all the same I feel *very very* homesick and I can't get the thought of 'Home' off my brain. Darling to please me will you write to Mr. Bent and tell him that I *am* homesick and won't he do something ?—otherwise I shall run away—I really shall. I am not bullied—just homesick. Darling please do—I know you don't want your own little Son to be unhappy. Or if you do not want to *write* to Mr. Bent, come down and take me out and then talk to Mr. Bent and tell him, but that will cost you expense so please don't do it.

"Anyway because I am depressed *you* won't get depressed will you?—Darling *don't*. I must end now. Best love my own darling.

"from your own loving son,

"x x x RONALD x x x"

He found things easier in time but he was always miserable at the end of the holidays, dreading with something akin to terror the day he must return to school. But he worked hard to please his mother knowing that in wasting time he was wasting money. One thing which upset him was that he wasn't allowed to read when he woke up in the morning. It was the only available time in a busy day, and already he loved books more than anything else. In a letter to his mother written during his last term at Parkfield, he mentions both the ban on his reading and the unceasing need for economy. He was then thirteen.

"I was glad to get your letter—it cheered me up wonderfully. I was feeling so depressed. That will be lovely—we'll have lunch together and then Barclays and Dewar can come to tea. That'll be lovely if you are quite sure it won't *cost* you too much.

"What do you think? We played a cricket match yesterday and I scored for it. It's a pretty good honour as you have to be very neat. We won the match!

"Yes, isn't it sickening about the reading and it doesn't look as though I shall read until the hols. Anyway I didn't mind—I shall write letters to you all the time, darling. The half term reports will be out soon. I do hope I have done well, darling, my last term. I am afraid I have not done well in Latin but you remember last hols I told you I was bad in Latin and you were going to let me have lessons. Then you couldn't."

At thirteen Ronald was somewhat of a prig. Just before the end of the term he wrote:

"Am writing in bed with my Onoto pen which is not allowed but that's a minor detail. Isn't it lovely to think that in fourteen days time I shall see you and Barbara and Tony. It is a lovely thought. My dear, what do you think a *new* boy called C . . . (he's in my dorm) said to a boy the other day. 'Curse your d——d soul.' He's the most awful little bounder. Tells lies to everybody and even to masters. He has not sworn in dorm yet. Well Dewar, my friend, reported him to Mr. Bent. He had only got halfway through the reportation matter when Mr. Bent shouted out, 'Send him to me.' C was sent to him and got 9 pretty hard ones. Of course its a good thing. But it seems rather a lot to give a little new boy of eight years old.

"I do hate old Bent, darling. When ever he can snub me he does. I get depressed sometimes. Your letters are the only things that cheer me up. So write often won't you dear? I am hoping to get a letter from you to-day. I do hope I shall. All my love darling. There goes the bell to get up."

Ronald took his Common Entrance Examination and on July 17th his mother received the following:

"PARKFIELD,
HAYWARDS HEATH.

"MY OWN DARLING,

"Have just heard that I have passed. Isn't it just topping? The letter from Charterhouse to Mr. Bent was as follows:

"'DEAR MR. BENT,

"'Your boy Cartland passed very satisfactorily especially in French and English.'

"The other boy, Richardson, failed unluckily. But I don't mind. I got in.

"All my love, I'm so glad I got in darling. Ever your loving son,

"RONALD."

At the end of the term Ronald gained the right amount of marks to entitle him to a prize for Scripture, but the Headmaster made an excuse for him not to receive it. This made a deep impression on him and he was to loathe injustice all his life. Parkfield left another mark on him due to the years of his defiance of Mr. Bent

—he was almost to invite antagonism by the unflinching assertion of his beliefs and creeds. He would not prevaricate or pretend and this desire to speak the truth as he saw it was to develop year by year until it became one of the strongest factors in his character.

Holidays were a joy and a happiness only dimmed by the knowledge that every day brought him nearer to the moment when he must leave his mother again. His adoration of her was growing year by year. As a baby he had cried when she left the nursery, now it seemed as though a kind of radiance enveloped mother and son when they were together.

For his father Ronald had admiration and affection but he saw very little of him. They had a few holidays all together when Bertram Cartland was invalided home and for a short time appointed Garrison Adjutant at Seaford, but he had returned to France as Instructor at the G.H.Q. Cadet School at Blendecques and by 1917 was back in the trenches with the 1st Battalion Worcestershire Regiment.

In March, 1918, he had fourteen days' leave, returning to France on Good Friday. Acting Colonel, he took the regiment into the line at Berry au Bac when, on May 26th, orders were issued to the troops of the 8th Division to man their battle stations. The Germans, with their unfailing faculty for discovering a weak spot, had unknown to the Allies moved three thousand guns in position to support a concentrated attack which started the next day, May 27th —the last phase of their great gamble for victory.

Everywhere companies and platoons made a fierce and gallant resistance, holding their ground so long as their ammunition lasted and men survived to shoot. But the Battalion was surrounded and was attacked in front, flank and rear. There was no surrender —all fought to the last. Bertram Cartland was killed in the trenches with his men. One by one the platoon posts were overwhelmed. Only a few stragglers came back.

The shells and trench-mortar bombs rained on the British trenches left the ground as though it had been ploughed—there were few identifiable bodies and no personal belongings which could be returned to relatives.

Mary Cartland was stricken with grief. She had always believed that her husband would return—she had been so sure that the end of the war would bring the realisation of her ambitions for him. They had decided he should enter politics as a Member of Parliament, they had planned so many things which now only sharpened and intensified her loss and sense of loneliness. They had been together for seventeen years—years of trial but years of love and unity, one with the other.

Ronald, aged eleven, wrote to his mother.

"PARKFIELD,
HAYWARDS HEATH.

"MY ANGEL,

"Thank you so very much for your two letters, Darling. I know I am the eldest son, I must be everything for you and Pray God I shall never offend him who is dead or you my darling. I shall soon be with you Angel and then I hope I shall be able to cheer you up. I am enclosing a few cuttings I have got from *The Times* and other papers. The cutting you sent me is very nice. Poor 8th Division. I see *they are* cut up.

"Of course darling I will follow Daddy but will you please explain to me in your next letter what you mean by this—'I want you to start where your Father left off.' I do wish I could be with you for the Memorial Service but I will pray earnestly that day for Him! Poor Tony! He will feel terribly wretched but he will soon feel all right.

"I wish I was at home to help you answer your two hundred letters. Darling, where shall we live now? I, being the son who should and will look after you, must know, for you, darling, are alone. There is no Daddy to keep us alive. But God will keep us.

"Forgive such a short letter but I have 4 others to write Darling. I will be your right hand, my dearest one.

"All my love Angel,
"I am ever,
"Your very loving son,
"RONALD."

"Love to Tony."

The lack of survivors meant many difficulties and mistakes in compiling the huge casualty lists. On June 17th, the day fixed for Bertram Cartland's Memorial Service, his wife received a second telegram from the War Office which informed her that "Major Cartland was now reported missing not killed."

Happiness raised its head, hope sprang into being, widow's weeds and mourning were put away. Mary Cartland had interviews at the War Office and with the Red Cross organisations, visited wounded soldiers in various hospitals, seeking news of her husband.

The months went by slowly but hope remained. A telegram could start her heart beating. A pile of letters on the breakfast table would be hastily scanned for a German postmark, every imaginable source of information had been tried.

Brigadier-General Francis Davies had now become Military Secretary to the War Office. Through his personal investigation information was finally received from the Adjutant of the 1st Worcestershire Regiment—a prisoner in Germany—that Bertram Cartland had been killed as originally reported on May 27th at Berry au Bac. In October, 1918, his name appeared once again in the Roll of Honour.

Colonel Scobell had been dead some years. His widow was living at Walton House, near Tewkesbury and Mary Cartland, anxious to save money, stayed with her mother during term time, renting various small houses in the neighbourhood for the holidays.

Financially, things were very difficult. Her entire income, including the pension paid on her husband's death, was now about £600 a year. On this she had not only to support herself and Barbara, but to educate Ronald and Tony, who had their names down for Charterhouse. Fortunately, war memorial schemes were being prepared at all big Public Schools for the sons of old boys who had fallen in the war. In the meantime Ronald was still at Parkfield.

In the July of 1918 Barbara became eighteen and left school at the end of the term. Her mother asked her: "Where do you want to live? I don't mind where I go—you can choose." Barbara had no hesitation—she wanted to live in London. She had only been there once in her life—those memorable two days at Queen's Gate.

While pointing out that she knew very few people in London, having lived all her life in the country, Mary Cartland accepted Barbara's decision and took a furnished house in Nevelle Street, South Kensington. There were first, however, the summer holidays to be arranged for, and in August the family went to Bembridge, where Barbara "came out" at the Club dances and where Ronald and Tony played on the beach with a small boy called David Niven.

They arrived in London on September 25th, 1919, to find 20 Nevelle Street was a tall, dingy house, identical in every particular with those on either side, its rooms one-front, one-back, on three floors opening off steep dark stairs. After supper Tony was put to bed and Barbara and Ronald left their mother unpacking and went out into the streets. They walked through the quiet squares until they came within sight of the South Kensington

Underground—then there were lights, the hum of traffic, the bustle of passing pedestrians.

They stood some way off—this was London! It all seemed very big, very impressive, and rather frightening. They both felt this was the start of a new era. What would they achieve?—what would they make of their lives? They were both ambitious for themselves—they were well aware of all that their mother hoped for where they were concerned. What would they do?

A feeling of insignificance at the vastness and size of the world overpowered them. Instinctively each clasped the other's hand. They had not realised one could feel so lonely in a crowd.

Then Barbara spoke defiantly.

"I shall get to know everybody—everybody in London."

"I shall be Prime Minister," Ronald said quietly.

They walked home almost in silence to the shabby respectability of Nevelle Street.

CHAPTER THREE

1920-1925

"Every man should give to Society as a whole, more than he takes from it."

In 1920 Mrs. Cartland found a small house in Eaton Terrace which she took unfurnished, her furniture was brought up from the country, and the beautiful things which had been chosen on her marriage for the big house at Peopleton and which had graced the simple walls at Amerie Court once again surrounded her. She

She made the house very charming, most of the rooms being almost completely lined with books. Besides her husband's quite considerable library Barbara had a passion for reading and Ronald had already begun his own collection. If the Cartland children were asked what they wanted for a present the answer was invariably "books."

After the summer term Ronald left Parkfield and went to Charterhouse in September. He was in Lockites and his House-master was Mr. J. R. N. Wilson. His entrance examination had shown such a high standard that he passed straight into the Upper IV. Mr. Fletcher, the Headmaster, wrote that Ronald had been assigned the Charles Hugh Tempest Whitehead Scholarship—the value of which was about £100 per annum. It was a Memorial Scholarship for sons of Carthusians killed in the War.

After he had been at school a month Ronald had begun to enjoy himself, to find his feet, and to challenge the authorities! He wrote to his mother:

"It's awfully nice here and I love it except the way everybody cheats, but I suppose that's only natural in a public school. It's fine to be here though. You have so much more freedom.

"My work is going on all right I think. Also the games. Sad to say the Master who takes me in History is awful, he actually taught us last time that Alfred started the *Anglo-Saxon Chronicle*. After the lesson I *gently* informed him that he was making a big mistake, because Bede wrote it. We had rather a discussion and it ended 'all square,' though I could show my authorities for it, while he could only show me a person called Morris (whose book we read) who is in my mind hopeless!! However such is the world!"

By half term he had settled down, but as he said himself, the excitement of new surroundings had worn off. He was desperately anxious to please his mother by doing well and he wrote to her in October:

"I manage to have plenty of time to read here. I'm now reading every one of Arnold Bennett's I can get hold of. The jam you sent me is still going strong. It's awfully good. The Tuck Shop here is a wonderful place. But so much of your money goes there that it takes away the nice feeling of friendliness towards it!! When we first came here we were never bored. Everything was so new. But now we know everything it's so boring.

"We come home on December 17th for 5 weeks' holiday. How lovely that will be!! And just to think it's only just half-term. It's awful. Never mind, the time soon goes. I wonder whether you'll find me greatly improved. I don't expect so. I don't get very squashed here. You'll get my mid-quarter report soon—I do hope it's good. I *do* want to be good at work darling, since I'm not good at games.

The mid-quarter report was good as Ronald had hoped. His Form Master wrote—"Will, I think, do well." His Housemaster's signature was under a sentence—"A conscientious boy and promising well."

The years passed uneventfully for Ronald. But his mother was never without money troubles. Barbara published her first novel in 1922 which was luckily a success and made her about £150. She immediately started another and after meeting Lord Beaverbrook she began to write articles and later paragraphs for the *Daily Express* and *Evening Standard*. But Mary Cartland, determined that the two boys should always have good holidays in the country, found the expense of a house in London was really beyond her tiny income.

In May, 1923, when knitted clothes were most fashionable, she opened a Knitwear shop with a friend, Miss Margaret Munn. They each put in a capital of £100, and due to hard work and Mary Cartland's many faithful friends they made a profit the first year of £300 after all expenses, including the rent of the shop over which they lived, had been paid. The second year the profit was £600, and the third £800.

The shop premises were on the first floor at 6a Pont Street, and

Barbara, her mother, and Miss Munn lived on the floor above it. Holidays were always spent in Worcestershire, Mary Cartland renting small furnished houses. During the months her sons were at home she gave her whole time and attention to them. Often she missed her husband's help and guidance unbearably, but she had no difficulty in disciplining the boys or in making them obey her.

Ronald was quick-tempered at times, but both he and Tony were always as quickly sorry if they had been irritable or rude. The Cartlands had been brought up from earliest childhood not to "let the sun go down on their wrath"—they very seldom disobeyed the maxim.

Their mother was most insistent about appearances and manners. Her sons got to their feet when she came into a room, opened the door for her, tidied themselves for meals, and always changed their clothes for dinner however meagre the meal, or even if they got it for themselves and helped wash up afterwards. It was a discipline which stood them in good stead in later life.

Ronald took a pride in his appearance and all his life he preferred to polish his own shoes rather than have them badly cleaned. Manners extended to being most punctilious about letters of thanks. Hospitality as well as presents, Mary Cartland insisted, deserved gratitude, and all three of her children wrote automatically to their hostess after a dinner party and to any one who was helpful to them in any particular way. Ronald's good manners were in consequence a subject of comment both then and in the future.

Everything was made easier for Mary Cartland in the upbringing of her family by their unswerving devotion to her personally, and the friendly rivalry which existed between her children for her attention. Ronald, particularly, was actively jealous if his mother paid what he considered too much attention to his brother and sister. "I want you all to myself," he would tell her, striving to coax her to spend an afternoon with him alone, or to leave the others out of some expedition.

Happy and carefree as these holidays were, Ronald was very concerned that his mother was working too hard. She was not strong and had, since her husband's death, suffered from severe heart attacks. Only her indomitable spirit kept her going, and the knowledge that she must keep alive and well for her children's sake.

In October, 1924, when he was seventeen, Ronald wrote his

mother from Charterhouse a long and passionate letter on the injustices of labour.

"I've been talking to some of the men working on the road here," he said, "and they have almost convinced me that Socialism is the right policy. Every man should give to Society as a whole more than he takes from it. Until that is carried out England cannot be saved—peace will never come nor prosperity. I believe that every man should have a living wage—not a paltry dole of 18/- for which he in employment has paid 1/2 a week. It is wrong for boys of 14 to be cast into this world with no future and less education. I am most fearfully worried about England's state and we do need a *Broad* policy."

He could not, however, eventually reconcile himself to the overthrow of tradition. The best and most ancient traditions of England he felt were an intrinsic part of all British people as of himself. But deeply ingrained within him was the conviction "that the majority must be considered if England is to be, once again, happy," and in the years to come he was to adhere to the principles and ideals set forth in this letter from school. He was not, however, without followers and opponents during the transition stage when he questioned the policy on which he had been brought up and strove to express his own instincts and convictions.

One report read: "His keenness is an asset, and he has set an excellent example to the House which has borne fruit. If he can curb his revolutionary tendencies I expect him to do well as head of the House next quarter."

Mr. Wilson's hopes were never to be realised—Ronald was to remain revolutionary until his life's end.

Ronald was unusually able at work, having taken the School Certificate in 1924 when he was seventeen and gained six credits. In January, 1925, he was eighteen and should have left Charterhouse, but the Headmaster, Mr. Fletcher, wrote to his mother suggesting that he should stay on another term. He told her that Ronald's influence in the school was so excellent and his industry so remarkable that though he paid few boys the compliment of asking them to remain on over the age of eighteen he would like Ronald to be one of the exceptions.

That February, Miss Dodgson, the Matron at Lockites, in a letter to Mrs. Cartland, wrote:

"I wanted to tell you how very pleased I am at Ronald doing so well as temporary head monitor, and, in fact, altogether, and now being made a school monitor. I feel very proud of him. I can't tell you the help he now is to me, so thoughtful and so splendid as regards anything to do with the house, most keen and business-like, and showing such good tact and judgment. He shows great promise of leadership. . . .

"I have always loved the boy, he was the first Lockite I ever spoke to, and in his usual friendly way at once tried to make me feel at home and less strange! It is so splendid the way Ronald has made himself felt and come to the top, but of course he is a boy of unusual character and ability."

In the summer term Ronald started to make money for himself by the joint editing of a magazine. It was Ronald's original idea, the title being *First and Last*, and as its name implied was intended for one issue only, but it was such a success that it was succeeded by *Plus One*. That term he was also Captain of the Shooting Eight, coaching the Charterhouse team for the Ashburton Shield at Bisley. On June 7th, in the letter he wrote to his mother, these conflicting interests were striving for pride of place.

"You will be pleased to hear that the paper has turned out a most enormous success. The three editors have made £5 11*s*. each, altogether we made £18 clear profit. Printing cost us £22 10*s*. We took £21 in advertisements, Sales came to another £20. Altogether we are very pleased with ourselves! I myself do not think it at all a bad effort. We sold about 450 copies.

"The Ashburton on Thursday and I am just a little nervous. To coach two pairs and shoot last *is* rather a strain. I do not for one moment think we shall win it. If we have luck we may be in the first five. I will send you a telegram immediately the shoot is over. Pray God I shoot well. To-day the eight have all been taking furious exercise. 1½ hours training. To-morrow we just rest. Bisley Wednesday and 'der tag.'"

In spite of all Ronald's hopes of winning the Ashburton Shield, Charterhouse was only ninth, Ronald himself making 59 out of a possible 70. He had thrown himself heart and soul into the effort and he received both sympathy and commendation, the authorities liking his enthusiasm and noting, incidentally, that it was the highest place Charterhouse had gained in the Competition for six years. Mr. Wilson's report said:

"He shows good judgment, some leadership and tact, and has

the gift of getting things done. In the special department of shooting he has raised the standard in the House very high."

For the summer holidays Ronald and Tony and their mother went to stay at Dumbleton Hall. Mrs. Eyres Monsell was not there, but she lent them the house. All through the years she had been Mary Cartland's best friend and a kind of fairy godmother to the children. She was, in fact, Tony's godmother. They called her "Aunt Sybil" and were devoted to her and her husband. During the war the latter returned to his old service, the Navy, and had reached the rank of Commander. He was now Chief Conservative Whip. Ronald admired him enormously. His quiet dignity, his charm of manner, and attractive smile were all noted and even imitated. He was extraordinarily kind to Ronald as a small boy and was to continue his kindness through the years to come.

Also staying at Dumbleton was a cousin of Mrs. Eyres Monsell, a boy of sixteen. Ronald and he went out partridge shooting together on the 1st of September, and climbing over a fence the younger boy's gun went off. Ronald was only a yard away from him and received the entire charge in his leg. He was carried back to the house on a gate, the doctor was fetched from the village, and his mother took him into Cheltenham to a Nursing Home.

He was operated on immediately, several hundred pellets being removed and a large amount of bone. The surgeon told Mrs. Cartland that the leg could be saved but that had the wound been a tenth of an inch higher amputation would have been unavoidable.

After many weeks in the Nursing Home Ronald went to his grandmother's house near Tewkesbury to convalesce. He suffered great pain, but in October he was well enough to return to Charterhouse on crutches.

His first letter after his arrival there was to his mother.

"LOCKITES.
20th Oct., 1925.

"MY DARLING,

"I am really a perfect fool. I wanted to say such a lot to you and I never did. I felt *so* miserable at leaving you and I wanted you to be brave that I never told you again how much I love you and how very very wonderful you had been all through this rotten time.

"Here life's all right, but I do miss you so, my darling. I *do* want you. I miss you every minute. There's nobody who can understand. I do hope you got back all right and found the flat not too bad. It must be so terrible for you there. Do try and go away as much as you can. I hate to think of you living there.

"I feel tolerably well but I know *you* did my leg ever so much better than these people. I get rather tired in the evenings but every one is very nice and sympathetic. The Headmaster condoled with me to-day and Mr. Wilson is always hopping up and talking.

"I've got my study fairly nice now and your light you sent me is wonderful. It makes all the difference to the room.

"Every one is so kind and the House seems very happy. I can never thank you enough for everything. Darling, I should hate to die. I love you so so much. Take care of yourself—you are the only person that matters.

"All love,

"RONALD."

His second letter told how his passion for organisation had asserted itself, and he had made alterations in the traditional rules of the House. It also spoke of a quite formidable amount of mental if not physical energy.

"The House seems excellent, but with Wilson's permission I have carried out numerous alterations in the fagging—abolition of fines, etc. The new system comes into operation on Monday but already it has proved very popular.

"With regard to the school I have been elected to two committees. Shop Advisory and Library—both committees of five—so I am greatly honoured. I look after 600 boys' feeding and reading! I am the president of the Debating Society. The first debate is next Saturday on 'Ghosts,' which seems to me a poor subject, but I expect I shall have to say a few words from the House. The following Saturday I believe I am introducing a motion against the British Fascisti. Also I have been elected a member of the Shakespeare Society—an august band of 14 in which are numerous masters. Last night we read *A Midsummer Night's Dream.* I read *Puck*—what irony on crutches!"

Ronald had already made his mark in the debating society, the *Carthusian* reported him frequently as being "vigorous" and "startling."

In 1924 when he was seventeen he had spoken passionately on Unemployment and Housing. A shadow of "coming events" eleven years later.

CHAPTER FOUR

1925-1926

"I pray God I shall do well!"

IN the meantime a difficult situation had arisen. Since 1916 it had been arranged through Captain Dick Coventry that Ronald should enter the Shell Oil Company, but when they heard about his leg they said they couldn't take him into their employment until the doctors passed him as absolutely fit. This was a bitter blow, as not only was there every likelihood of Ronald being on crutches for a year but there was also the possibility that another operation might be necessary later on.

However, once again Mary Cartland's good friends were not to fail her. The Countess of Rothes introduced Ronald to Sir Harold Snagge, who, after an interview, offered him a job in Edward Boustead & Co. As Ronald couldn't move about very easily he was to go into the Cashier Department.

This meant three years training then being sent out to Singapore. It was not ideal, but employment was hard to get, public school boys were a glut on the market, and there was nothing for it but to accept the offer gratefully. Other employment was offered him in Jardine, Mathieson & Co., but that meant an even speedier parting—China at the age of twenty.

In the Autumn Mary Cartland gave up her partnership in Knitwear and the auditors decided that a fair price for her interest in the business was £1200—a marvellous return for an investment of £100 over two and a half years.

Ronald left Charterhouse at the end of the Winter term. His Housemaster, Mr. Wilson, in a letter written to his mother enclosing his report, said:

"You see we all have something nice to say about Ronald. It is a real regret to us that he has to leave but that is one of the things that we have to get used to and fortunately is not the end– as the interest of watching the careers of the boys goes on. I am not going to add to my report of him. I hope he will get a job which gives him a good chance of making the most of his abilities. I expect political life would be his taste and I should think that he is cut out for such a career—he has some gift for debate and fluency in speaking."

Ronald's report was pleasant reading. Mr Wilson had said:

"The steady improvement in his character during the years he has been here has been pleasant to watch, and he has earned the best opinion of all with whom he has come into contact. He has a high sense of responsibility and has put his heart into the work of keeping a healthy tone in the House and of raising the standard of efficiency, taste and good manners throughout all sections. The unfailing cheerfulness with which he has borne the burden of his accident has been a good lesson to grumblers."

The Headmaster, Mr. Fletcher, wrote:
"I cannot recall any boy whose development and improvement during his school years has given me more satisfaction. His character has strengthened and deepened, and the qualities he has developed will not, I believe, fail when the responsibilities of school are over. He has intellectual interests which I hope he will maintain."

Christmas was spent as usual in the country, then in the second week in January Ronald and his mother came to London to move into a new house, No. 6 Royal Avenue, Chelsea. It was a delightful little house, built two centuries earlier, when Royal Avenue was the fashionable dwelling place for the famous "or infamous" ladies who were under the protection of the gentlemen of the Court. Now respectable young married couples and retired colonels with limited incomes sought the houses as being cheap and easy to run.

Mary Cartland planned their new home with care, she believed in giving her children as much freedom and independence as possible. There was a sitting-room for Barbara where she could write and entertain her friends, there was also one for Ronald where he sat at his father's desk surrounded by book shelves reaching from floor to ceiling.

While Ronald was waiting to enter Edward Boustead's, he was offered temporary work with his uncle, R. C. N. Palairet, the famous cricketer, who was the Secretary of the Oval. In the meantime, in spite of having to walk with the aid of sticks, Ronald was enjoying himself. He was invited to many theatres, he dined out a great deal.

In March he paid his first visit to the House of Commons.

He was also thinking seriously about his future, not so much in the immediate present, but as a whole. Ever since he had been a small boy his thoughts had turned continually to politics. "I must be Prime Minister one day," he told his mother, "because only in such a position can one effectively help and guide the country. It's no use talking from the street corners—one must first attain authority."

For some time in his teens he seriously considered entering the Church—he had always been religious—but on thinking it over he decided that the call was not strong enough. He always had very definite ideas as to his own mission in life. He believed absolutely that some day the way would be clear for him and he would have the power to help others. He talked it over very often with his mother and with Barbara. He stressed the point continually that he knew that no one could succeed ultimately if they worked for a selfish motive. Personal achievement must be gained only because the main goal was unselfish.

In March he started work with Edward Boustead at 149 Leadenhall Street. On May 4th a General Strike was declared. All normal transport services were at a standstill, but like millions of other men and women that morning Ronald was determined to get to work. He accepted the offer of a lift from Geoffrey Pritchett, a friend of his, on the carrier of his motor bicycle.

They started off gaily from Royal Avenue, but crossing Westminster Bridge a car swerved unpleasantly near them. Instinctively Ronald drew in his long legs, his foot touched the wheel of the motor bicycle and the spokes cut through the leather of his shoe and sliced the back of his heel from his foot. He was carried into Westminster Hospital, where they sewed on his heel and sent him home in a taxi.

For two weeks Ronald was in bed, suffering really acute agony, after which his mother took him down to Eastbourne to convalesce before he returned to work.

There was no money for a summer holiday this year; the Cartlands stayed in London, but Ronald spent the Bank Holiday weekend with his great-uncle—Major Howard Cartland, the head of the family who lived at The Priory, King's Heath, Birmingham.

The Priory had belonged to the children's great-great-grandfather; a large grey stone house with a tessellated roof, it was surrounded by lawns, flower gardens, shrubberies, and adjoined by a farm. Once it had been in open country but in the passing years Birmingham had encroached nearer and nearer. Now what Uncle Howard and his maiden sister, Annie, who lived with him, called "the village" was the busy shopping centre of King's Heath, where trams rattled their way through miles of congested suburbs into the heart of Birmingham.

Out of sight of the house where the green paddocks sloped down to Hazelwell station there was a vista of unending rows of smoke blackened houses, increasing year after year to feed the great factories of King's Norton. Only the Priory and its occupants remained unchanged. One stepped off the noisy, tarmac road into a wide avenue of huge trees, past the lodge which had housed Abbey, the groom, for forty-five years, up the gravel drive which was bordered with daffodils in the spring, until one saw the clock on the ivy covered stables and above it, carved in stone, the Cartland crest.

Inside the house things had not been altered for over a century although gas lighting had been introduced as a concession to progress. "Uncle Howard" himself was a character. He had, in his cavalry days, commanded the B Squadron of the Worcestershire Yeomanry; he had been a keen polo player and a hard rider to hounds; and up to the age of eighty-eight he was not only to ride every morning of his life but to show his horses at the King's Heath Horse Show and invariably win a prize.

"Kingfisher," his most famous pony, was almost as well known in Birmingham as he was himself, for although he possessed cars he invariably drove to Birmingham in his smart sprightly dog-cart. Policemen knew him, grinning and saluting as he came trotting up Newhall Street towards his club, the harness polished and jingling, the groom in a uniform of the family colours and cockaded hat, sitting stiffly behind him. When traffic lights were introduced they disconcerted and infuriated Major Cartland, and in nine cases out of ten he would disregard them, to the horror and terror of any passenger he carried.

The Priory was crammed with trophies, for not only had Howard Cartland been a sportsman all his life, he had also been a great traveller. Polo and racing cups jostled Mexican daggers, heads of wild game which had fallen to his rifle, African humming-birds stuffed behind glass, statues dressed in the uniform of Japanese warriors, trumpets from Lhasa, and a tarpon of 98 lb., caught by him in the Gulf of Mexico.

In his study "Uncle Howard" had a store of Hawaiian, Japanese, Indian, and Burmese souvenirs—sandalwood boxes, ivory elephants, carved knives, novelties and necklaces of beads, and some of these were picked out and presented to his nephews and nieces every Christmas. He always wore loud check trousers, had an enormous sense of humour, never hesitated to call a man "damned fool" if he thought him one, and could offer his guests a glass of 1835 brandy.

His cellar was remarkable, for the wines had been put down by his father about the time Queen Victoria came to the throne, and added to every succeeding year. Unfortunately it had not been drunk quickly enough and when Ronald was living at the Priory ten years later he was to find forgotten pipes of ancient port too old to be palatable, champagne of the '80's, while only the brandy remained a nectar beyond price—the last bottle being finished in 1938.

The servants at the Priory were part of the atmosphere. Dixon, the butler, had been there before Barbara was born, and as a little boy Ronald had his meals in the nursery with Miss Gill who had nursed his great-grandfather in his old age and been Nanny to his grandfather, to great-Uncle Howard, and to the latter's brothers and sisters. To the children's delight she never referred to their father save as "Master Bertie."

Ronald loved the Priory—when Uncle Howard died he would be head of the family—but he had not yet begun to dream of living there, of being a citizen of the great city of Birmingham, and of playing a part in its affairs.

He returned to work. There were other week-ends spent at Dumbleton Hall with the Monsells, at his grandmother's in Worcestershire, and in September he took his brother Tony back to Charterhouse.

On September 14th Ronald attended a political meeting in Paddington. Mr. Patrick Hannon, M.P. for the Moseley Division of Birmingham, was the speaker. A week later he went to another meeting, this time of the 1912 Club, and heard Mr. Hannon again. A friend, Geoffrey Pritchett, accompanied him, and through him Ronald was to become a member of the Young Conservatives' Association. On October 1st he spoke for the first time at a study circle, and the following evening he went to a meeting at the Polytechnic Hall at Kingston.

From then onwards he went from meeting to meeting, he heard Sir John Power, M.P., at Fulham, Sir Henry Page Croft at Kingston, Mr. Hannon once again at Peckham Spa, and continually spoke himself at the Y.C.A. debates. He suddenly knew beyond any doubt that the aspiration which had been his all through his childhood was now a force which could not be denied. Whatever the consequences financially he must follow where his inclination led him.

He saw Mr. Patrick Hannon, an old friend of Uncle Howard, and had an interview with Sir Henry Page Croft. Both were sympathetic; they promised to try to help him. He had also met that month Colonel H. F. Williams, who was a director of the Conservative and Unionist Educational Institute—a Department of the Conservative Central Office. Ronald went to the Central Office for particulars of a speech he was to make at the Y.C.A. Study Circle. Colonel Williams, impressed by his ideas, hinted that he might be able to offer him something later on but could say nothing definite.

In December Ronald was told by Sir Henry Page Croft that a place would be found for him in the Empire Industries Association, and joyful, almost fearful of his good luck, he gave in his notice at Edward Boustead's. They were sorry to lose him. He was told that they had never had a public school boy who had worked so hard or done so much. Sir Harold Snagge promised Ronald that any time he needed employment they would make an opening for him in their business.

On December 24th he said good-bye to the office for good. In his diary he remarked "sensational leaving!" At the end of the same diary he wrote a short summary of the year.

"Looking back on 1926 it has been an extraordinary year for me. Now on 1st January, 1927, I feel nervous with the prospect. Shall I prosper—I wonder? I pray God I shall do well. I have read much in 1926, I have seen a number of good plays—*The Constant Nymph*, I think, taking the first place, tho' *Mozart* was probably the better play. In politics I have learnt a lot. Socially I have enjoyed myself. Politically too. In literature—no. I have tried to write and failed always tho' my MS. of a book of essays was actually finished.

"God grant 1927 be a good year and a happy one."

CHAPTER FIVE

1927-1929

"I am happy but never contented, and I never will be while there is suffering, injustice and inequality."

EXCITED, apprehensive, and full of enthusiasm, Ronald's diary for 1927 starting on his twentieth birthday tells its own story.

Monday	Jan. 3rd	E.I.A. Start career.
		North Lambeth, 6.0.
Tuesday	Jan. 4th	South Kensington, 2.0.
		Norwood, 3.0.
		Southwark, 4.0.
Wednesday	Jan. 5th	Fairly slack morning.
Thursday	Jan. 6th	Go B'ham morning Hannon.
		Stay at Priory.
		Meet a few people.
Friday	Jan. 7th	Wandered round, tried to make work.
		Feeling depressed.
		Meeting 8 p.m. Morland Club, Moseley Division.
Saturday	Jan. 8th	Bulsale Hill, 8.30.

Memoranda.—It seems to me Hannon doesn't know exactly what he wants me to do. I'm really fed up generally and shall accept Colonel Williams if he asks me.

He was staying at the Priory, King's Heath, with his great-uncle, and wrote his experiences fully to his mother.

"I came up here yesterday with Hannon by the 9 a.m. train. I left my luggage at Uncle Howard's club. Hannon took me to his—the Conservative—and 'made me known' to various odd men —nobody in particular. I lunched with him and another man who is enormously rich and a very big subscriber indeed to the E.I.A. After lunch I was introduced to the Conservative Agent for Birmingham and Hannon's Division Agent. But nothing was discussed at all. I just said how-do-you-do and that's all. Apparently,

Hannon says, there is heaps of time and I am to get really well known first. But I'm all for quickness. I can't go on staying at the Priory for ever and anyway slowness is always boring.

"Actually, I don't think I shall be in this job very long. Last Wednesday I met in the bus my old friend Colonel Williams of the Education Department of the Central Office. He told me he expected within two or three weeks he'd be able to offer me a job—that he was very keen to have me with him and the job he had in mind was his own personal secretary, acting, as it were, assistant-director of the department. Would I take it? I said yes—and I think I should be a fool to refuse if he *did* make the offer as there is a much bigger future in that.

"At the moment I expect to be here for ten to fourteen days and if I am dead at the end of it don't be surprised. I'm too hatefully depressed—but I think it's only lack of work at the moment."

The next day he wrote again from Empire House which housed all the political activity of Birmingham as far as the Unionist party was concerned.

"All the Birmingham agents work here in our building so it's easy to meet anyone I want. I spent from 3.15 to 6.15 here and did, I believe, a fair amount of work—have fixed a number of meetings up. I've no definite orders (as usual). Hannon, however, is coming up next Friday and will probably send for me. I'm just dying to get away into Colonel William's office, tho' more than anything else I feel the E.I.A. should hand itself over to the Central Office. If it did that I shouldn't leave them. But to be non-party is not going to help me much so I think if I can I must make the move. Anyway, I shall be glad to work again in London. And I certainly shan't talk any more about the joys of being a bachelor and living alone. No, thank you. My home and hearth and family to look after me."

His next letter continued the story—but nothing one learns by experience is ever lost. Ronald was to remember nine years later what he had considered then was the only way to raise money in Birmingham. If for nothing else those weeks of frustration were to prove of inestimable value; but at the time everything he did seemed fruitless and disheartening. His next letter, written on January 13th, was from the Union Club.

"Just a line to welcome you home. I wish I were there to greet you in person. God knows when I shall get away from this place, but I am writing to-morrow to Hannon to tell him that I do not think I can stay on at the Priory after next Wednesday. Actually, I do not think Uncle Howard would mind—but really *I* can't go on living here free like this. It makes me feel most uncomfortable.

"If only Colonel Williams would make me a definite offer now it would simplify matters so much. But I expect I'm fated to wait. I don't think I've done *so* badly here. But certainly not as well as either they or I hoped. What I didn't realise nor they—and they should have—is that there is *no* hope at all for subscriptions, etc., by my touting round. Manufacturers don't give like that. The only way, I believe, is to get thirty to fifty of them at a lunch, have a couple of good speeches, and then try to get £ s. d. by making one outbid the other.

Of course the Clubs and the press I've found easy. But unless they are prepared to spend money, to have a big public meeting or get someone to give a lunch as I say, I don't think myself they will raise any money in any other way. If you were a manufacturer and I came to see you, would you send a £5 note to London because *I* said an organisation of which you haven't ever heard was going to help you? Of course not. It would take me three to six months to get to know the right people properly —and I've given three weeks.

"I spent last night at the Clubs and altogether I've fixed up about twelve meetings, and both the *Birmingham Mail* and the *Midlander* have agreed to advertise us. But my total subscriptions *promised* are £2 2*s*. 0*d*. which won't cover *my* fees. I'm doing three or four more Clubs to-night and then I've done the lot."

His diary continued:

Monday	Jan. 17th	Went into Birmingham but had nothing to do.
Tuesday	Jan. 18th	Lunch at Club.
Wednesday	Jan. 19th	Golf in the morning. Grocers' Exhibition Bingley Hall afternoon.
Thursday	Jan. 20th	Go into B'ham though there is nothing to do.
Friday	Jan. 21st	Heavy snow. Hannon 6.15 Conservative Club. Go London 8.0.

Memorandum.—Fog. Terribly depressed at news of another three to four weeks in B'ham. Marvellous week-end.

It could not continue. Even as a schoolboy Ronald had loathed inaction, hated not to be busily employed. He didn't know what to do with his idle hours. Grateful as he was for the efforts Sir Henry Page Croft and Mr. Hannon had made for him, the idea of doing nothing for an indefinite period was abhorrent. But Colonel Williams had not forgotten him and on March 21st gave Ronald the definite news that he would be employed in the Education Department of the Conservative Central Office.

There were thanks, letters of apology and gratitude, once again sympathy and understanding from Sir Henry Page Croft and Mr. Hannon, then on April 4th, with a light heart and bursting with enthusiasm, Ronald entered the dingy portals of Palace Chambers, Westminster, which were to know him for eight years.

There was much to do, organisation, ability, and hard work were all required of him, and he was completely absorbed and completely happy. Even on Saturday afternoon he was not always free—there were reports to be finished for the printers, letters, pamphlets or instructions which could not wait until Monday; Ronald welcomed it all with open arms. At last he was working at what really interested him, and working "all out."

On April 23rd, 1927, his sister Barbara was married to Alexander McCorquodale at St. Margaret's, Westminster, and the reception was held at Commander and Mrs. Eyres Monsell's house in Belgrave Square.

The summer of 1927 passed in routine fashion, the office absorbing all his thoughts and interests although he saw a good deal of the Monsells who took him to many parties and theatres. Unfortunately, his leg was giving him great pain—the wound had become inflamed and was discharging. By July the doctors were of the opinion that a small piece of bone must be removed and Ronald went into Sir Douglas Shield's Nursing Home at 17 Park Lane, and was operated on. He was in bed for nearly five weeks, then went to Dumbleton Hall to rest. Luckily it was holiday time at the office and he was able to return comparatively fit to work on September 5th.

Faced with the expenses of the operation, Mary Cartland decided to give up the house in Royal Avenue, which was really too big for their requirements now that Barbara was married, and she also thought that it might be to Ronald's advantage to have complete a small legacy from the estate of his grandfather, James Cartland. Accordingly she found for him a tiny bachelor flat at 2 Pont Street, and she planned, while Tony was at school, to store her furniture and live at her Club while in London or visit friends.

Ronald was rather thrilled at being on his own. He now had a great many friends and he could, if he wished, lunch and dine out practically every day of his life. He did not, however, have too much time for social gaieties. In February, 1928, he told his mother how busy he was, starting the letter with a reference to the Budget introduced by Mr. Neville Chamberlain.

"Thursday I dined with H.F.W.[1] and we came back here afterwards—mainly discussing work because Neville's axe had fallen that afternoon. I've never been so busy as I am at the office these last few days. I've not got away till 7 and worked without a stop from 9.45 to then. I am delighted. I find the finance takes a bit of looking after. I couldn't have done it if it hadn't been for Edward Boustead & Co."

A crisis arose in the office in the next month owing to lack of funds. Ronald's letter to his mother on February 6th started:

"I have been bad about writing to you lately, but since I joined Williams I've never been so busy. Rarely was anything (except a child) brought into the world more hardly and with more pain (and here I believe the child is less painful, being physical) than our present scheme.

"First, there was Neville[2] supporting us and making us wait while he got the P.M. Four months wasted waiting for Baldwin. Then Neville throws us over. Buchan,[3] this week, writes saying 'Throw in the sponge. I can't get any money. Sack the staff, get rid of the offices, and creep back to the Central Office—beaten—with our tails between our legs.' What a Chairman! I ask you? The result—we've spent a week intriguing—playing the Central Office off against Buchan so that we can do what we want. H.F.W. has been really wonderful—he is always at his best when we are badly up against it. His diplomacy has been superb—his schemes never better, and I think (though I'm touching wood all the time) that the worst is almost over. H.F.W. has now taken into his own hands the raising of funds and I think should be successful.
independence, especially as he had inherited on his coming of age

[1] H.F.W. was Ronald's chief—Colonel Williams.
[2] Rt. Hon. Neville Chamberlain.
[3] John Buchan, M.P., Chairman of the Executive Committee.

"Finally, and this the hardest blow of all, the Liberals brought out their Industrial Report on Friday—one of their suggestions is for a General Staff of Economic Experts—a thinking machine. Our idea! But not carried as far as we suggested as theirs does not go beyond the question of finance. However, we are hoping we may be able to use this as a weapon to induce our party to give us its blessing. I hope Neville will feel a fool. But Cabinet Ministers never read anything that they should so I don't expect he'll see. They have always said H.F.W. has been up in the air. To be vindicated by Keynes, Simon, Lloyd George, etc., is rather a victory!

"You can now imagine what my life has been up here this last week; scheming, planning, typing, writing, besides all the ordinary office routine which must go on. Anyway it has been very exciting. Pray Heaven we pull through. I have read nothing. I'm glad 'Wilson' intrigued you. But what an insight into politicians! I'm in the dirtiest game in the world—but I don't regret it."

A month later the crisis was passing. Ronald wrote:

"At the office we've not had a spare moment—working every night. Things here are not too bad and H.F.W.'s final diplomacy has been consummate and ended in a complete victory—Davidson[1] writing to Buchan and saying he will give the Institute £12,000 a year if we can collect on our own an additional £15,000 to £20,000. With D.'s letter this should be fairly easy, because rich men will see that we are not likely to go smash—and by supporting us they will not be wasting money."

During this year Ronald made a close friend whom he met in the Office. This was Lord Knebworth, who was working in the same Department. Antony was a gay, lovable person, idealistic but not entirely convinced that politics were the right medium through which he could work. Ronald and he argued, disagreed and agreed with each other—both alike in having an inexhaustible fund of vitality, and an unquestionable sense of adventure. Life was to both of them something to be lived fully and completely. Barbara gave a party that spring at her house in Mayfair. Antony and Ronald dined together and went on to it together to be the gayest, gladdest people there.

Another young man came into Ronald's life that year. Their friendship was not to be a close one until later on, but they met at a week-end party at Dumbleton Hall. This was J. P. L. Thomas.

[1] The Rt. Hon. J. C. C. Davidson, C.H., C.B., M.P., Vice-President

Good-looking, charming, and intensely loyal, "Jim" was to mean a great deal to Ronald in the future.

That June Ronald went with Colonel Williams to inspect Ashridge and stayed three nights. Through a generous legacy this property had been purchased by the Conservative Party and was to be known as the Bonar Law College. This acquisition was to supercede the Education Department of the Central Office. In July, however, the personnel of the Department heard only rumours of what was to happen but were told nothing definite. That month Ronald noted in his diary:

"The criticism in the Office regarding Ashridge developed all this week and made life very difficult."

A week later the entry reads: "In the office we are at a standstill."

Holidays began and Mary Cartland took a charming house in Worcestershire for the first three weeks; then in the middle of August Ronald and Tony went to the Orkney Islands, where Barbara and her husband had a shoot. There was plenty of sport and Ronald enjoyed himself enormously. He proved himself quite a good shot, not only at grouse but at the more wily rock pigeon. There was bathing in Scapa Flow and trips to the various islands in a motor-boat.

He returned to the office which was still wondering apprehensively about its future, but not until November was the announcement to be made that the Education Department would close down in six months.

During the summer Ronald had made a friendship which was to have far-reaching effects in the years to come. Derek Studley-Herbert introduced him to Patsy Hastings, the second daughter of the famous K.C. Through her Ronald was to meet Sir Patrick and Lady Hastings, Barbara, Nicky, and Pip, and to fall in love with the whole family. Unconventional, brilliant, vivacious and entirely original, they fascinated him and he had for Sir Patrick a young, eager hero-worship. Another friend made that year was the Countess Portarlington, whom he met at a luncheon party given by Barbara. She was to prove kindness itself, while her son, Viscount Carlow, was later to be one of Ronald's greatest friends.

In December, however, all other interests were swept aside by the crushing news that the Education Department was to close on January 1st, and that Ronald's services would no longer be required. Once again there was the desperate task of trying to find a job—and a job in politics. Ronald tried the Primrose League, but there was no opening for him. In the past year he had found time to write a novel. It was sent to an agent but proved too Disraelian in style, and a political theme was not at that moment particularly saleable.

In the previous November before the office closed down Antony Knebworth had accepted an invitation to contest the Borough of Shoreditch. It was a Labour stronghold and he had no hope of winning the seat, but it was considered all good experience. Ronald was delighted that his friend should have a chance to prove himself, but he longed and ached for the same opportunity. He talked to Antony of trying to get nominated as a candidate, of risking everything he possessed or might possess in one desperate attempt to get into Parliament. But even while he talked he knew it was impossible—at this Election he could only be a spectator.

The first four months of the year Antony visited his constituency daily and Ronald frequently accompanied him. He wrote to his mother on February 5th, saying:

"I continue to starve. Honestly, at last even my optimism is beginning to fade I have had no word from the Central Office and it is a week now since I saw them. I don't know what to do. Except that my life has been lately so full I should have become desperate. I don't think I can face the city again. Journalism, though I'll own I've not yet tried my hand at it, seems a closed way, and as for politics——!

"Last Wednesday I went to Shoreditch to this Club and I go there again to-morrow. I hope I shall get on all right. They're a rough crowd, of course—most of them, I'm told, in private life are burglars—but they all strike me as very nice. Next Tuesday I am addressing 20 to 30 Conservatives at the London School of Economics on 'A Division of Political Thought.' I am not quite certain what that means but I have no doubt I shall be able to convince my audience of my overwhelming brilliance!"

Ronald was shocked beyond words at the conditions he found in Shoreditch. A flaming desire was born within him to improve the lot of the working people. His hatred of injustice flared up into a blaze of anger. He knew then that he would never rest until he could bring hope and faith to the people who most needed it. He believed that for all men there must be security for their old age and freedom while they were young from the terror of unemployment.

Some years later someone accused him of being discontented.

"Of course I am," Ronald replied, "and I thank God for my 'divine discontent.' I am happy but never contented and I never will be while there is suffering, injustice, and inequality. The more one knows of these things the more discontented they should make one. In fact the most discontented man in this country *should* be the Prime Minister."

In the meantime nothing was being left undone that could be done to get him a job. Ronald's idea now was to get into the Conservative Central Office itself, and Lady Portarlington spoke to Lord Stanley, Deputy Chairman of the Conservative Party, on his behalf and Ronald saw Commander Eyres Monsell and asked his help. The Commander promised to do what he could and Ronald, greatly cheered after seeing him in the House of Commons, wrote in his diary—"I think that at last something may happen—B.E.M. was so nice."

The very next day Sir Patrick Gower, Chief Publicity Officer, sent for Ronald and a week later he was offered a job in the Library of the Central Office. Pleased beyond all words, Ronald started work on March 11th, 1929. In the following months he spent much of his spare time in Shoreditch helping Antony, particularly with the Clubs and the Junior Imperial League.

On the evening of the General Election, May 30th, 1929, he watched the results come through at the Carlton Club—results which showed Mr. Thurtle, the Labour Candidate, returned for Shoreditch, Antony at the bottom of the poll, and a heavy Conservative defeat over the whole country. Two days later Antony wrote to him.

"KNEBWORTH HOUSE,
KNEBWORTH.
June 2, 1929.

"DEAR C.,

"Here is a fine PS. to your great political novel. I can give you a lot of 'copy' if you want it. . . .

"I have learnt more about the Labour party and about the working of the Labour party than I ever dreamed of, and also of the Conservative party. I am clinched for ever now in my fidelity to the latter. I have also learnt that none of this knowledge is of any avail if you want to guess the outcome of an election.

"Nothing will ever get right in this country until there has been a strong Labour government, and then it will probably take twelve years as in Queensland. I have seen first-hand the thing we are fighting and haven't been able to see it even though I did.

"I was more cheered and better received everywhere in Shoreditch even than Thurtle. But the Xs were not put against my name. It is forces without any doubt that win or lose elections and not people. Forces can be calculated in offices, whereas on the spot people eclipse them. At the same time, and this is what offices don't know, people create forces though they take twenty, thirty, fifty years to do so.

"It may amuse you that one of our Imps Committee was working outside the polling-booth for the Liberals!

"And thank you, by the way, for your telegram.

"The only thing in which I have done right for the past two years was in advising you not to risk all and stand at this election. No one had a chance, because we were fighting not Ramsay but John Burns, not Ll. G. but Laissez faire, not for Baldwin but for Ld. Liverpool!

"Yes, and thank you for helping with the Imps such a lot,

"K."

The summer passed, Ronald was happy in his work. Barbara took a house in the Surrey hills and Ronald spent several week-ends there and several with the Hastings in the New Forest. After one of these visits to the latter when he bathed, rode, played tennis, golf, and laughed a great deal, he wrote in his diary: "Perfect weather the whole time—the best week-end I've ever spent in my life."

Friends, congenial work, good health, and a lot to do—on the surface everything was perfect; but actually Ronald was desperately worried. He was living beyond his income; the rent of his flat ate up his small salary, getting about in London was expensive, even delightful week-ends cost money in fares and tips. As usual he turned to his mother. Together they agreed that he must give up his flat and she would take a house near London from which he could travel daily to work.

Also, until his most pressing debts were paid off, Ronald decided to hand over his entire monthly salary to his mother, letting her give him an allowance of the smallest sum possible for petty expenses. Mary Cartland found a quite attractive house at Newnham, near Basingstoke, for sale. She bought it very cheaply and spent a little money on alteration.

In the September Barbara produced a daughter. Ronald was now an uncle and Major Cartland a great-great-uncle.

CHAPTER SIX

1930-1932

"High-souled ideas of saving the nation do not give one bread and butter."

1930 found Ronald working hard, his mother gradually paying off his bills and putting his affairs in order. Ronald was quite hopeless where money was concerned, not because he was consciously a spendthrift but because money bored him and he hated to have to think about it. His one extravagance was books—he could not resist them. He would go without food to buy them and, like all real collectors, he had to possess the volume he wanted to read.

He belonged to the London Library, but when a book was published which interested him he was quite unable to withstand the temptation to buy it in its first edition. He bought, too, every book written by or about Disraeli, and like so many young, ambitious, would-be politicians, the great Lord Beaconsfield was not only a hero, he was a model on which life could be fashioned, built and sustained. By 1939 Ronald was to own over 2000 books—mostly on political and spiritual subjects.

A year or so later his mother gave him a book plate—the Cartland coat of arms engraved with his name. Ronald could never open a book without reading the family motto—Loyal Devoir. This had been handed down to him from the eleventh century, yet it was becoming essentially personal. Loyalty to his duty as he saw it, was a foundation stone on which he was gradually building his philosophy of life.

In the meantime, financially, he was gradually getting straight, although it seemed to him to take a long time. It did him good, too, to be at home, getting regular meals and sleeping in the fresh air. When he wanted to be in London for some particular evening there was always a bed for him at Carlow's home in Chesham Place. From there he wrote to his mother in June.

"Do please know I *am* grateful to you—terribly grateful. I loathe not being able to pay you anything—and I hate living on you. But I do love living with you, and I've never regretted coming back to you—if ever you have. Really this last year at Newnham has been the saving of me. I am sure I'm much better in every way than I was—thanks to you.

"Money is foul. I'm so depressed at my beastly bills—I feel I shall never get straight. I know I ought to economise in every way—and I don't. I really will try."

In another letter he wrote:

"I'm everything in the world despicable so far as finance is concerned. But I know I'll never get straight or keep straight unless you simply look after me like a child and give me 3d. bits from your purse. I think I'm the worst son in the world. But I am devoted—at least that and not merely because you're the most spoiling and best mother in the world."

In the previous year, 1929, he had made yet another friend who was to play intellectually an important part in his life. He went to the Opera with Carlow to see *Parsifal* and met there for the second time Rom Landau, the clever young Polish author who was already well known in the literary world on the Continent and who was to become famous in England with the publication of his book, *God is My Adventure*. Ronald had met him the previous year at a dinner, and had written to his mother:

"There was one other man there—a Pole, Rom Landau. He lives in London and earns a living by writing for continental newspapers on Art, Literature, and Politics. He is about 29, clever and interesting because he has travelled a lot and talks well. We dined at Chez Taghoni and went to *The Crooked Billet*, which is, I think, the worst play I have ever seen. Then we went to the Nightlight—then Victors—and so home. Fancy me in a night-club, but they were, of course, the ultra-respectable ones. Mr. Landau said I am one of the few young Englishmen he has met whom he considers really interesting—wants to meet again, and who appears to have thought about things."

With this second meeting their friendship developed rapidly. The two young men found an association of ideas and a unity of interests which influenced them both in their separate spheres. Rom Landau helped Ronald to clarify his views on comparative religion and on Germany. Ronald assisted Rom Landau by correcting his biography of Paderewski and later was his mentor and teacher in public speaking.

In August, 1930, while staying in the Orkney Isles, Ronald

corrected Barbara's fourth novel. In the next ten years he was to correct sixteen novels for his sister.

In the autumn Mary Cartland sold her house at Newnham, making a good profit on what she had paid for it. She wanted to return to Worcestershire, the county she knew and loved. It took her some time to find a house, but finally she found the most beautiful little sixteenth century black and white building, called Littlewood House, at Poolbrook, a tiny village on the outskirts of Malvern. It had a nice garden and was surrounded by orchards and grazing fields, and as a background there was the bare, rounded beauty of the Malvern Hills.

The house was rumoured to possess a ghost, but Mary Cartland had the house blessed before living in it and after that the ghost rested peacefully Certainly no one saw or heard it and the atmosphere of the house was a particularly happy and peaceful one.

Once again the dear, familiar furniture was arranged in new surroundings. The collection of Toby jugs which had stood in Bertram Cartland's smoking-room at Amerie Court now decorated shelves filled with his books. The flowered linen curtains which had been altered to fit five different drawing-rooms looked as fresh and attractive as they had thirty years before at Peopleton. The grandfather clock stood in yet another dining-room, only the silver had disappeared, having been sold at different times to pay school fees or for the necessities of life.

Mary Cartland made a new house charming but, what was more important, she made it a home. For as far as the children were concerned they never grew too old or too busy to want "to come home." If Barbara had domestic difficulties, was unhappy or perplexed, she rushed to her mother; Ronald said openly he could do nothing without her; and Tony, just about to leave school and enter the Army, shared all his interests, ambitions, and heartaches with the person he, too, loved best in the world.

Ronald stayed in London for some months, and went to his mother for week-ends. Barbara had moved to 37 Green Street, and having a latchkey of his sister's house, he would very frequently drop in late at night, walk up to her bedroom, and sit talking to her until the early hours of the morning. All the Cartlands liked talking after they had gone to bed; Mary Cartland was generally in her children's bedrooms until after midnight when they stayed with her, for every time she made an effort to leave they would cry, "Don't go—don't go," and start another subject.

These talks, they declared, were essential to them—they clarified their thoughts, their creeds, their ambitions, and so much of their lives was decided and planned this way. Most mothers flatter themselves that their children tell them everything, but for Mary Cartland this was literally true. Whatever they confided or confessed she was never shocked, never horrified, only anxious to understand their motives and guide them by her sympathy and faith.

In the autumn of 1931 there was to be another General Election. Ronald wrote to his mother from a tiny flat he had taken near Portman Square.

"This week-end I am spending here in London, my first week-end for over two years that I haven't been away, but I'm thinking there'll be a good many more of them before this month is finished. The election is, I understand, quite definite. Anyway, our rush has begun in earnest. I left the office to-night at 7.30, yesterday at 7, Wednesday 7.15, Tuesday at 7, and Monday 7.15. Next week 8 will take the place of 7 and once the Election comes we'll be well into the 9's and 10's. I hear there is to be no increase whatsoever in staff for the election which, in a way, I am very pleased about—temporary workers usually take all the pay and most of the time off—but it means, of course, an extra burden on our shoulders and as most of the work in the Department is already done by Willis and me God knows how we shall feel on Polling Day! Still, if and when it comes, a bonus for all my work will be very welcome. It is very much needed.

"No news. The mobs up here last week were very bad—much worse than the papers said—5000 people in Parliament Square one night—nearly 10,000 in Bond Street and Oxford Street the next day. The police had to use their batons pretty freely. It is the start of the Revolution which I have predicted for over a year, usually only to be laughed at. If we don't get back at the Election England is finished and we can all pack up and go to the Dominions. And if we do I feel myself unless a miracle happens it is only postponing the evil day.

"The office is optimistic about the election results. I am not. I lunched with Jim Thomas on Thursday and Ted de Clifford on Wednesday and with Barbara on Monday. She had Edward Hulton and Bob Holland there. I've dined here every night as I've felt too tired really to go out and I've been hard at work on our play which we have finished. I am now polishing it. I am very pleased with it. This last act has eventually worked out very well—all quite witty though not much action.

"There is no truth in the rumour that Pat Hastings is to fight MacDonald at Seaham. He was asked, but refused. I've talked to him on the telephone but not seen him. I may dine with them on Sunday night."

Jim Thomas stood at this Election for Hereford. He had unsuccessfully contested the Llanelly Division of Carmarthenshire, in the Conservative landslide the previous year, but this time he won his seat. Ronald wrote to his mother and asked her to help Jim on Election Day in her car.

For August, Barbara, who had planned to go to Scotland, had asked her mother to stay at Hayling Island where she had taken a house for her two-year-old daughter, Raine. Mary Cartland agreed, thinking it would also be nice for Ronald and Tony to have a seaside holiday. At the last moment Barbara's husband decided not to open the house in the Orkneys and Barbara came to Hayling Island as well. They had a jolly family party, only damped for Mary Cartland by the knowledge that Barbara was desperately unhappy in her married life.

Immediately after the summer things came to a crisis, and Ronald moved into 37 Green Street, to be with his sister. Realising what she was up against, he went to see Sir Patrick Hastings, who agreed to take her case. Barbara filed her petition for divorce and Mr. Norman Birkett was briefed against her. For a year a bitter legal action was fought by solicitors, the costs mounting higher and higher. Ronald threw himself heart and soul into working for his sister's interests. They had always been close friends, but now they entered upon a new and more united relationship.

Barbara won her case but unfortunately the huge solicitors' fees and the economic slump of 1931 were to swallow up the whole of Alexander McCorquodale's personal capital. When everything was cleared up she was left with only a few hundreds a year and a delicate child requiring constant care. She had moved in the spring of 1932 to a maisonette at 24 Half Moon Street which her mother had found for her, and Ronald had also moved into one bed-sitting-room in the basement of Clock House, 8 Chelsea Embankment. He had been worried by money all through the year. In a letter to his mother at the beginning of March he asked:

"What is going to happen to me? I've been wading through my bills. Everything much too strictly in order. I've got £30 worth of pressing bills like the telephone, etc., and total assets nil.

"X, anyway, has definitely offered me a job on his new paper, which I have accepted. So in a few months' time I may be making a bit more money. A little busier in the office but still too slack for my liking. I wish now I had gone to Singapore! High-souled ideas of saving the nation don't give one bread and butter, while very soon the want of it drives one to bitterness."

In another letter he asked:

"Darling, what am I going to do about my rent? I must pay £35 somehow—in fact I shall have to draw a cheque for that to-morrow. Then there's another £10 for three pressing creditors. I am really feeling at the end of everything. Will you once more—and I swear for the last time—come to my aid?—then for God's sake take over my finances and manage them. I'm so much in Queer Street that really sooner than I know I shall be in Carey Street. Please, dear, do forgive me once again and see what you can do. I am the most hopeless person in the world so far as £ s. d. is concerned—a system of pocket money is the only way I shall ever get along. What a foul letter when you're worried yourself—I'm a cad and you're so good to me."

His mother asked him for particulars, and in his next letter he told her:

"I am writing out my bills for you in plain simple form and will send you a list to-morrow or Thursday. It is good of you to say you'll pay £30 of them. I'm sure I'm not worth it! But I hope next week-end to have good news for you. I have been feeling most terribly ill—I don't know what is wrong with me—but so unsettled and nervy and quite unable to concentrate, which is not at all satisfactory. Yesterday afternoon I went to St. Paul's and for a long walk round—then to the British Museum. Tony came up to-day and we lunched with Barbara."

Once again Mary Cartland agreed to put her son's affairs in order, to divide his salary among his creditors until they were paid off, keep a strict record of expenditure, and do her best to prevent her son from exceeding the minute amount of "petty cash" he might expend on himself.

After writing several pages of thanks for taking his troubles on to her shoulders again, Ronald said:

"I don't know how to thank you, darling. If only our play could be taken or someone die and leave me money, with what joy should I give you £300. I will one day, darling—I do promise you that—but I hope soon for your sake as well as mine.

"No news as I told you. I did enjoy the week-end. I still can't get over all that you've done to the house. It's unbelievable. And I'm thrilled by it all. I'm longing for the spring and summer. I shall do a lot of gardening I *warn* you.

"I shall be down on Friday if that suits you. Littlewood makes me more and more in love with it every time I see it. All my love, darling—I can't thank you but you are always in my thoughts."

CHAPTER SEVEN

1932

"None of it has been spent on riotous living."

RONALD had a great affection for his brother Tony although they had few tastes in common and the six years' difference in their age was, at their particular time of life, a wide gulf. Tony was so many things that Ronald was not—contented, easy-going, tolerant and social. He had no desire to reorganize either the world or his school. He was popular both with his contemporaries and the masters, but he was not particularly outstanding and his mental development was slower than Ronald's had been.

Ten years later he was to be ambitious within the limits of an Army career; in the meantime he took life as it came, with sunny good-humour and a charm of manner which made him friends wherever he went.

In May, 1932, Ronald went down to Charterhouse to take him out. They spent the day among the beauties of Hindhead, hours of happy companionship only disrupted by that invariable and to most people annoying practice among English hotel-keepers of using the scenic effects of nature to their own advantage. Three days later Ronald wrote to his mother.

"I did really enjoy myself with Tony. I went down by train to Farnham, he came on by bus, and we walked to Frensham where we sat in the sun by the water and ate the lunch I had brought down. I bought two of those snack lunch boxes from Paddington and we bought *6d.* ices from a Walls bicycle man! Then, my dear, we walked all the way to Hindhead where we had a delicious tea for 2/6. And so home—partly by bus—to Farnham. We found dinner was 6/- each at the Bush and we had to eat there as there's nowhere else, and we'd left the box there in which I'd brought down the eight volumes of my Encyclopedia that Tony wants to see for his exam. We made a hell of a row and eventually had steaks and potatoes and ices—4/- each. They charged Tony *6d.* for a roll and butter! I said I thought everything in the hotel was charming but dinner was preposterously expensive. 'We've a very good French cook,' they said, to which I replied that I didn't come to the English countryside for French cooking!

"However, the whole day all told cost us 10/- each which was cheaper than my coming to you. And I had to get the Encyclopedias to Tony somehow and I believe it would have cost nearly that to have sent them on their own. It was a glorious day—so hot. Tony was in marvellous form; myself very happy and we'd a lovely time altogether. Got back about 11 p.m."

This walk from Farnham to Hindhead via Frensham Ponds was about 8¾ miles. Ronald loved walking—to him it was the best "sport," for it was the only one in which one could use both body and brain. If he was with a companion the exercise he was taking did not distract his attention. If he was alone he could exercise and do what he called "mental stocktaking."

But he also enjoyed sightseeing and walking took too long, although for Whitsun the previous year he and Barbara had done a three days' walking tour in Yorkshire. When the summer holidays began Ronald, anxious to see the country round Stonehenge, persuaded Tony to join him on a bicycling tour. Tony hired a bicycle locally and they set off on August 8th and returned to Littlewood four days later. As was to be expected, the ride was not without incident, but nothing and nobody could stop Ronald once he had made up his mind to a thing, and he saw Stonehenge despite the opposition put up by Tony's bicycle. Incidentally to be disappointed at his journey's end, even as Barbara was when he took her there a year later. From Wilton he wrote to his mother.

"We got on splendidly as far as the Canning Arms—so much so that we should have got to Gloucester by a quarter to nine. At the Canning Arms there was a noise like a pistol shot and Tony's left pedal broke. But not just the pedal. The whole caboodle—the shaft and all shot away from the frame. So there we were. However, at that moment up came a man who said there was no shop before Gloucester, and then Willcox in Westgate Street was the one to go to.

Tony got on and I pulled him along by his arm the whole way to Gloucester. Of course he had to walk the hills, but anyway we pegged on—fortunately it's fairly level or down hill and we reached Gloucester at 9 a.m. Not bad—up to time after all. Willcox said the job meant a new spindle—it had been rotten for some time obviously—and would take at least 1½ to 2 hours. Then they had no bicycles to lend. But eventually the good woman relented and produced a bike which brakes on the pedal but otherwise excellent. And off Tony rode on it. We left the other there. But this new one means 5/- a week!

"An excellent breakfast at the station and then by train to Swindon. As we were getting out of the town, walking up hill, along comes Cynthia Radcliffe in a car—stops and we converse for some time. She seemed to think us both mad! We ran into Devizes dead on time 1.15 for lunch, where we sent you a P.C. and then on to Stonehenge, which was my intention. I was struck by its smallness. We had an excellent tea there and then came on here.

"The weather was warm but no sun—cloudy all day till Stonehenge—at which and since it was perfect and coming into here about six o'clock quite beautiful. The country was lovely and we were both struck by the charming way everybody treated us. We are tired but not unduly so, and both feel we could have done another twenty miles—which, after 62, isn't bad. Tony is keeping up well tho' at times he lagged a bit! No disagreeableness. All very rosy and affectionate. The road's excellent and very little traffic.

"And now goodnight to you, my dear—off to-morrow at 9."

That summer money had had to be considered at every turn, the expenditure of every penny calculated. In the same letter in which Ronald had written a description of his day with Tony at Hindhead he had told his mother that he was completely penniless, dependent for luncheon on a cake made by her maid, and unable to afford a taxi to Admiralty House where he had been asked to dine by Lady Monsell's eldest daughter Diana. Sir Bolton was now First Lord of the Admiralty.

"Will you send me 10/-?" Ronald asked. "This seems like a continual drain on you. But I'll give you a full account. None of it has been spent on riotous living! At the moment I have 1/9. Thank goodness for Steer's cake. It's my regular lunch from now on; because I can't afford anything. I must keep something for buses. I dine to-night at Admiralty House with Diana and a party. Hope to manage to get there by bus. This terror of rain and the necessary taxi is appalling."

Finances were, however, to improve a little by the autumn. Ronald was commissioned to write weekly for a political newspaper which had just started. He was paid three guineas for each article, which were published anonymously. Unfortunately the paper had a short life.

Barbara was also seeking work and had been lucky enough to

have a lot of articles commissioned on various papers. The play she and Ronald had written together in 1931 had not been accepted, although they still had hopes for it. They had started another. The plot was planned in September when Barbara, on her doctor's advice, spent several weeks at Brides-les-Bains. Much of her trip was paid for by friends and she had saved enough for Ronald to come out and join her for a short holiday. They did everything in the cheapest way and enjoyed themselves enormously. This was the first of their annual trips abroad.

Ronald's letters from France show, as do all that he wrote, his extraordinary attention to detail. He set down his travels as meticulously as he made notes in his office or planned the organization of a campaign. He had an eventful journey to Brides-les-Bains, his description of it to his mother pictures vividly not only his gift for making friends but also his capacity for making the very best out of every situation, however unexpected.

"HOTEL DES THERMES,
BRIDES-LES-BAINS.
August 7th, 1932.

"DEAR DARLING,

"My journey started off well—a perfect trip to Southampton and to find on board a lovely cabin engaged for my sole use. I was in bed by 11.30 and slept peacefully like a lamb the whole way across—to awake to find we had had a very rough crossing indeed. Everyone very ill bar me!—and worse, to find we were two hours late. We'd left Southampton half an hour late and ran into bad winds, etc. So instead of getting to Havre at 6.30 we arrived at 8. Got through the Customs O.K. and found my seat engaged on the Paris train, but alas! it didn't leave until 9.30, arriving Paris 12.16 so I knew that meant the day there as the connection to here left 11.18 and there was no other day train. I got to Paris all right and across to the Gare de Lyons in a taxi. It was a lovely day—so hot—and I enjoyed the drive—much interested but rather depressed with the thought of spending eight hours alone in a city I don't know.

"As luck would have it I'd spoken on the boat to a man and his wife called Blunt who were going to Chamonix—the same train as I and therefore they were stranded too. At the Gare de Lyons they couldn't get a porter. I had one so they shared mine. From there we consulted trains to find mine left at 9.20, theirs at 9.53 and they then asked me to lunch with them. He about 28, she 25, both *so* charming and intelligent.

"We lunched at a little estaminet near the station, then after lunch wandered down all by the river to Notre Dame, which I was rather disappointed with, very poor chapels I thought. After tea on the boulevard we sat for an hour or so in the Luxembourg Gardens to go to dinner to a funny little place he knew of near-by—having spent some time in Paris when he was a boy. The weather was perfect and I was quite entranced, but of course my two good friends made all the difference to my enjoyment as you can guess.

"I caught the 9.20, sitting up in a second class the whole way here. A couchette, you see, was 185 francs extra—much too much. I folded a rug for a pillow and there was only a man and a woman in the carriage with me—so we were very comfortable and all slept. In a way I was rather glad in the end to come as I did as we ran into the Savoy district by day, and that is perfectly lovely—it would have been dark if I'd come as I originally meant to.

"I can't begin to describe to you how beautiful Brides is. Hills on all sides of you like Malvern, but masses of trees and in the distance those enormous mountains covered with snow. Blazing sunshine and masses of flowers, rushing water all through the village. It is very small—one little street. We've lovely rooms and I am sitting on the balcony now in hot sun after lunch, B. lying down on her bed reading. It is so hot I've to wear glasses. The views are marvellous. I'm not certain it'd agree with you as the air is very strong and I sleep all the time. Food excellent. People are beginning to go. September is supposed to be cold. Lord knows what it's like when it's hot.

"Yesterday we went in a char-a-banc on a Mountain Tour. B. and I terrified and vow never again. You've never seen such roads !—all at 90 miles an hour—we screamed with terror the whole way. . . . I am having such a lovely time. It's all so wonderfully quiet and peaceful and the weather's so marvellous.

"You have all my love and thoughts,

"RONALD."

He was always ready to learn even from the most unlikely people. A week later he wrote:

"Our days continue as I pictured to you in my last letter. Very very lazy mornings—and we spend the afternoons energetically. Thursday we walked up to a village called Les Allues about 4½ miles from here right up the hills. Such glorious views. B. really did the journey well—but we were both tired out in the evening.

The air is so terrifically strong that after 9 miles walking—one way all up hill—one feels good for nothing.

"Yesterday we walked into Moutiers—where the railway station for Brides is, about 3 miles. An attractive little place. On the 12th there is a big cattle fair there and already there were many hundreds of cows brought down from the hills and they are continuing to come down still. Unfortunately the cows all wear bells round their necks and as they pass fairly near to the hotel we were all awakened this morning at 4 a.m. to the sound of a carillon that had Westminster Abbey and St. Paul's beaten to a frazzle! B. filled her ears with cotton wool and slept again. I suffered.

"Last night we dined with B.'s doctor and his wife. Both very charming and talk fluent English. They gave us an excellent dinner in the French style. We started at 8 but didn't say good-night till 11. So you can imagine we enjoyed ourselves. He talked politics to me and I got to know perhaps a little of the French view of Germany —full of war talk! and distrust of Germany's intentions."

As they walked over the hills Ronald talked to Barbara incessantly of politics. He believed that a universal code of international behaviour as set forth in the Covenant of the League of Nations was the only formula for lasting peace, but our days of being "policeman of the world" were over—the question was could we succeed as peacemaker? To Conservatives the first concern must always be the preservation of the British race.

Once Barbara asked him to explain the difference he found in the three policies from which an elector might determine which party he would support.

"Socialism," Ronald replied, "would destroy the individual for the State; Liberalism would destroy the State for the individual; Conservatism stands for a media via; for the continual growth of the individual, which must inevitably lead to a growth of the State. The prestige and prosperity of the one is bound up in the prestige and prosperity of the other."

CHAPTER EIGHT

1933

"We watched all sorts and conditions of people."

RONALD ended December, 1932, with the note in his Diary—"Not feeling too well."

He hated illness and had his own way of curing it. On January 2nd, 1933, he wrote to his mother:

"On Friday night I definitely felt unwell and on Saturday morning rather worse. However I went to the office and determined afterwards to effect my infallible cure of 'walking it off.' I left the office at 12.30 and after a snack at Waterloo Station I set off over Blackfriars Bridge to St. Bartholomew the Great. I had, of course, been there before but I had forgotten how lovely it was. Thence into Ludgate Circus where I inspected Wren's church on Ludgate Hill—I do not mean St. Paul's Cathedral—and then on down into the City, looking in at every church en route.

"I think I have found the most beautiful little Anglo-Catholic Church in London—St. Nicholas Cole Abbey. It was the first Church Wren restored after the great fire. Very beautiful and also very 'high.' Reservation—a crib, etc. I got into conversation with a charming woman who was cleaning!—fat and cheery—she lives at Wimbledon but comes in always to Church there. She said the congregation every Sunday was always about 70 or 80. *I* should be made most welcome! One Sunday if we're in London we must go there, you and I—or at least I must take you down there—Queen Victoria Street—to look at it.

"After a thorough do of the City I wended my way homewards up Fleet Street into the Strand where I had a cup of tea and some toast at Slaters! Price 5*d.*!—then on again right up Oxford Street to take a bus to Paddington where I bought a 1/- snack box. I walked home from there, buying en route a pork pie, a mince pie, and a buttered roll—to arrive home about 8 p.m. rather tired but definitely better. I ate my delicious dinner and had meant to go to Molly Mount Temple's but in the end the fag of changing into fandangos was too much for me and I went to bed instead and read the *Life of Lord Oxford* which is fascinating and which I am simply delighted with.

"The Old Year was sent out with a noise such as you can hardly conceive of—sirens from the river, whistles from Victoria Station, bells from the churches, and what I took to be African War Dances from the flat above! It was all very inspiring—so I took two aspirins and went to sleep—to be awoken at nine the next day by Mrs. Fleming, with the tea which, beginning from the New Year, I have substituted for my coffee (Mrs. F.'s ideas of coffee and mine are vastly different) and the compliments of the Season. I read my *Sunday Times*, I lolled in bed, and I came to the conclusion that I felt grand. So I dressed and was off at 12 noon in the rain for Victoria Station from where after my usual snack I took a bus to Richmond.

"I arrived at Hampton Court about 1.45 p.m. to have the place almost to myself. I did the whole place thoroughly. It was a free day and I revelled in it all. I had forgotten it and came to it quite fresh. What amazed me was how much of it is *not* Tudor but "William and Mary" and designed by our old friend Wren, who was vandal enough to pull down the Tudor block by half to erect William's palace. Still I was enchanted, though shocked. I did not visit the maze, though I went and looked at it and walked all over the Gardens. Of course at times I wished I had a companion, but I would rather sight-see alone than not sight-see at all. And at least I was my own master.

"At four o'clock I caught a bus back to Olympia where I got off and walked to the top of Church Street, Kensington. In an A.B.C. there I had my usual tea and toast (and needed it by this time) price 5½*d.*! and thence up Queen's Road and Bishop's Road to Paddington for a 'snack' box. And so I walked home again to get in at 7.15—my 'flu gone. I spent a quite peaceful evening reading—early to bed, and this morning I arose hale and hearty and entirely sound."

In spite of this "cure" severe attacks of pain were to become more and more frequent and eventually Ronald consulted Barbara's doctor and a very dear friend, Sir Louis Knuthsen. The latter, after overhauling him, announced that he was suffering from duodenoclitis brought on by insufficient and the wrong type of food. Ronald, saving money, ate only a sandwich or a piece of cake for luncheon, had a cup of tea in the office, and on his way back to Chelsea as he showed in his letter he would buy himself a snack box, a cold pie, or sometimes only a glass of milk.

He was working hard and was often wet through when he walked home to save a bus fare and was seldom in bed until long after midnight. It was a mad way of living and Sir Louis told him so. Ronald had to promise to have at least one hot meal a day whatever it cost.

He was, however, in good spirits because he was busy. In April he went down to see Tony who was stationed at Dover with his regiment. They spent a happy day together and Ronald wrote:

"I *did* enjoy myself. T. was charming. His real self. In excellent form. Looking so well. We had a long talk about everything —money, women, etc. Tony very sensible."

Ronald's financial affairs were getting gradually straight, thanks to his mother's bookkeeping. He was also making a certain amount of money from anonymous articles commissioned by an Editor who was a friend of Barbara's. These political articles, clever, witty, provocative, caused a good deal of comment. No one had any idea as to the author, even on the paper itself. The payment cheques were made out to a nom-de-plume and were sent to Barbara's address.

The latter was also working hard and doing well. She was writing regularly for several newspapers, publishing two novels every year which Ronald corrected, and had just made a success of the famous Embassy Club by redecorating it and putting it on its feet again.

Brother and sister telephoned each other every morning and every afternoon after Ronald had finished at the office he walked across the Park to Half Moon Street. Barbara believed in Ronald's future as firmly as his mother did. The whole family, closely united, were never happier than when they could all be together at Littlewood. Ronald and Barbara would argue and spur each other on to oratorial flights, while they both agreed that Tony was "the perfect audience." Ronald could be extraordinarily funny, at least the family thought so, and often they would laugh until the tears ran down their cheeks, especially at his impersonations of well-known political and social personalities.

Mary Cartland had built a swimming bath at Littlewood in the garden, having it dug by her gardener with the help of out-of-work men so that the cost was infinitesimal compared to most people's baths. It was a joy to Ronald, who loved swimming, and that summer he asked many of his friends down from London for week-ends.

But what he loved best was to walk on the hills. He would often go off for the whole day, taking sandwiches to eat. Unless his walk was to be an abnormally long one, like the day he did thirty-two miles, he would always take his mother's small cairn terrier with him. Rags was an old dog and once he had a kind of seizure. Ronald said—

"He lay stiff, with his legs in the air, only his eyes moved and looked at me beseechingly. We were miles from home. I rubbed him but it seemed to have no effect, then I picked him up in my arms and prayed over him. Quite suddenly he was all right—he tried to lick my face. I put him down and he frisked along beside me wagging his tail as if nothing had ever been the matter."

Ronald always spoke quite simply and unaffectedly of his faith. Another time with Barbara on the top of the Beacon, it was a dull grey day with a promise of rain and the hills were deserted. The Vale of Evesham below them faded into a deepening blue horizon, the undulating Herefordshire country was veiled in a mist. Suddenly the clouds opened directly overhead and a shaft of sunshine —brilliant, dazzling, golden, held them spellbound. For a few seconds they stood in the light—then it was gone.

When they got back to Littlewood their mother asked, "Did you have a good walk?"

Ronald replied quite seriously, "When we got to the top of the hill we had a vision of God."

At times, however, he grew depressed when it seemed to him he was marking time and getting nowhere. His ambition never let him rest. When the pamphlets and reports he wrote at the Central Office were praised or the notes he made for various speakers, from the Prime Minister downwards, were used without alteration, an aching desire would consume him to be able to play an active part himself.

He was very upset by his friend Antony Knebworth being killed in a flying accident at the end of May. He wrote to his mother:

"The death of Antony was quite ghastly. Bob Holland who was in his Squadron telephoned us the news that night. I was terribly upset for tho' you know I have a complacent regard of death K. was one of the few men I really admired and respected. I am so glad to think I have kept all the letters he wrote to me. They are remarkable. I wrote to Lady Lytton. I fear she will take a long time to get over it—she simply adored him, as indeed they all did. What a tragedy and what a useless end of such a perfect life, so full of possibilities. How I do hate aeroplanes."

After a tiring summer Barbara was determined to take a holiday and left it to Ronald to make all plans and arrangements. He was very keen to visit Austria and on the 9th of August he and Barbara set off, clutching small Woolworth books of German sentences. He wrote from Vienna to his mother.

"HOTEL MEISSL & SCHADN,
VIENNA.

"DEAR DARLING,

"On Wednesday Barbara and I caught the 3.20 boat train to Paris, 2nd class, but only two American females in our carriage. It was pretty hot and hotter still in Paris. We had two hours to catch our connection from the Gare de l'Est but drove straight there. On arrival the taximan having charged me 11 francs was immediately arrested by an officious gendarme for overcharging me 20 centimes! Huge crowd, my name taken, me rather hot and bothered battling with a foreign tongue, terrified of being arrested myself but not wanting to get the poor man into trouble. Finally we seized our luggage and went off, but what adventures! We were so overcome by all this that we put our eight pieces *à la consignee* and repaired for ices to the Station Café.

"The Arlberg-Orient Express was very exciting—all sleeping cars and a restaurant car and no ordinary carriages at all. B. and I found ours, packed our things into it and were off. We had some dinner and then to bed, I on the top bunk. The heat was pretty bad but we had a fair night and awoke to find we had already crossed the Austrian border. *Petit dejeuner* in our sleeper about ten and got up leisurely. Scenery very like round Brides-les-Bains, but more magnificent—huge mountains with snow on top, many of the hills fir covered, Swiss chalets, etc. I've never had a hotter journey. It was *terrific*. Over lunch I nearly expired, but afterwards with my coat off and no braces I felt better, and of course no one in your carriage is a help.

"After the Tyrol with the mountains we ran into country more like Wiltshire—huge rolling down—all very extensively cultivated—wheat and vegetables. The men in the fields all working stripped to the waist, copper coloured; whenever we passed a stream or river always people bathing in slips.

"We got to Vienna 6.40 and a taxi brought us here. Rom Landau had, as you know, written to the Manager to say look after us, but I was surprised when they showed us into the most magnificent suite which B. and I feel sure was used by the Archduke himself in years gone by. Sitting-room, huge double-bedroom for B., large single for me, bathroom, 2 lavs., 2 extra washbasins—besides those in our bedrooms—extensive passages!

"We washed and unpacked and went off to the Stadt Park where Rom had told us to go and which was also recommended by our waiter. Imagine a restaurant in Hyde Park on a terrace where the élite sit facing a bandstand. Below the terrace, at tables, the middle classes drink beer or coffee; farther out the *hoi polloi* may stand, listen and look for nothing. The food was excellent and we had a marvellous dinner while the band played just the sort of music one expects in Vienna. A lot of people sitting in shirtsleeves it was so hot—none in evening dress. All the men wear belts so they can take their coats off. We had a waiter who spoke English and told us he had been at Colchester before the war, and was also at Frascati's in Oxford Street but hadn't been back since and was now married with two children. The place was packed. All very nice people; a few Foreigners.

"We walked home and the next morning after breakfast, which in Austria is *petit dejeuner* with whipped cream for the coffee and jam, walked down the Bond Street of Vienna. Its shops are lovely, B. says better than Paris. Things are about the same price as London. Then we went to the Stefans-Dom—the Cathedral, the most beautiful church you can imagine. Magnificent and superb, so full of atmosphere—nothing tawdry or French. We came in for a Mass and heard the whole thing through. Over the altar is a picture of the Madonna supposed to be miraculous. A copy is put in the Nave, all day people come in and touch it and pray.. We watched all sorts and conditions of people from those who were obviously praying for a new young man or a good business deal, to mothers hoping for sons and heirs and a poor broken old woman obviously wanting bread.

"We are both thrilled with Vienna. I can't describe it to you. It is much more beautiful I think than Paris because it is much more English; though there is nothing to compare to the Place Vendome or Place de la Concord. The Opera House, Palace, Parliament, all look on to the famous 'Ring,' which is a street with trees going all round the inner city—a sort of Mayfair for about three or four miles. The people are enchanting. Most talk English, but B. is excellent with her little book, *How to get on in Austria*—the sort of thing Daddy took to France. I am a coward and always ask who speaks English, which infuriates B. who says I should try!

Actually the language is very like English in manyof the words. The money is all shillings and groschen—100 to a 1/. Taxis pretty cheap, no one presses you to drink with your meals and you are always given glasses of water after your sweets, the water being marvellous and we can drink it out of the taps in our rooms! No common 'tin-huts' in the streets—nothing to offend the eyes or nose. No man wears a hat, many in shorts, women not very beautiful but no 'following' or staring at B. as in Paris.

"We made the rule to come home in the afternoon from 4 to 7 to rest and bath before going out in the evening. It is very hot indeed then and it's no use being exhausted. Last night we dined out at a place called Kobenzl, high up in the hills above Vienna; all the lights below. We went by tram and motor bus. Very lovely. The smartest place we've been to but not expensive. We picked up an American youth called King Harold—undergraduate from Harvard—who told us he was motorbiking round Europe.

To-day we went and saw the Summer Palace of the Emperors—like Versailles but only ten minutes out—much smaller and less pretentious but lovely rooms and furniture. We saw the actual bedroom he used and the iron bedstead the old Francis Joseph died on, also his washbasin--they had no running water. Lovely chandeliers, nice gardens, statues and fountains, but nothing so magnificent as Versailles.

"There are splendid parks and grass everywhere and trees. I adore it as much as I hate Paris. It's not half so exhausting, much cleaner and better kept. To-night we go to the famous Prater—a sort of Hyde Park with Shaftesbury Avenue combined! I'm afraid this letter has been rather like a Baedeker (which, by the way, I use all the time) but I knew you'd like to know what we've been doing and seeing.

"Much love to you. You seem a long way away. I wish you were here with us because you would love it so, and we'd all have such fun together.

"Always your loving son,

"R."

Ronald had been deeply impressed by the Stefans-Dom. To Barbara he said, "I feel as if the spirit of Austria is there—there is an atmosphere of tense desperation, of faith strained almost to breaking point yet remaining faithful because without it there is only the hopelessness of utter despair."

But despite an undercurrent of fear for the future and sudden glimpses here and there of a poverty near to starvation, they found Vienna lovely—"a city of love and laughter." The people were so delightful, childlike in their invariable desire to please and to take Barbara and Ronald for a honeymoon couple.

They only stayed a few days, then went to Millstatt Ersee, a warm lake situated in the southern part of Austria. On their arrival after a long journey they didn't like Millstatt itself, which was quite a small town with a bathing beach, music from loud speakers, and crowds of young people, so they hired a taxi and drove round the lake until they found the tiny village of Seeboden. Here a few villas were clustered round the lake, most of them advertising "frei zimmer."

In the garden of the Villa Undine there was a tiny little wooden chalet built on the water's edge. It consisted of two rooms one above the other. Ronald and Barbara both knew that this must be theirs. They were handicapped by the fact that no person in Seeboden spoke English—the young Fraulein at the Villa stammered a few words but understood one in ten. The main difficulty was to explain that they wanted two rooms. Everyone took them for a married couple, reiterating over and over again, "You want nice room—two beds—yes."

It was some time before they discovered that accommodation in Austria is reckoned by the bed not by the room. Five or six people would share one room on a holiday, each paying 3 marks for their bed. Finally after a great deal of arguing and shameful overbidding of the present occupants, the Chalet was theirs. The tenants of the upper room which was to be Ronald's—"an engaged couple"—moving with the uttermost good-humour into the boathouse.

"Is there a bath?" Barbara asked the Fraulein when they had moved in. "But why? There is the lake," was the reply, and next morning they saw the other boarders at Villa Undine going down to the lake with large cakes of soap.

The holiday was ideal. Ronald and Barbara swam before breakfast, then had coffee with cream, hot rolls and wild strawberry jam on the verandah of their little house. Breakfast was the only meal served at the Villa; for the others they walked down to a lakeside restaurant where the food was cheap and delicious. Long walks occupied the afternoon and evenings when they roamed over the tree-covered hills, discovering tiny villages where even the humblest hostelry would offer them the most perfect coffee.

The churches thrilled them, so different from the Catholic churches in France. In contrast to plain whitewashed walls the altar and pulpit would be decorated with the most wonderful wood carving, done by loving hands through the centuries and generally coloured. Everything was in perfect taste and after saying a prayer in such surroundings Ronald and Barbara would leave feeling they had been both blessed and invigorated.

After a fortnight's rest they returned to England, leaving Spital, the railway terminus, just ten days before the first uprising of Austrian Nazis caused fighting in the streets with machine guns. On the Arlberg-Orient Express there was some trouble over tickets —the collector couldn't speak English, Ronald couldn't speak German.

Barbara walked up the corridor of the train asking for an interpreter. A young man offered to help them and they made their first acquaintance with the Hon. William Astor, who was to gain his seat at West Fulham at the next General Election.

CHAPTER NINE

1933

". . . to the uttermost strength in my power, I shall devote myself to the service of you and of our country."

RONALD returned to the office. On Tuesday, October 16th, 1933, after he had finished his work he walked across the Green Park for a late tea with Barbara. "What do you think?" he asked her. "I've heard to-day that Major Beaumont-Thomas will not seek re-election at King's Norton! The seat I've always wanted."

Suddenly Barbara knew what he must do.

"You must put forward your name," she said.

"Are you mad?" he asked.

"No, I only know that you must get it. It's the right thing for you. I am as sure of that as I am of anything in the world!"

Ronald thought she had gone crazy, he laughed and pointed out that he would need nearly a thousand pounds for election expenses. "I must be independent—I could never be a party hack paid for by the Central Office—my hands tied. If I am ever a Member of Parliament I must be free to follow my conscience."

"Money doesn't matter," Barbara told him. "This is your opportunity. I know it and I know that it is the right moment for you to stand. Money will come—all our lives our Faith has never let us down—it won't fail us now."

They argued for nearly two hours—Barbara in tears with the intensity of her feelings. At last Ronald was convinced. He agreed to put forward his name.

The next day Barbara left for Scotland to stay with Lord and Lady Stonehaven at Ury. In the house-party was the Rt. Hon. Leo Amery. Barbara told him frankly Ronald's story and asked his advice. His words were characteristic—"Never let money stand in the way of opportunity."

When he returned to London he met Ronald at Barbara's house and was so impressed by him that he offered to give him a personal recommendation to the King's Norton Association. He was to be a wonderful friend to Ronald in the House and to write to Barbara in 1940:

"I think the one thing I regretted most at the time when the Chamberlain Government fell and the new Government came in was that Ronald was not there to share in our effort. He cared so tremendously about it all and, I know, sympathised so heartily with all that I felt and thought. Of all the younger members he stood nearest to me and I had the greatest affection for him."

In the meantime Ronald had put forward his name and had broken the news to his mother. She also had been in Scotland and he wrote saying he must see her at once as he had something very important to tell her. She thought he must have got engaged to be married and was quite stunned by the truth. But although worried as to ways and means her belief in Ronald's future made her not only agree but, as her son had expected, promise to do everything in her power to help him.

Letters of recommendation were also given Ronald by Sir Bolton Eyres Monsell, First Lord of the Admiralty, Captain David Margesson, Chief Conservative Whip, and Mr. Patrick Hannon, M.P.

On Friday, November 3rd, Ronald and his mother went to King's Norton to meet the Selection Committee, who had already turned down no less than twenty candidates. Ronald was nervous but there was a feeling of inevitability about it all. There was, of course, the question of private means. It was the Selection Committee's business to inquire into that. Ronald's actual assets were a small allowance from his mother, promises from Barbara, and prospects from Major Howard Cartland.

Many years earlier "Uncle Howard" had told Mary Cartland that the boys were his legatees, but as a great-uncle there was no obligation for him to leave them anything save for affectionate and sentimental reasons. They were, with the exception of one nephew, John Cartland, the only members of the family left bearing the name.

Ronald's association with Birmingham was, of course, of great importance. Not only was there the Priory standing on the boundary of King's Norton and King's Heath, where Cartland Road ran down into the constituency, but there was the Vault in King's Norton Church where his grandparents were buried, and standing as a perpetual memorial the works, buildings and institutions erected by James Cartland during his lifetime.

There was, however, luckily no need to explain to the Selection Committee exactly what Ronald possessed in the bank. He accepted the obligation of giving £250 a year to the Association, and stressed the point that he would never give large subscriptions to the constituency. Apart from the impossibility of this at the moment Ronald very much disapproved on principle of Conservative Candidates outbidding in hard cash their Socialist opponents. Had he been a millionaire his subscriptions and charity in King's Norton would have been on exactly the same scale of generosity.

King's Norton was luckily a "cheap seat." The £250 a year contribution by the Member to the local Association, of which a third was appropriated by the Birmingham Unionist Association, was a small figure compared to the average Birmingham seat in the Caucus. The Caucus consisted of eleven out of twelve of the Birmingham seats—one had broken away in the past. At Empire House, the Headquarters of the Birmingham Unionist Association, there was a centralised organization and a head agent, but every constituency had its own local organization and agent.

The interview passed off well but there was no knowing what the result would be. Ronald and his mother went home to wait apprehensively for a letter, but both in their hearts felt that the verdict would be a favourable one.

Ronald went back to London and wrote to his mother,

"God bless you for Friday. You *did* help me, not only in being there looking like a Duchess but also in keeping me happy and calm and collected. King's Norton, if all goes well, will be too good to be true. I want you always to share in any triumph I shall have and I mean to have many. You are the most wonderful mother in the world. My life—I can't imagine it without you. You do mean so much in it. You know that. I tell you *everything*. I can really say I have not one single secret from you."

On Thursday, November 7th, Ronald heard that the Selection Committee was recommending him to the King's Norton Unionist Association and asking him to attend a meeting of the Executive Committee on November 23rd. He prepared his speech with hours of careful thought and then took it to Barbara. She heard him over and over again until he was word perfect and drilled him in elocution and gestures. He was amazingly patient, inviting her criticism on every point until at last she declared "There's nothing more I can do."

On Thursday, November 23rd, Barbara and Ronald and their mother had dinner at the Queen's Hotel, Birmingham, with Major Pritchett, the Chairman, and Mr. R. H. Edwards, Head Agent of the Birmingham Unionist Association. They went on to the meeting of the Executive Committee in Cotteridge Schools. A nerve-racking ordeal but Ronald, although pale, appeared outwardly confident. He spoke well and only once referred to his notes.

After telling the sixty members of the Executive present about himself and his association with Birmingham and his years in the Central Office, he spoke of disarmament and unrest in Europe, adding these words:

"But if we are concerned with the peace of the world, how very much more are we concerned with the peace and prosperity of our Empire. In this city there is no need continually to be holding up what the Empire might mean to us here, to the Empire itself, and to the World at large. But it is essential that the Vision of Empire should not be allowed to grow dim through the difficulties and obstacles of daily politics."

And he ended:

"If you give me the opportunity to fight for you and for your interests, to serve you and through you, I hope, the nation, you will not be choosing for your candidate and for your Member some political weather-vane. But I promise you that to the best of my ability and to the uttermost strength in my power, I shall devote myself to the service of you and of our country."

He was adopted unanimously.

After this meeting Ronald returned to London. His mother and Barbara went to Littlewood. He wrote to the former:

"CONSERVATIVE AND UNIONIST
CENTRAL OFFICE,
FRIDAY, *November 24th*, 1933.

"DEAR DARLING,

"Just a line before I see you to-morrow to thank you for all your help yesterday. I was so glad to have you with me in what was naturally a very trying time. Thank you, darling, for being as always a tower of strength. I'm sure your prayers helped me. It's marvellous, you know, to feel that we've always you with us in our joys and sorrows, strengths and weaknesses.

"God bless you always,

"R."

The Central Office on hearing the news agreed to let Ronald stay on with them until the Election. He was very anxious not to lose his salary and grateful to them for letting him remain, although the benefit was not entirely one-sided, as they were delighted not to lose him or his ability for getting through an abnormal amount of work.

Two weeks later he spoke to a big meeting of the Association where he was finally adopted. In his speech he reminded them that the 7th December was a day all Members of the Unionist Party might well remember, for it was on that day "96 years ago that Mr. Disraeli made his maiden speech in the House of Commons."

He spoke again of the Empire.

"I hope we shall do something more to promote Imperial unity. Ottawa was a beginning. But it was not enough and I do not only want industrial agreements, I want political, financial, and social agreements as well. It seems to me that they are essential if we are going to preserve our English standard of living. But our standard of living is not merely a standard of comfort. It is a standard of life. Sometimes I wonder whether amidst all our daily problems we are not inclined to forget that the real, great contribution which this country has given to mankind is not reckoned in pounds, shillings, and pence—but in what I would call a way of life. Other countries strive towards the same goal—we lead the way. You know how Greenwich time is known throughout the world. Well, in this, too, our way of life—our standard—is the Greenwich standard for the world.

"I want to see England remain the greatest country in the world. But if she is to, it means that all of us whoever we are, whatever our age, our position, have got to do our bit—all the time. It's no good waiting for others to start. Let us be pioneers. Let us lead the way. And if you decide that I am to go into battle with you, then I know that together you and I will be victorious in the end."

Again he was adopted unanimously.

Ronald, his mother and sister went back to the Priory where they were staying; they were too excited to feel tired and sat talking until after 3 a.m. At last Ronald could see ahead the first glimpse of those high mountains beyond which lay his journey's end.

CHAPTER TEN

1934

"It's the spirit of the people which is really of vital importance."

AFTER Christmas children's parties, meetings and dances at King's Norton began to occupy a lot of Ronald's time. He was in the best of spirits, sure about the future. Only his mother worried a little as to how everything would be paid for, but he wrote to her early in the New Year.

"Thank you so much again for coming to King's Norton. I was pleased to have you with me. I am really so terribly grateful that you have agreed to do so much. And you were splendid the other night. "I was so sorry you never had the chance of saying anything. I wish now I had insisted on your saying a few words at Stirchley. I am so glad that the Chairman said so many nice things about you.

"I don't want you to feel in any way at all that what we are doing is a pretence. After all if you look at it squarely it is *not* and there is no need for it to be. The only pretence is if we pretend we are richer than we are. But there is no need to do that! All I say is do not let us *volunteer* the information as to quite how poor we are. And again, looking at it largely, are we *so* poor? In so far as I can see my way ahead I think I shall be able to manage it all right —and as you have so often said, if the worst comes to the worst we *can* always raise money by selling the house.

"Anyway, please darling don't get worried over the business. That is the one thing I want to avoid. The whole joy of all that King's Norton means disappears if you are in the slightest upset. And do know that I thank God every day for giving me such a wonderful mother. I think really, you know, I grow more grateful and know how lucky I am every day."

At the Selly Oak Annual Dinner in February, 1934, Ronald spoke of patriotism and tradition, on which he had always felt very strongly.

"The characteristics of the English people which have gone to build up this country, which you will find steadily accumulating all down the ages, illuminating our own history and giving a lead to the whole world, are the characteristics of self-reliance, faith in our destiny, and courage. For hundreds of years English men and English women, nothing remarkable, just the ordinary people whom you and I know and live amongst, have lived their lives with those characteristics to guide them. Because of them they have attempted the impossible over and over again, attempted and been victorious. You get, of course, great names standing out in history, Clive in India with 800 men winning a battle against fifty thousand. You get Wolfe conquering Canada, by that feat of scaling the Heights of Abraham which would have seemed lunatic to anyone who was not determined and fearless. You get Florence Nightingale. You get Cecil Rhodes. All great names and every one of us can add to them. But the same instincts which have made those men and women heroes are the same instincts which have inspired the millions of people who have just stayed at home and done their own jobs. They are heroes too."

At Northfield Annual Dinner he struck the same note in another motif—"the spirit of the people"—saying:

"You can take it as a general rule that if the Nation is sound, the Government is sound, and I believe that where you have to begin is with the nation and not with the Government. The people who matter are not your Cabinet or your Members of Parliament but the men and women who go to make up Northfield, King's Norton, Birmingham—this country. It's the spirit of the people which is really of vital importance; not something special which is kept locked up for four or five years and only produced at Election times, but something which ought to direct us every day of our lives.

"It is by the effect that they have on the spirit of the people that I think we should judge a Government. Are they building a stronger, freer England; are they preserving our liberties; maintaining that vigour of body and dignity of mind that are our greatest traditions? These are the questions which we must ask ourselves and answer."

He was getting about the Division, getting to know it and the people. King's Norton was the largest constituency as regards area in the Birmingham caucus. At the Election Ronald found it meant 32 miles motoring to get round the Committee rooms. Included in his constituency were the Austin works at Longbridge, the Cadbury works at Bournville, and two huge housing estates—Weoley Castle and Allen's Cross, the residents of which had been transplanted there from the slums in Sir Austen Chamberlain's constituency.

King's Norton was by no means a safe seat. As Ronald explained in a Memorandum written for the contributors towards the Educational Fund:

"The Division consists of three wards, Selly Oak, King's Norton, and Northfield. The Northfield Ward, the largest in area in Birmingham, runs the entire length—north to south, of the Division. Until a few years ago it was entirely countrified with only a number of villages and farms making up the electorate. The Austin Works situated at the extreme end of the Ward, and a small housing estate near to—that was all. To-day an almost unbelievable development has taken place. Two vast Corporation housing estates (of over 2000 houses each) have been built in the Ward, and private enterprise has built and is still building not only along the main roads, but in the villages and in what seemed almost inaccessible spots. The character of the Ward has completely changed. From being a Tory stronghold with 5000 local electors it is now with its 15,000 electors a Ward where the strength of Unionist and Socialist is about equal. But the most extensive development has taken place since 1931. Thus we can have no exact knowledge of the Ward's political allegiance. There are still a few farms and country villages left: but the Austin Works and the housing estates are the over-riding factors in the Ward. Not only has the growth of Northfield altered the character of the Division, it has upset the political balance and made what was formerly the least important Ward the most important, and the one where political activity is most necessary.'"

Ronald went systematically to work. To begin with, on finding that the organization of the Association was in a weak state, both as regards finance and enthusiasm, he had entirely replanned and reconstructed it. He soon grasped, too, that the people must be taught to be interested in seeing their candidate and future Member, it must not be left to chance. In a letter to his mother from London he said:

"I stayed up on Thursday and wrote my speech for the dinner. I was dissatisfied with all I read to you, so I re-wrote the whole thing and considerably improved it. Actually it was rather good. Wednesday, I lunched with B. and she and I set off for Birmingham. The dinner was awful. Everyone terribly refined, all much too 'upper class' to laugh or applaud. They were attentive and B. made a nice little speech but no one thanked us for coming and we were left to drift about talking to people who didn't want to talk to us! The whole affair made me determine to alter the whole attitude towards me. I asked Hodge up on Friday and B. and he and I lunched at Browns and talked it all out. I told him how I must be officially greeted on arrival and departure, be thanked, etc. and you and B. and I were never to appear all together. It is a waste of us and they become blasé as to whether we are there or not."

Mr. M. F. Hodge was the agent for King's Norton. He had worked in the constituency since 1913 and although it had been altered both in name and area under the Representation of the People's Act of 1918 his position had remained unchanged except that his duties for a few years included the Moseley Division. It was invaluable for Ronald to have such an agent. Mr. Hodge knew the place and the people—he could anticipate most problems that were likely to arise. He also knew enthusiasm and vitality when he met it, he liked Ronald and appreciated him. With extraordinary and exceptional flexibility he accepted what seemed revolutionary ideas with goodwill and unswerving loyalty. He grasped these new suggestions at once, saw that with a big and difficult electorate the most must be made of every opportunity, and promised to work with Ronald on the lines he suggested.

It was to prove an unqualified success. From that time onward Ronald and any of his family on entering a meeting or party were escorted, looked after and introduced by "officials" until they left the building.

In the midst of so many new interests Ronald's family affections were not forgotten. For May 27th—the anniversary of Bertram Cartland's death—Ronald wrote to his mother:

"I always think of you each year as the 27th comes round—and I realise increasingly how you must miss Daddy and how terribly little we children can ever make up to you for him. You do know, though, how much you mean to all of us—all the more as the years go by—and how more and more you play the biggest part in our lives. Most families drift as they grow up. We have, I think, done just the opposite—we've drawn even closer to you.

"My darling, if happiness is deserved it should be yours. What we reap—you and Daddy have sown. I feel I am only at King's Norton the fulfilment of all his hopes and ambitions. And you know what *you* are up there already. I pray you won't feel unhappy on Sunday—always remember at least you have wholly the devotion and love of us children—and particularly of me."

Mary Cartland, who had undertaken to be President of several Branches of the King's Norton Association, gave parties at Littlewood that summer to which the members came as an outing. Thirty or forty women would arrive by charabanc, have tea on the lawn, play games and competitions for which there were prizes, and drive home in the cool of the evening.

Ronald was also busy with the Junior Imperial League which had always been dear to his heart. Jim Thomas came to King's Norton to speak at one fête which was opened by Sir Herbert Austin. At this gathering Ronald said there had never been such an opportunity as existed at present for the youth of this country to demonstrate to the world that, whatever happened in other countries, the younger generation of England would remain loyal to the national traditions of law and order.

"Events abroad," he said, "are proving the tragic results which are bound to follow when young people are led astray from the natural path of the Nation's progress. Let the sense of responsibility for their country's reputation be undermined and hooliganism and bloodshed are bound to follow."

He concluded by advocating the recently started camp for unemployed men, deploring the attitude of those who had tried to make trouble by calling them "concentration camps."

"Such camps are giving the unemployed a new outlook, a fresh hope. I would like to see many more of them, especially for young men, run jointly with those who are in work."

He had a large number of letters following this speech and one man who signed himself "Unemployed but not Downhearted" wrote to a newspaper saying how pleased he was with Ronald's remarks.

"I've never had a holiday like it since I left the Army," he wrote. "There are fine chaps in these camps and good sportsmen."

This year Ronald couldn't spare the time for a long holiday with Barbara. He went with her for a few days to Pourville near Dieppe, then he returned to make arrangements for a big open air campaign in the constituency. This was the first of his autumn campaigns, an innovation which took a lot of organising but which well repaid him.

In ten days he addressed 28 open air meetings, while a cinema van gave free demonstrations. The meetings were in the evenings—during the day Ronald put another idea of his into operation. He introduced a mass canvas. This was arranged by 300 members of the Association being enlisted to co-operate with him. Starting down a road canvassers on either side of the street would knock on the doors, hand the householder a letter, and pamphlets from Ronald, remarking:

"Here is a letter from the Unionist Candidate, Mr. Ronald Cartland, if you would like a word with him he is here in the road."

In this way Ronald visited 150 roads and came in contact with approximately 14,000 households, an impossible task had it been tackled in any other way.

Ronald also thought of a novel way of showing his constituency that he was in the Division. He had to have a car and his mother gave him as a present a second-hand Austin. It was what he called a "bolt-upright" vehicle, distinctive in itself. Barbara paid for it to be painted white with a black hood. It was impossible not to notice it. This was good propaganda, and the residents of King's Norton grew to know it well, and with somewhat obvious humour called it the "Whisky-Car."

It was also to be expected that Ronald should be nicknamed "Ronald Colman," but all these things meant that the people were beginning to know and talk about him. Mary Cartland was marvellous in the constituency, she worked unceasingly starting a Mother's Union in the housing estates and spending a great deal of time in the Division. Ronald wrote to her for her birthday:

"CLOCK HOUSE,
CHELSEA EMBANKMENT, S.W.3.

"DEAR DARLING,

"Many many happy returns of the day. I do wish I were going to be with you—but one must be thankful for small mercies—and to spend last night with you and have our delicious dinner together was something to be thankful for. Every year I tell you I cannot imagine our life without you. But every year you make it more obvious than ever.

"You are, I think, the *most* perfect mother in every way and no one could have been so wonderful to me as you have been—all my life and especially so in the last twelve months. The constituency of course adores you—I'm not surprised—but I *do* appreciate you.

"Darling, all good things to you for 1934-35. You deserve all the best. Sometimes it must seem to you you are waiting a long time for these good things of Life! The only thing I do pray for is that you shall be happy.

"God bless you always, and please for ever take great care of yourself.

"I kiss you, good wishes,

"R."

For Christmas, 1934, the family were all together at Littlewood, Ronald, Tony and Barbara and her small daughter, Raine. All wrote afterwards and said it was the best Christmas they had ever spent. Ronald was as gay as any child, swore that he had no presents for anyone.

Then on Christmas Eve when they were all arranged in the hall preparatory to a grand opening on Christmas morning, he appeared with not one but half a dozen presents for everyone, all wrapped in coloured paper and tied with holly ribbon from Woolworths.

CHAPTER ELEVEN

1935

"*We believe that character is more important than cash.*"

RONALD, on enquiring into the finances of the King's Norton Association, had been horrified to find how very little money they had in hand. The Election was obviously going to be bitterly fought on the part of the Socialists who were working energetically in the Division and something had to be done to counteract their activities.

He drew up plans for raising money by various methods throughout the Division, but knew that these, however successful, would only raise a comparatively small sum. Remembering his experience with the E.I.A. he decided to call together the chief industrialists of King's Norton, put the case before them, and ask their co-operation and help.

He told very few people of his idea but those he spoke to were not optimistic of his attaining much success as Mr. Neville Chamberlain had made more or less the same sort of appeal just before Christmas and raised only £300.

Ronald, however, was undaunted and Sir Herbert Austin gave a dinner for him on January 7th. Twenty-four of the leading citizens of King's Norton were present. Ronald told them of the hard fight that lay ahead and asked for their help.

Approximately £2000 was subscribed that evening and more was given afterwards. This money was, however, on Ronald's direction, not given to him but incorporated in an "Education Fund" presided over by several trustees, including Major T. B. Pritchett, Chairman of the Association, Mr. E. L. Payton of Austins', and Mr. Graham Cunningham of Triplex.

This meant that the Birmingham Unionist Association at Empire House could not claim a third of the fund. The latter had, of course, neither been consulted nor informed as to what was taking place. And when the rumour got about they applied for a third share of the money to be informed it was outside Ronald's jurisdiction. Mr. R. H. Edwards, the Head Agent, was unpleasantly surprised by Ronald's success where he and his organization had failed.

Ronald drew up a full agenda of the proposed expenditure of the Education Fund for 1935. He wrote:

"The purpose of the Fund is to provide for propaganda, but perhaps it may be pointed out that propaganda falls into two distinct classes—offensive and defensive. One can afford to neglect the education of one's supporters no more than the attempt to counteract or convert one's opponents."

The Education Fund was to operate, of course, in connection with the Executive Committee of the Association but to be directly responsible for:

1. Posters to be put up immediately and to be changed every six weeks.
2. Cinema propaganda during advertisement time.
3. Organization to assist branches in forming, maintaining and extending their Membership with its own sub-agent.

Ronald finished his Agenda with the following remark:

"Before summarising the proposals put forward I might remark that it appears to me that to make full use of our resources with the object of winning the seat at the Election, we have to use our propaganda—

"1. To 'plug' our policy—with one carefully chosen slogan.
"2. To 'plug' the candidate—who at Election time takes over the slogan and becomes identified with it.
"3. To attack; both in method and matter."

All these ideas were put into operation. The posters were original—messages written in Ronald's own handwriting and signed by his name met the eye everywhere in the constituency.

In this Agenda Ronald also said:

"The Juniors have always lived from hand to mouth and their financial position is the principal cause of their decline in Membership. We should have in the future for some time to carry the Junior branches, but it is, I think, a case of 'casting our bread upon the waters.'"

In a Message to the Junior Imperial League of King's Norton he wrote:

"England and all that it stands for in the world to-day, with its history and traditions of British character, is passing into your keeping. When you in your turn have to pass it on what sort of place will you have made it? Will you have led it along the road to a higher and a nobler civilization?—or will you, through neglect and indifference, have let your country and your fellows down?

"You have to decide now and delay means disaster.

"We believe that character is more important than cash; that class warfare can only end in the destruction of the race; that love of our own country and the desire to preserve it is the surest guarantee of peace; that a Nation of independent men and women, and not a soulless slave state, is the goal to aim for.

"We mean to uphold these ideals, we intend to put them into practice. Because we believe that we can solve the difficulties which face us if we stand true to our principles, it does not mean that we believe in standing still. We will experiment and reconstruct and build, but on sound foundations, We put practice and common sense before theory and false mass suggestion."

"Campaign Hints" were also issued to the Junior Imperial League written by Ronald and printed with his photograph on the leaflet. It set out clearly the scheme for operations in King's Norton. It told of a general meeting "with the object of roping in every member as an active Campaigner." It asked that days and hours when members would be available should be noted, so as to use those who would do jobs with maximum efficiency.

Streets were to be selected for "an intensive house-to-house canvass," bus stops to be "picketed" by literature distributors, shopping centres "raided," and "concentrated attacks" to be made on particular works where large numbers of young people were employed. Members were to work in groups starting and ending from an arranged centre.

Not only were the details worked out with careful, thoughtful efficiency, it also was attractive and appealing to the young reader. And the campaign itself was to be run with enthusiasm and Ronald's own particular vivid vitality.

Adults were being prepared too, and newcomers to the constituency were not forgotten. Ronald sent a letter to every person who had been registered as a voter since the last Election. He asked them to get in touch with the nearest branch of the Association, then added:

"I have often found that many electors like to discuss their views personally with the Candidate. If you send me a postcard at any time I shall do my best to come and see you at your home."

In May Ronald had a second big campaign in the constituency—a week of open-air meetings—and another new idea was introduced to the Electorate. This was the distribution of pamphlets headed "What's going on." In short concise paragraphs which anyone could understand the voters were told about the situation at home and abroad. These pamphlets were to appear every month, the first page written and signed in a reprint of his own handwriting and signature, so as to synchronise with the propaganda posters.

Already he was warning the people of a powerful Germany. The pamphlet began:

"1. The whole situation, at home and abroad, has been upset by Germany. Her re-arming threatens the peace of Europe. Her air force already is nearly twice the size of our home defence force; she has now announced her intention to build a navy; her army is over half a million strong.

"2. The first duty of a Government is to protect the lives and the homes of the people. Any Government that neglects to take adequate steps for the safety of the nation betrays its trust. In England we have always taken our security for granted because of the sea. But our natural frontier has no difficulties for aeroplanes. If we were attacked to-day could we be sure of our safety?

"3. What are we to do? We are a civilized nation. We hate war. We do not believe that might is right. As a civilised, Christian people our duty is to try every possible method to obtain peace; but we must preserve at all costs our faith as a nation in Christianity, in individual liberty, in a moral and ordered society. Aren't these things worth defending?"

One of his last paragraphs spoke of what he personally felt so keenly—the preservation of a high moral standard in public life, so that the people of England should be assured of hearing the truth, however unpalatable or unprofitable. Ronald wrote:

"As citizens we must demand to hear the truth. Religion, freedom and peaceful society can only survive if the men in public life are men with sound principles and high ideals."

That spring Ronald was to miss his younger brother who, now a subaltern in the Lincolnshire Regiment, had been appointed A.D.C. to General Sir George Weir, G.O.C., Egypt. Tony had become exceedingly good-looking, six-foot-four tall, and was just as sunny-tempered, charming and delightful, as he had promised to be as a schoolboy. Strangers often confused him with Ronald and *vice versa*, although the family themselves saw little resemblance bar a kinship in voice, manner of speaking, and humour. Tony was twenty-two, very young to be an A.D.C., but he had extremely good reports from his Regiment and Sir George was anxious to have him. He sailed for Cairo in April.

In the next month came the Silver Jubilee. Barbara took a window over the Cheshire Cheese in Fleet Street and Ronald with the family watched the procession from there. Always stirred by tradition and the great pageantry of England, he cried like a child as King George and Queen Mary passed by among the cheering, waving crowds.

The same month Barbara published a small book on her own philosophy; this was the result of many talks with Ronald when they clarified their beliefs by discussion. It also put briefly the advice they gave to anyone who, questioning fundamental issues, felt depressed. Ronald jokingly called this "uplift—lesson one"! He corrected and edited the book and was with difficulty restrained from being carried away by his enthusiasm and rewriting a large part of it.

He was also working very hard at the office, and the strain of routine and campaigning at times overwhelmed him, and he wrote to his mother after T. E. Lawrence's death:

"Madly busy at the office but mainly with King's Norton stuff! I seem to have a great deal to do and little time to do it in. I feel depressed about the money side of it all, too. B. optimistic—but alas I'm not. I feel sometimes like giving it all up and going into a monastery. Lawrence was right, of course, in eschewing the world —Carlow will naturally be desolate."

T. E. Lawrence had been a close personal friend of Lord Carlow. Ronald was seeing a great deal of the latter. A brilliant linguist, a Grade A Pilot, his own wireless transmitter, an amateur printer, Carlow was an unusual person. He also hated society and he and Ronald would often dine alone at some quiet restaurant and sit on there talking to the early hours of the morning.

In August Barbara insisted on Ronald taking a holiday. He had been working too hard and she knew that the months before the Election must be particularly arduous, apart from the Election itself. She refused to take no for an answer but left their destination and the arrangements for their holiday as usual in Ronald's hands. In August they left Southampton on the *Bremen*, disembarked at Bremerhaven, and took the train to Berlin.

Ronald wrote a long description of Berlin to his mother. He was particularly struck at finding all the churches closed—even in the Catholic Cathedral one could only look up the aisle through a grating in the door. Ronald met various Nazi officials and ended his letter:

"You shall have my impressions later on. They're much the same as B's—ugly women, masses of uniforms, crowds of fat, aggressive people, etc."

From Berlin they went south to Bavaria where they spent a fortnight at a hotel situated by itself on the Eibsee Lake which is directly under the Zug-spitz, the mountain which marks the Austrian border. Like a scene from *Lohengrin*, it was incredibly beautiful, but spoilt by crowds of tourists and by the German army manœuvres, the armoured motor-bicycles of the German Army being most impressive. And what struck Ronald as sinister was the fact that the single line railway track over the Austrian border was being increased to a four-line track—men working on it night and day.

Outside every village Barbara and Ronald saw the huge notices not only warning Jews against entering the place but describing atrocities and horrors in terms which in English would have been unprintable. Ronald's general impressions were very clear cut. They were:

1. That the Germans hated the English.
2. That they would annex Austria.
3. That ultimately, and sooner than anyone expected, they would fight Great Britain.

He expressed his opinions freely on his return to England and they were greeted with laughter, derision, and anger. Many people at that time were strongly pro-German and anti-French and Ronald was condemned not only as an alarmist but as a "warmonger." Immediately on his return he received an invitation headed "Der Führer" inviting him to the Nazi festivities in Nuremburg in September—this he refused.

CHAPTER TWELVE

1935

"I am certain of only two things: my faith in God and my faith in the British people."

In the next two months there were an almost overwhelming number of meetings to be held in King's Norton besides another large open-air campaign. The Socialists were confident of winning as for over four years their candidate had been nursing the seat. His name was Mr. G. R. Mitchison, M.A.

Aged 45, Mr. Mitchison had a distinguished war record, was a well-known barrister, had travelled extensively, was the author of several books on economics, and the husband of Naomi Mitchison, the historical novelist. It was little wonder that his party felt optimistic against an opponent aged 28, with few obvious qualifications.

Ronald met Mr. Mitchison for the first time at a public meeting where they and the former Liberal Candidate, Mr. A. P. Marshall, had been invited to discuss the political situation and the responsibility of Christian citizenship.

The idea had been promoted by the Vicar of Bournville, the Rev. Gilbert Molesworth, an avowed Socialist, who was to become one of Ronald's most fervent friends and admirers.

Mr. Mitchison spoke first on opportunity for everyone. Mr. Marshall wanted the elevation of the whole race through the fulfilment of the Liberal policy. Ronald came last. He began:

"Our duty to-night on this platform is to make a profession of faith; but, as far as I am concerned, it must be partly a profession of my religious faith as well as of my political faith. I don't think you can divide the two. And the fact that people have tried and are still trying to keep religion out of politics seems to me to be one of the causes of the troubles in the world to-day."

After speaking of how far we were from our ideal of a Christian country, he went on:

"Our philosophy, as Unionists, rests on the belief that a man's life in this world is a preparation for the next; that the soul of man is more important than his body and that as far as is possible in the state of society in which he lives a man should be allowed to work out his destiny in his own way.

"We have our ideals; but ideals, we say, if they are to have a real influence in our lives must be related—closely related—to the world in which we dwell now. We live in the world as it is; we strive to better it, but we realise that the Kingdom of God is above and it is man's soul that will attain to it—not man's body. No Government can change men's souls.

"As individuals our duty is to harmonise our own personal search for God with the need for living in the world with other men, and doing what we can to help them.

"As a Government our duty is to harmonise the personal development of each individual in the nation with the spiritual growth of the nation as a whole.

"We are the beneficiaries of the past, we must never forget that we are also trustees for the future. We attempt to strike a balance between the life of the individual and the life of the nation. This is why Unionists lay so much stress, on the one hand on the rights of the individual, and on the other hand on history, on tradition and on patriotism. We believe the rights either of place or of property—and the responsibilities they bring—develop man. Tradition and patriotism are a call to man's higher feelings, something beyond his own immediate self. Love of country breeds service.

"We believe in the divine purpose in life. We think that every man and every woman has something to add to the stream of a nation's life; and every nation has its particular part to play with the other nations of the world in the general advance of mankind. As persons, as nations, we have different talents, different characters. Taken all together they make up the whole complete pattern of life —as many shades go to the making of a single colour. Our duty, we say, is to develop our own nation—the nation to which, only by God's will remember, we belong—and thus to make our fullest contribution to man's general progress.

"These are our principles.

"We have no cut and dried programme—'no complicated abstract plan of life,' as Browning says. So long as it agrees with the general principles we will put anything into practice. The only criterion is the national wellbeing. As for methods, we ask where does the balance of advantage lie? Hence our support of private enterprise and private ownership, and along with them State-managed and State-owned concerns.

"As for the time factor—the balance of advantage to be settled then is between the claims of the immediate present and our duties as guardians for the future. We die and are buried. The English people go on. We neither expect nor desire always to see in our own lifetime the fruits of our labour.

"This is our approach to the two main problems of to-day—unemployment and peace.

"Unemployment is both a social and an economic problem. It is only by tackling it from both sides that we can solve it. What is the difference between unemployment and leisure? It is very slight. And it may well be that by increasing leisure, which is voluntary unemployment, we shall help to solve unemployment, which is involuntary leisure.

"We are aiming at making a man's leisure hours a blessing, not a curse. It is no use abusing people for spending their leisure as many do until we have provided, or rather helped them to provide for themselves, something better and more attractive. The cultivation of gardens, of allotments, the development of craftsmanship, adult education, and so on—these are the lines we are working on.

"We have to face the hard facts of lost markets, high tariffs, the fall in emigration. We are aiming at a permanent policy and the prosperity of our industries must be the main approach to the economic solution. But in a wider expansion of capital, an increase in each man's share in the business in which he works, lies, I believe, another approach.

"And there is one thing more—perhaps the most important of all. Industrialism, for a time, submerged the real values of mankind. Cash was put on a higher plane than character; material advantage, which could be measured, above spiritual endeavour, which could not. I believe those true values are rising to the surface again. We have got to lower the inflated expectations of what money can bring; we have got to increase the attractiveness of leisure occupations, and by using any and every method we have got to encourage invention, increase production and develop and improve industrialism.

"What is the use of our talking of other problems, even of unemployment, when there is still to be settled this one great problem of peace. 'Peace on Earth and good will towards men'—the one essential task for all men and for all women at all times. It is not a task merely for statesmen—it is our task—yours and mine—and each one of us has our responsibility.

"And when war breaks out, as it has broken out now, we have to decide, you and I, not between our duty as Christians and our duty as citizens—I believe they are the same thing, but between our own personal interests as individuals and our loyalty to the men and women in the world to-day—and to the men and women of the future, growing up and yet unborn.

"The League of Nations does still offer not only the best, but I believe the only hope for the future permanent peace of the world. There have been failures. There have been mistakes. In what man-made machine have there not been failures and mistakes? But the very strength and purpose of Christianity comes from the belief that the failures of mankind will eventually be overcome.

"And other people's failures do not absolve us.

"As a nation we are pledged. We have given our word—to the Covenant—as it stands. It may be we shall revise the Covenant, but now, at this moment, we cannot stop to argue and suggest alterations in it. The world contains Mussolini and Hitler; this is the world we are dealing with, and until the nature of man has changed we shall be forced to fight, perhaps to die, for what we believe to be right and good. There are worse things than death. To draw back now—even from war—in face of Mussolini's aggression—would, I believe, be a betrayal not only to the honour of our nation, but to the principles and the faith of Christianity.

"Ladies and Gentlemen, you cannot explain faith. You cannot analyse it or dissect it. You can't really argue about it. It is within you—or it is not.

"In this uncertain, dangerous, difficult world I am certain of only two things; my faith in God and my faith in the English people. There is an instinct in us—our greatest heritage—for what is right and for what is noble. In times of trouble, and in times of happiness, it has never failed us. We have so much to be thankful for, so much to do. God grant that you and I—and England—will never fail."

It was a strange evening, a unique gathering, and one which those present will never forget.

The Election was drawing near and the ominous problem of finance had to be faced. But Barbara and Ronald's faith was to be justified. Barbara herself had had a good year and she was able to give Ronald his deposit of £150 and to guarantee him an overdraft of £300. Ronald, taking his courage in both hands, approached "Uncle Howard" who, pleased with what he had heard of his great-nephew's activities, promised to guarantee a further £500. Ronald's own friends, who knew the circumstances, contributed smaller sums, and eventually he could start the election with a light heart.

There was, of course, the future to be faced if, and when, he won the seat. His job at the Central Office would come to an end, and a salary of £400 a year as a Member of Parliament was not going to be sufficient for his needs when £250 a year had to be paid to the Association. But there was no point in crossing new bridges until he came to them—with deep gratitude Ronald accepted what was "sufficient unto the day. . . ."

The election Campaign opened on November 4th. Ronald could stay at the Priory, but his great-aunt, Annie Cartland, was seriously ill following a stroke and there were two nurses in the house; there was, therefore, no room for his mother and Barbara who stayed at a small hotel in the constituency.

Ronald had to make a difficult decision just before the Election. Mr. Mitchison was being supported by many of the big names in the Socialist party—Mr. George Lansbury and Sir Stafford Cripps—to mention two. Who was Ronald to have? The Cadburys, due to their growing friendship with him, had decided not to run a Liberal Candidate and Ronald was anxious to get the Liberal vote. Birmingham is a difficult place politically—the people are not Conservatives as Westminster know them, they are Unionists, and their beliefs were laid down by Joe Chamberlain—at heart Birmingham is radical.

After a great deal of thought Ronald decided to have no big political personalities to help him. Whoever he asked was bound to antagonise some portion of the community. To keep the meetings going there was his mother, Barbara, and several young friends who came up to Birmingham for one night to give Ronald a hand—two of whom had never spoken on a platform before.

Barbara and her mother canvassed all day, then opened the meetings at night, being followed by one of the amateur speakers. As soon as Ronald arrived they left the hall, rushing on to the next meeting and holding the audience there until the Candidate arrived. There were, of course, local dignitaries to help in this game of "My leader follows" which worked very well.

Ronald made one rule from which he never swerved; he would never attack his opponent personally—he referred to his party and his politics, but never descended to personalities.

He soon proved himself excellent with hecklers. On November

9th the *Birmingham Evening Dispatch* carried headlines:

HECKLERS SILENCED IN 3 MINUTES

One method he employed was always to allow time for questions and when rowdy meetings seemed unavoidable he cut his speech altogether and devoted the whole time to questions. His long years of research in the Library of the Central Office was to prove itself now—his quickness was abnormal, but his knowledge was phenomenal. He was, too, always courteous to his questioners. One man at Weoley Castle gave an unsolicited testimonial to his fairness after a meeting which had started by being hostile and excessively noisy. This man rose to say:

"Labour man as I am, I admire Mr. Cartland for his fairness and because more than at any Unionist meeting I have been to, he has answered questions."

When Ronald left the meeting the audience sang "For he's a jolly good fellow."

On another occasion a heckler complained that "ten minutes was too short a time for questions to a candidate who wanted a job for five years." Ronald immediately offered to take him on in his car to the next meeting, so that he could continue his interrogations. The questioner—a Scotsman—accepted the invitation.

Friday, November 14th, was Polling Day—a day of drenching rain, and the Cartland family started their activities in low spirits. They had been warned over and over again that "Labour goes to the polls in the rain, our side can't be bothered—pray for fine weather."

They hardly saw Ronald, as Barbara and her mother made one tour of the Committee rooms, Ronald another. Enthusiasm was most evident on the Housing Estates where feelings were running high. The Labour Party were in tremendously high spirits, they were backing themselves for an easy victory and made no effort to disguise the fact.

Ronald, his mother, Major Pritchett, Barbara, and Mr. and Mrs. Hodge, reached the Town Hall about midnight. They watched the Tellers at the long tables, keeping to one side of the narrow room, while on the other side Mr. Mitchison strode up and down and his wife, hatless and in high Russian boots, sat on a bench beside their Labour agent.

Everyone was tired and tense. When the result was announced at ten minutes to one it seemed almost impossible to believe that the goal had been reached and that the fight was over. Ronald had a majority of 5,875 votes.

Ronald had ordered some food at the Conservative Club where all the Birmingham Members traditionally congregate on Election night. Outside the Town Hall only a small crowd was still waiting for the last result of the night. But they made up in enthusiasm what they lacked in numbers. They burst into cheers as Ronald appeared and, rushing across the Square, lifted him high on their shoulders. It was raining and the streets were damp and greasy, but they carried him all the way to the Conservative Club, rushing up the steps of those dignified precincts before they could be stopped or halted.

The other members were about to leave. Mr. Neville Chamberlain was standing in the hall, his hat in hand, the not yet famous umbrella on his arm. He gave way before a noisy excited crowd—he stood aside while the "baby" of the Birmingham Members spoke a few words of thanks from the doorway of the Club.

Newspaper reporters were waiting inside. Ronald, asked for a statement, said,

"I have told the truth throughout the campaign. As long as people tell the truth and have a real love for their country, England will never fail."

There was still the long drive back to King's Norton, a call at the Chief Committee room where the news was being celebrated by members of the staff—and then, at about 5 a.m.—bed.

Ronald had wanted to be with his mother that night, and had moved to the hotel where she and Barbara were staying. Their first visitor the following morning was Major Cartland, with tears of pride in his eyes.

CHAPTER THIRTEEN

1935-1936

"*Are we dealing with this problem in the right way?*"

THE SESSION opened on November 26th. At last Ronald fulfilled his mother's wish in the letter she had written to Parkfield telling him of his father's death—"I want you to start where your father left off."

Ronald wrote to her that evening:

"I wore Daddy's links to-day—I thought I'd like to my first day in the House. Went down about one o'clock. Found my way in all right and to the cloakroom. Every Member has a peg with his name on it and an attendant. Then up the stairs into the Inner Lobby. About three policemen asked my name—that was all. Every one very charming and helpful, and Jim there who took me rapidly round—showed me the Library, smoking-room, etc., and we had lunch together in the Member's dining-room. Before that I put my name on a card and in my place. So I had a seat all right. Went and sat down about 2.35. The House packed!—had a new Member next me, Keeling for Twickenham. I didn't go up to the Lords. Most of the House stayed behind in their seats. You'll read the accounts in the papers of what happened. All very impressive, but the atmosphere is much more homely than one expects. We got out about 3.30. Had a word with Page-Croft, Stanley, Duncan Sandys. The only Birmingham Member I spoke to was Simmonds.

"So that was that. Most of the House seem *old*. No one looks as young as I, but I shall get over that, and I really don't think when I get started I shall have much to get over. But I shall go slow for a bit. I send you for the cutting book my first 'Whip'—I thought you'd like it. I shall go down to-morrow about one and get a place again—thereafter it should be fairly plain sailing.

"Got up all right on Monday to find B. with the news of a flat. Went off and took it. Rather small—two rooms, but nice and spotlessly kept—with service £90 a year. Petty France, Westminster, a small street near St. James Park Underground—Bachelor's Chambers. I share a bathroom with another M.P.—Robert Bernays.

Meals as you like—1/3 for breakfast, 2/6 for lunch, 3/6 for dinner. They will re-decorate. I've not received the confirmation yet but hope to to-morrow—start alterations at once and hope to move in about the 20th."

Ronald's new flat was only five minutes' walk from the House and he was to be very comfortable there.

Jim Thomas, who had shown him round, was to be one of Ronald's greatest friends both in the House and out. As Member for Hereford Jim lived a distance of only twenty miles from Littlewood. He often motored over to spend the day or stayed for the week-end. He was intelligent, vivacious, and full of charm, he and Ronald had much in common and the latter was often to ask Jim's advice and to be invariably certain of his sympathy. Jim was at this time Parliamentary Private Secretary to the Secretary of State for the Dominions—his namesake but no relation—the Rt. Hon. Jim Thomas.

On December 4th, Ronald wrote to his mother again from the House of Commons.

"No news. I am thoroughly happy here—intensely interested. Every one is exceptionally charming. The *Morning Post* has asked me for an article to be published on Friday. So I shall be working hard on it to-morrow morning. Dined with Jim last night, the House rose early and we went to a play. Saw Bobbie Monsell take his seat in the Lords to-day—very impressive—he was actually nervous."

Sir Bolton Eyres Monsell had received a Viscounty in the New Year's Honours List. Ronald's article in the *Morning Post* duly appeared the following Friday. In it he wrote:

"The Socialist Opposition as I see them from a back bench on the Government side of the House, give me the impression of a group just ready for the photograph on 'Parent's Day.' They are ready to cheer any remark, or laugh at any joke at which they wouldn't even smile if they had paid for their own seats at a Music Hall."

Immediately after Christmas Ronald gave a large Victory Party in the Austin Works at Longbridge. Over a thousand workers in the Division were entertained. Sir Herbert Austin made a speech, Ronald said a few words, there was dancing until midnight and a cabaret which included Douglas Byng—an old friend who was in

Pantomime in Birmingham. Altogether a party on a gigantic scale and arranged as only Ronald could arrange a big show.

In February, after watching the funeral of King George V from the Horse Guards Parade with Ronald, Mary Cartland went to Cairo to visit Tony. Ronald wrote to her air mail of his first "All-Night Sitting," and the letter reached her at Marseilles. The remarks at the end of the letter mention Lord Lloyd. Ronald already admired the latter and later saw a good deal of him.

"HOUSE OF COMMONS.

"DEAR DARLING,

"I write this at 11 a.m.—we have been here all night—an all-night sitting and it is likely to go on until two or three this afternoon. But I have my week-end school engagement at Cheltenham, so shall have to be off about twelve in order to catch the 2.10 to Birmingham. I was going by the 11.10 but of course have had to cancel and stay here. I was on a Committee yesterday morning—started at 11—so I have been here now just twenty-four hours. No sleep—not a wink. The House is not at its best I can tell you! The Socialists frantic—we spent most of the time in the library or smoking-room. We had eggs and bacon and at 8.30 I had a delicious breakfast with Duncan Sandys!

"Very little other news. I spent last week-end with Basil Bartlett. Motored down to Dartmouth with him and spent the night, then a long drive back all across Dartmoor. Quite lovely.

"Went up to Birmingham on Wednesday to the British Industries Fair.

"Lady Astor has asked me to dine next week and Lord Lloyd is dining with Alan Lennox-Boyd, Bill Astor, and me on Tuesday night to talk about Egypt. I stay this week-end with the Crohans and the week-end following with Philip Dunne—he is a Member, much the nicest new one here. They live in Warwickshire."

Ronald was speaking at the Political Week-end School at Cheltenham on "Social and Industrial Conditions One Hundred Years Ago and To-day," and managed to be exceedingly interesting in spite of his lack of sleep.

Now he was in the House there was to be no relaxing of Ronald's efforts to keep King's Norton interested and alive; at a meeting to which he had invited Miss Florence Horsbrugh, M.P., he said:

"You are proud in this city of what you call the Chamberlain tradition. I wonder how many of those who so glibly use those words, who are so pleased to reap the benefits that result from that tradition, understand what it means or do anything to keep it alive in the changed circumstances of the times. I am appalled by the lack of volunteers in the city for social and public service; I am dismayed by the seclusion from public services of those who are most fortunately situated."

The Labour Party were to protest that summer against Ronald being invited to open a fête when no other political representatives were there. Ronald once and for all made his views on the matter clear.

"Since my election I have consistently maintained in the Division as great a degree of impartiality as my known membership of a party permits. I regard myself as representative of every person in King's Norton, quite irrespective of their politics, and in acting for my constituents I have never for a moment stopped to consider what their political views might be."

All through the succeeding years he reiterated this until the Labour Party eventually believed it and did look on him as their representative and not only the representative of a party organization.

On April 8th, the *Daily Dispatch* made the following observation:

"A valiant band of young Conservative M.P.'s is 'hotting things up' for Ministers just now—and making a good sound job of it. Its Members are Mr. 'Ronnie' Cartland, Mr. Sandys, Mr. Donner, Mr. Wise, and Mr. Lennox-Boyd, and it is apparent that their staff work is well thought out.

"They have selected certain aspects of defence and of foreign and Empire policy for their 'ginger' efforts, and their 'nuisance value' is increasing steadily.

"I notice that junior Ministers in particular are paying respectful attention to the little group. They are wise, because deftness in putting awkward supplementaries is becoming more and more apparent with practice."

Three weeks later the *Sheffield Telegraph* headed a paragraph:

MANDATED TERRITORIES
MR. CHURCHILL SUPPORTS YOUNG REBELS.

"The Government is facing a revolt from a number of its young supporters, Mr. Duncan Sandys, Mr. Wise, Mr. Cartland and others, on the question of possible transfer of mandated territories."

On May 1st, the *Morning Post* carried a letter asking for its support for—

"It is our hope and desire that H.M. Government will see their way to give a clear and unequivocal pledge that they will not entertain demands from any quarter for the cession of British Mandated Territories."

After quoting the legal position and suggesting that the cession of territories to Germany on her agreement to return to the League of Nations and an acceptance of disarmament might well prove a vain sacrifice, the letter alleged that Germany's demands rested on a desire for raw materials and "the determination to secure strategic advantage."

It went on to say that the only compensation the British Empire received after the Great War, when other European nations acquired valuable increases of territory, was a measure of security in Africa and the Near East. "Is our only indemnity for the loss of so many lives and the expenditure of so vast a treasure to be thrown away?" was asked.

And the letter ended: "Our title to Empire is challenged. Are we prepared to meet the challenge? Or have we lost faith in ourselves? Are we afraid? Has virtue gone out of us? This is the issue which British people have now to decide."

Signed: RONALD CARTLAND
PATRICK DONNER
CHARLES EMMOTT
ALAN LENNOX-BOYD
DUNCAN SANDYS.
House of Commons.

Ronald had not yet made his Maiden Speech—he was waiting deliberately on the advice of Sir Austen Chamberlain, who was a friend and adviser to Ronald as he was to hundreds of young men, both inside and outside the House. Ronald said of him once—"He is the Elder Statesman; the back benches have given him what the Front Bench never did—disciples."

Ronald had written to his mother in February: "I am not going to speak. I had a long talk with Austen Chamberlain yesterday, and he advised me most certainly not to. So that's that."

But May 7th was to give him a great opportunity. When the

Special Area's Reconstruction (Agreement) Bill was read for the Second time. He rose at 4.45 p.m.

"I feel that I must apologise for choosing the present occasion to intervene for the first time in debate. I am afraid that many Members with a much more intimate knowledge of this subject than myself may well wonder why it is that I, who have the good fortune to come from one of the most prosperous areas in the United Kingdom, should not have kept silent on such an occasion as this. But this is not a local problem ; it is a national problem ; and anxiety about particular areas is not confined to these areas.

As the Chancellor of the Exchequer knows, there is in Birmingham grave anxiety about the depressed areas, and I feel bound to say that there is a very general feeling that the Government are not facing up to this problem. There is, I believe, in our people a very acute social conscience, and the social conscience of the nation has been very deeply stirred by what is happening in the depressed areas. This Bill does very little to relieve the idea that the problem is being trifled with. If the Government had brought forward the Bill as an item in a general programme, whether a long-range programme or a short-range programme, it would perhaps have been better.

"Are we dealing with this problem in the right way? Is it really a problem of depressed areas? Is it not rather a problem of depressed industries? It seems to me that one can envisage a situation arising in a few years' time of industrial depression—depression in certain industries—which has nothing to do with areas, but which has to do with industries. We may be faced with identically the same problem of depression, and, unless on this occasion we attempt to deal with the problem on correct lines, we shall have no idea how to deal with it if it arises in the years to come.....

"The Chancellor of the Exchequer has told us nothing this afternoon about the effects of the Bill. We have not been told whether there are industries waiting and anxious to start in these areas, or how many are waiting for the word 'Go.' As soon as this Bill is on the Statute Book, will the industrialists start industries in these areas? We have been told nothing about that, nor have we been told anything with regard to the employment that is envisaged as a result of this Bill.

"I venture to ask the House to consider whether we are dealing with the problem in the right way. My right hon. Friend said some time ago, 'We expect losses,' and it is provided for in the Bill. But

I would ask the House to consider the psychological effect on a man who has been out of work for a number of years—say a coal miner—and who gets occupation in one of these new industries, if six months later that industry, which was going to give him a chance of life after many years' unemployment, fails. What is the psychological effect, not only upon him, but upon his family and friends, and, in fact, upon the whole area? If a new industry comes in and then fails, that is bound to have an appallingly tragic and depressing effect on the whole circle of those who know that this new industry has failed, as the old ones have failed.

"Like many other Members, I have taken some trouble to try to find out why these light industries have not gone to the Special Areas. I have in my division a trading estate. Hon. Members opposite were inclined to laugh at the idea of trading estates, but I can assure them that these trading estates are extraordinarily successful. Knowing that this Bill was coming on, I took the opportunity to ask them to give me their opinion as to why it was that the light industries were going to the trading estates, particularly those at Slough and at King's Norton, and why they are not going to the depressed areas. They gave me their opinion, and I give it to the House for what it is worth, because I feel that we are bound to consider these questions in deciding whether we are dealing with the problem effectively.

"The first reason they gave was that of proximity to markets, the importance of which every one admits. The second was that these light industries are both manufacturing and selling industries. They are a combination of the two, and at least 50 per cent of their effort is spent in selling. There is a big saving both in effort and in finance if they are placed near to their biggest markets. The third reason was that many of them are run by small employers. They are owned and organised by the small man, and he, apparently, prefers to live either in the Midlands or in the South. I do not say that that is right; I am only saying what is the opinion of the trading estate. The fourth reason was that nowadays it is generally considered to be both cheaper and more convenient to bring your raw materials to your manufacturing establishment, rather than, as previously, to take your manufacturing establishment to your raw materials; and I am told, though I was not able to secure any figures, that there is a definite advantage in freight rates. These are circumstances which we have to take into account in considering this Bill.

"A feeling has often been expressed that the concentration of new industries near to their markets, and the resulting concentration of population near to big towns, ought not to be encouraged, but it is a perfectly legitimate and normal trend for industry to go as near as possible to the big centres of population.

"In 1921, when the balance was more towards export than towards domestic trade, one-half of the population of Great Britain lived within 15 miles of the ports, which, after all, were the gateways to their markets. Since the balance has gone over, and now the domestic market is on the up-grade and the export market is on the down-grade, it is natural and obvious that population and industries should be concentrated near these centres. The only thing which interests the House is the action of the Government in relation to this trend, and I venture to put to the House the suggestion that the duty of the Government, and the only way in which a government can assist industry, is to accelerate the natural trend of industry, rather than to take some artificial means of stimulating what I might call unnatural development.....

"In trying to find a solution of the problem of the distressed areas, we have to look at the problem from two angles—first, from the point of view of the relation of the State to industry, and, secondly, from the point of view of the relation of the industry to the people who work in it. As regards the relation of the State to industry, I would take the point with which the hon. Member for Hamilton (Mr. D. Graham) concluded his remarks, namely, the question of national defence. My right hon. Friend the Member for Epping (Mr. Churchill), in the Defence Debate, made a great point about skilled labour and national industry in connection with the whole question of defence, and I would ask the Government whether they can afford to let the docks fall into disrepair, to let the shipbuilding industry break down, to let the miners drop out of work? Can they afford to allow any body of skilled labour which they may find it necessary to draw upon in the future to run to seed? Some of the most tragic passages in the Commissioner's report are those in which he deals with the decay of craftsmanship, and I think it is deplorable from the moral point of view as well as from every other point of view to allow craftsmanship in any volume of the population to run to seed.

"In considering the industry and those who are dependent upon it for their livelihood, we are bound to accept the fact that, in what I would call the essential, the great trades of the country, labour has a definite vested interest, just as much as capital has. It is essential that we should realise that in these essential trades capital and labour have equal interests. Capital has some form of protection through its mobility, and we can only balance that by giving some sort of protection to labour.

If one accepts the points which I have submitted to the House—and, unless one accepts them, one can find no solution for the problem of the depressed areas—one is forced to the conclusion that in the essential industries there must be some form of public control. With that there are very likely, and, indeed, bound to be subsidies, increased wages, better conditions and so on. It seems to me that in this Bill we are subsidising, and subsidising with very little control.

"I would like to ask my hon. Friend who is going to wind up the Debate where is the market for the goods which these light industries will produce? Are the Government looking solely to the depressed areas for that market? If they are, I am afraid they will be disappointed. If they are not, and if the goods are going to be sold in the ordinary industrial market, we shall have Government-subsidised goods competing with the goods produced and turned out in the ordinary way extremely economically by existing light industries.

"From that point of view the principle of the Bill is quite untenable. I am not against subsidies, but, if we are to have subsidies, we must have them with control; and it is far better, if there are to be subsidies, that they should be paid direct to the essential industries, where they would be far more useful than if they were paid to light trades.

"I must apologise for having detained the House so long, but I would beg leave to submit one or two more points. I think labour has to play its part. We have every right to ask the trade unions to look into the whole question of apprenticeship. Take the question of boys and girls in the distributive trades. I am appalled at the enormous number of boys and girls who are going into those trades. A quarter of the boys and nearly a quarter of the girls in work are in them. It is not very healthy, because many of them are blind-alley occupations. If we are to solve the problem, we have every right to look to the trade unions to give us their support in thinking it out. We are all in favour of some sort of transference, but I would far rather that it were family transference. Individual transference is of very little use.

"I see the hon. Member for Ebbw Vale (Mr. Bevan) in his place. Last week I came across two young men who came from his constituency and I discussed this problem with them. Their whole point was that, unless they were able to bring their families to Birmingham, which they would like to do, they must give up their jobs in Birmingham and go back to Ebbw Vale. I can see no way out of that unless we adopt the system of family transference.

I am certainly not against the Bill. By all means let us have it. There is an uneasy suspicion that there must be some gap in the financial machinery of the country to account for the introduction of the Bill at all. I should like to see it extended so that any small industry requiring money could come and demand it. It applies only to the Special Areas. Such as it is, we are bound to accept it, but let us not delude ourselves that it will assist the problem in any way. Above all, let us not delude with false hopes those men and women in the depressed industries who for too long have held out, their craftsmanship disappearing, their faith vanishing, against growing misery and neglect."

Mr. Kingsley Griffith who followed Ronald, said:

"I should like to congratulate the hon. Member most heartily on a speech which was not only attractive and informing but extremely courageous. He has faced not only the actual problems of the Bill but the problems underlying it with a comprehensiveness which has commanded the admiration of all who have heard it."

Sir Robert Horne began:

"I should like to add my encomium to that which has been so gracefully pronounced on the speech of the hon. Member below me. He displayed a facility which at the end of a long Parliamentary career I have not yet for myself achieved. The House will listen to him on many subsequent occasions with the same pleasure and admiration that we have felt to-day."

Mr. Harold MacMillan, who was to become a personal friend of Ronald's, in following Sir Robert, said:

"I hardly like to speak in this Debate without paying my tribute to an attractive maiden speech which was one of its features, and I should like to offer my congratulations to the hon. Member for King's Norton for his first contribution to our Debates. He addressed himself with great breadth of vision and clarity of argument to this problem on a very wide field, and he showed all the enthusiasm of youth which we like to see in this House. I am bound to say that it made me feel rather sad and old, and it recalled the enthusiasm with which 12 years ago, when I first came to the House, my hon. Friends and myself used to address ourselves to this problem. I am afraid that we have made little headway. There was in the hon. Member's speech a note of courage and critical observation on the Government of the day. I am afraid that he must learn to conceal that method, at any rate as long as the present control of our administration remains in hands similar to those which have controlled it in the last 40 years."

The newspapers next day were interesting. First and foremost Ronald was mentioned in *The Times* leading article. The *Birmingham Gazette* gave him big headlines:

KING'S NORTON M.P. HITS OUT IN MAIDEN SPEECH

The *Birmingham Post* called it "a bold declaration of his industrial ideals," while the *Sussex Daily News* said quite concisely:

THE NEW SOCIALISM
By a Conservative M.P.

CHAPTER FOURTEEN

1936

"Open your eyes a bit wider."

RONALD, in describing his reactions to the House, told Barbara: "The gap left by the lost generation—those killed in the war—is enormous, and it seems to me that there is an unbridgeable gulf between the young Members and the old die-hard Torys. The 'left' Conservatives are immeasurably nearer to the 'right' Socialists than they could ever be to the older Members of their own party." He believed that one day a split might come and the progressive thinkers on both sides of the House might unite.

He saw Barbara practically every day and they still telephoned each morning—now at exactly twenty minutes past nine. When he had to write an important speech his procedure was invariably the same, both then and through the years ahead. He would discuss it with Barbara, asking her for suggestions and listening attentively, then he would meditate on it for several days, and finally write out the whole speech during the week-end at Littlewood. When he had finished he would say to his mother—"Now, darling, you must listen to this and make comments."

Sometimes she would say—"That's not quite plain," and Ronald would exclaim impatiently. But he always altered it, remarking—"I dare say you're right. The average brain isn't too good."

Rom Landau said that what impressed him most was that "in friendship there was not a grain of vanity in Ronald and he would talk of his work, his speeches, his beliefs, with the greatest humility."

In the House of Commons Ronald usually sat next to Mr. Duncan Sandys—Mr. Winston Churchill's son-in-law and M.P. for Norwood. They worked together and one wag, noting the contrast of Ronald's dark head and Duncan's flaming red one, called them "Black Beauty and Ginger."

Peter Howard in the *Sunday Express* had another name for Ronald and his friends. On Sunday, May 24th, he wrote:

"I am glad to be able to give you the news of a new and keen group formed by five Government supporters. A sort of new Fourth Party. The 'Quins' of Westminster.

"These five Members meet in private every Thursday, the day when the business of the House of Commons for the following week is announced. They take counsel with each other as to what their attitude shall be towards the coming business. They do not sit together in the House. But they form an offensive and defensive alliance. They back each other up at Question Time and in Debate. They hope before long to become a powerful influence in the counsels of the nation.

"Here are the names of the Quins. And in alphabetical order, for so far not one of them has revealed himself as their leader. Ronald Cartland (King's Norton), Patrick Donner (Basingstoke), C. E. G. Emmott (East Surrey), Alan Lennox-Boyd (Mid-Bedfordshire) and Duncan Sandys (Norwood). The only new M.P among them is Cartland. He is an exquisitely dressed young gentleman of twenty-nine.

"Except for his clothes, he leads the simple life. He does not smoke. He rarely drinks; never when the House is sitting. And he is no great eater either. Except that he is fond of Cadbury's chocolate. He munches it as he drives along in his Austin motor-car, fitted with Triplex glass.

"Why not? Austin cars, Triplex glass, and Cadbury's chocolate are all produced by factories situated in his Birmingham constituency. He takes no exercise, and looks well on it. His white teeth gleam, his hair is oiled straight back from a brown forehead.

"He abhors noise, especially the noise made by gramophones or the radio. Books are his hobby. He has bought nearly 2000 of them. Politics are his passion. He came into them because a friend shot him in the leg by mistake. He was thereby disabled from taking a job in the City which was being kept open for him. And when he had recovered he hobbled into the Conservative Central Office where he remained for eight years.

"Cartland is ambitious. I should not be surprised if he hopes to be Premier himself one day He has got a better chance than many of the other young aspirants I know. For he has enthusiasm and firm purpose. Also courage. In his maiden speech he criticised some aspects of Government policy and was reproved by Captain Margesson.

"I think he is a first-rate Member of the House of Commons. He has a strong local connection with his constituency. His uncle lives there, an eighty-seven-year-old bachelor, one of the great characters of Birmingham.

"This old gentleman wears the loudest clothes in the midlands. He still enjoys the good things of life. He lives in a great thirty-acre estate in the middle of the city. The city has grown up around him."

The *Daily Dispatch* called the five young men—"The New Fourth Party," and added:

"Members of the Group are not hostile to the Government, but they believe that constructive 'ginger' applied regularly in small doses has a stimulating effect on the body politic and they purpose to act as practitioners."

Ronald was impatient with these remarks which he thought made him appear frivolous. He was, in fact, deeply concerned with the problem of unemployment. In June he decided that he must see for himself the conditions in the distressed areas of South Wales. He started on a tour of Maesteg, Merthyr Tydvil, Aberdare, Ebbw Vale, Dowlais, Maes-yr-haf, and parts of the Rhondda Valley. In the details of his visit he was helped by the National Council of Social Service while his cousin, Captain Geoffrey Crawshay (a nephew of Uncle Howard) who was District Commissioner for South Wales, arranged meetings with the leaders of industry and the Trades Union representatives.

Ronald returned from this tour sickened and horrified by what he had seen. He said, "I don't believe any one can realise how bad

"I don't believe any one can realise how bad conditions are in the depressed areas until they have seen them for themselves. Equally, I don't believe any one could realise the courageous fortitude of the people in these South Wales areas in face of great difficulties."

He was particularly struck by the character and outlook of the people, but in one market place he saw over 300 men sitting around doing nothing. In the centre someone was giving a religious address but no one paid the slightest attention. Those men were too despondent to be interested in anything—they were not even Communists. This scene remained in Ronald's mind indelibly; he would refer to it again and again; the pathos of it was to him almost a physical hurt. The Social Services he thought excellent as far as they went, but considered them only of a palliative nature.

"The Social Service activities," he said, "only touch the fringe of the problems and the Government must realise that South Wales cannot and will not revive and reach its former prosperity until existing works are got going, and, what is equally important, new industries established."

He stayed one night at the Settlement at Maes-yr-haf. He talked with the men there, many of them only boys. Barbara asked him if he thought he had done any good.

"Only in the fact that I showed them a Tory M.P. could be human," he replied. "They had never seen one before, and they expected a stout, pompous old gentleman with a heavy gold watch chain."

At a joint annual Conference of Occupational Clubs held in Edgbaston Ronald said that there was a strong feeling in South Wales that occupational clubs were dope, and he had a great sympathy with the men who thought that.

"However admirable the work of the clubs in the Midlands, are they dope in South Wales?" he asked. "Are they something to keep the people sufficiently happy to prevent the likelihood of a riot or revolution? Is there any way of making a Government face up to the problem of unemployment except by a riot or revolution?"

He went on:

"Club work is not enough. Open your eyes a bit wider. You've had God only knows how many reports and commissions. You must not be content to let people go on playing with this problem. Social service has come too late to South Wales."

He told his audience that there was a suspicion of Government grants. Men asked: "What is behind it? What the devil are the Government up to?" He had asked some of the men what they thought of free food and they didn't like the suggestion at all. They had always paid and always wanted to—they did not like things free.

To Barbara he said: "The only thing they have left is a fraction of their pride, a morsel of their self-respect. Take that away by your damnable charity and you have what?—a human derelict—a man who is little more than animal because you've destroyed his finest and best impulses of self-respect."

On July 21st the "Unemployment Assistance Act, 1934," came before the House. Ronald, attacking a speech made by Mr. Daggar, Member for Abertillery, said:

"He also made fun of the fact that in the Regulations the words 'flexibility,' 'discretion,' 'advice' and 'assistance' occur so frequently, and he said that no Government publication within his knowledge had ever contained words of this character so many times. No Government publication, however, has had to deal with such a vital social problem in which flexibility, discretion, advice and assistance were so necessary. When you are dealing with human beings this is exactly what we want. One of the troubles with the last Regulations and the reason they broke down was that they embodied a cast-iron, rigid, universal system. One of the reasons why many hon. Members on this side, who were apprehensive about those Regulations, find themselves able to give support to my right hon. Friend is that the new Regulations are now introduced with a great measure of flexibility, discretion, advice and assistance."

At the end of a frequently interrupted speech, he said:

"The public have a very acute conscience, not only for the unemployed, but for the employed. I am convinced that as these Regulations operate, and as people get to know more about them and see what the officers of the Unemployment Assistance Board are doing, they will realise that there is indeed truth behind that statement the Board is a trustee for the public conscience of the nation."

When Mr. Tinker (Labour) rose, he remarked: "I have not much fault to find with the speech of the hon. Member for King's Norton. As he was speaking one of my hon. Friends said: 'He means well, but he has never experienced what it is to be unemployed.' I think that that remark would apply to the great majority of hon. Members opposite."

The sitting on the Bill opened at 2.45 p.m. on Wednesday, and continued until 1.4 on Thursday morning—the longest session in the House since 1881.

Ronald spent a great deal of time during the summer helping with the organization of a huge meeting at the Albert Hall for the Joseph Chamberlain Centenary. He and Alan Lennox-Boyd were the Hon. Secretaries of the Committee, the President being the Rt. Hon. Leo Amery, the Chairman Sir Henry Page Croft. A party of constituents came from King's Norton to act as Standard Bearers and Barbara arranged the sale of programmes. It was a well run, impressive meeting and Ronald was to gain useful knowledge during the weeks of work he expended on it.

The House closed, and Barbara and Ronald left England for one of their quiet holidays. On August 4th, *The Times* leading article, summing up the Session, said: "Other back benchers did not get many chances, but Mr. Bernays, Mr. Cartland, and a few others have made their mark."

Ronald wrote to his mother from Begmeil, a tiny village on the shores of Brittany.

"Thank you for sending on Jim's letter. I expect you recognised his writing? He wrote to congratulate me on *The Times* leading article. I expect you saw it. I must say I was awfully pleased. It is a terrific honour to be mentioned in *The Times*. I'd rather that than any other notice—and in the first Session of my first Parliament. I was thrilled when I read it—more conceited than ever. Very nice of him to write.

"It is quite lovely here—the coast and the shore and the pines, trees go right down to the sand dunes. That bit is rather like the New Forest. One small store, two shops up to which every one walks at least three times a day. You *can't* spend much money.

"The beach is deserted. A dozen people seem a crowd! We are lucky. We are taking our tea on the beach this afternoon. We live in our bathing dresses except for meals, when in true British style we appear *decently* clad—I in linen trousers and shirt, B. in a variety of dresses which puts the French to shame."

In another letter he wrote:

"Every day B.'s and my voracious reading continues—a book a day being our average. Absurd? I agree, but we do enjoy it, and our taste varies from high spirituality to low sensuality.

"The day before yesterday we went to Quimper by bus—three-quarters of an hour journey. Quimper *is* attractive—a lovely old early Gothic cathedral, beautiful old glass, quite nicely kept. The Chancel built out of the straight from the Nave which is quaint. Old streets with excellent shops. We bought souvenirs and I tried to buy a pair of holiday shoes and a pair of bright red linen trousers (not that you'd approve but they're quite de rigueur here!). My size in foot and body were outrageous to French minds. Nothing of that size was catered for. Anyway, it led to a great deal of conversation about 'les grands Anglais—plus grands que les français,' etc., etc. The main street has trees all down it, shops one side, water the other, with bridges leading over it to gardens and private houses. Afterwards we seemed to have spent a lot of money—this franc business is fatal for economy—but we had a lovely time."

A week later his mother read:

"We adore your letters and there is great rivalry as to whom you write. I think B. and I are now all square. Last holidays B.

complained bitterly you wrote to me more often than you wrote to her. What it is to have such devoted children that they even fight amongst themselves and with you for your epistles.

"I wonder how your new dahlias have done. The hydrangeas here are a sight—enormous plants with 20 to 30 blooms on each. All blue. People have huge walks of them. The fuchsias, too, are very fine, and the dahlias—altho' common variety—grow luxuriously.

"Yesterday we actually had a bad day—rain, the first for ten days. We did nothing in the morning. Got up late in time for an early lunch and went off by bus to Quimper where we looked in all the shops. B. insisted on going into most of them, walking all round, fingering everything, and coming out again without parting with so much as 50 centimes. But it was all great fun. We bought a few more souvenirs and had delicious chocolate and ' gateaux ' at an excellent patisserie followed by ices! We laughed at Smart Mayfair and the Member—on holiday.

"Got back here at six and bathed—the only people on the beach—' the mad English '—but it wasn't bad. It had stopped raining and the sea was fairly warm. We felt virtuous and then we just had our dinner—to bed early."

Of course they talked politics. Ronald had a power of description which was always interesting, frequently witty. But if there was sometimes a criticism of individuals, he had always a reverence for all that Parliament stood for—"the instrument through which democracy works—the safeguard for our liberties." But mainly the conversation was of the future, of Ronald's ideas and ideals, and of the day when he might be in the position to put them into practice.

One aspiration he reiterated over and over again was—"the status of the worker in industry must be raised. The length of a working man's contract must be extended and defined. And he must be given a stake and a say in the industry in which he has invested his capital—which is himself.

The number of those who have a direct interest in their work is dangerously small; dangerously, because the best is not being got out of the system either for the nation or for the individual when natural interests are throttled. The workers in industry must have a share in profits, apart from their normal earnings and, either by holdings in the business or securities of some kind, be enabled to build up a reserve of capital for themselves."

He talked, too, of holidays with pay for every one, retirement pensions, a short working week, and that compulsory membership of the Trades Unions might become inevitable. He felt that the Unions had a vital part to play in the modern State.

He always tried to make his ideas practicable. As he said—"High ideals and noble aspirations are valueless without the industry and intelligence to translate them into the tough world of trade and political rivalries, social jealousies and human ignorance."

1 Ronald Cartland, 1934, aged 28

2 Ronald's father
Capt. Bertram Cartland, APM
taken in 1915

3 Ronald's mother,
Mary Cartland, taken
in 1920

4 Ronald, Barbara and their Mother

5 Ronald in a horse push-cart with Barbara aged 7 in 1908

6 Tony, Ronald aged 23, and Barbara, Christmas 1930

7 Ronald speaking at the Eccles Works, Birmingham, just before the Election, November 1935

8 The Unionist Candidates for the twelve Birmingham Parliamentary Divisions; standing (left to right) E. W. Salt (Yardley), Ronald (King's Norton), Capt. Arthur Hope (Aston), Oliver Simmonds (Duddeston), Geoffrey Lloyd (Ladywood), Comm. O. Locker-Lampson (Handsworth), J. F. Eales, K.C. (Erdington), Smedley Crooke (Deritend), and seated, Sir Austen Chamberlain (West Birmingham), Neville Chamberlain (Edgbaston), L. S. Amery (Sparkbrook) and P. J. Hannon (Moseley)

9 Anthony Eden at the Junior Imperial League rally arranged by Ronald at the Birmingham Town Hall on February 14th, 1938. Left to right, the Countess of Plymouth, J. P. L. Thomas (Parliamentary Private Secretary to Eden), Ronald, Mrs. Anthony Eden, the Earl of Plymouth, Anthony Eden and Lord Dunglass

10 Ronald with Winston Churchill when he visited the Austin Motor Works on July 3rd, 1938. Left to right, Ronald, Winston Churchill, Lord Austin and E. L. Payton

11 Christmas at Littlewood House, 1938. Ronald, Raine, Ian, Barbara, Tony

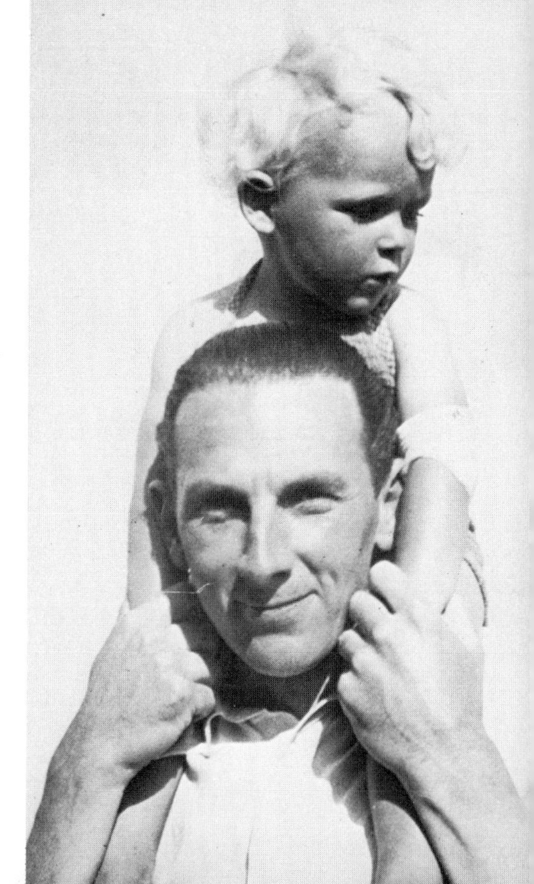

12 Ronald with his nephew and godson, Ian, at Pevensey Bay, August 1939

13 Ronald the day before he left for France, January 1940

CHAPTER FIFTEEN

1936

"Fancy a year gone by! Well, I'm content—I've enjoyed every second of it and tried to be grateful."

SEPTEMBER saw another campaign in King's Norton and a special message to the electors in the shape of a letter from Ronald on a pamphlet bearing his photograph. In it he said:

"Last November in my election address, I wrote, 'the greatest honour a man can have is to represent many thousands of his fellow-citizens in Parliament. That honour is a trust; so I shall regard it. I shall say what I believe to be true regardless of considerations or consequences and I shall do my best for all of you—always.'" At the end of my first year as your representative in the House of Commons I can say to you I have kept the pledge."

No one could deny that, any more than "regardless of consequences" he was to keep it for three more years.

He had been able to settle his finances fairly successfully during the summer. He was making a small but regular income by articles, Barbara was able to help him towards his rent, and a close friend who was interested in politics and believed in Ronald's future offered to give him an annual sum instead of contributing it to the Party funds. Ronald was exceedingly grateful for this relieved him of worry regarding the £250 to be paid to the King's Norton Association. But he still had to count every penny, to make personal sacrifices at every turn.

Immediately his autumn campaign was over Ronald went to a week-end school for "political study." He took an immense interest in these schools, this one being held at Stratford-upon-Avon under the auspices of the Midland Union of Conservative and Midland Association. The students were mainly wage-earners from the Midlands. Ronald was one of the lecturers, another being Mr. Percy Cohen, C.B.E., with whom he had worked at the Central Office.

In proposing a toast Ronald referred to the Prime Minister. "Mr. Stanley Baldwin," he said, "has his faults, and he has critics young and old, but when he talks of England he talks of something that brings a sob to the throat of every one who listens, because he is talking about the one thing which matters to every Englishman.

Mr. Baldwin has done more than any man who has held office to waken English people to what England means—the green fields, the Stratford-upon-Avons, and liberty."

Ronald had not seen much personally of the Prime Minister, who had for many years been a friend of his mother. But in 1941 Lord Baldwin wrote to the latter of a meeting with Ronald in the House of Commons, saying—

"The last two years I was in office were so heavy and so full of work that I had little chance of keeping in personal touch with the newcomers in that Parliament.

"Ronnie was making a mark, and in process of finding his feet in the House—never an easy task for the young Member. But I remember vividly what must have been our last meeting. We were washing in adjoining basins, and I asked him if he had heard from you and how you were. He brightened up immediately so I went on and told him of old Hunt Balls, and how every one admired you and wanted to dance with you, and it did my old heart good to see how he coloured up and his whole face irradiated with pleasure. I said to myself, 'That boy's all right,' and he was. There was a lot in him and it would have come out more and more."

After his lecture at Stratford-upon-Avon Ronald went to Birmingham, where he impressed the industrialists of that city with his speech to the Jewellers and Silversmiths Association and his suggestion of a "long range research body." He said that since the war there had been increased specialization and immobility of Labour.

"There is no conception where British industry is going, where we want it to go, and how we are going to direct it," he said. "There must be some form of general staff for industry—not an executive staff but an advisory body. If it is to work to the full it must not be a secret body, working for the Government alone, but one whose work is as well known as that of your Chamber of Commerce— or even better known—and as well known as that of the British Association. The results of its work must be known to the whole of industry, and we must let industry ask it: What is the future of this or that to be?'"

As a result of this speech Ronald was invited to open a series of debates on the wireless—the question being "Are Midland shops doing their job?" His opponent was Mr. Colin Clarke, a statistician. Ronald proved in this, his first talk, to have a first-class broadcasting voice.

He was much concerned with wages and working conditions,

and on the 9th November in the debate on the Address Ronald rose to say:

"As I have listened to the speeches of hon. Members of the Opposition I have felt inclined to remind them that not all the virtue and intelligence are to be found facing hon. Members who sit on these benches, and that not all the 11,000,000 people who voted for the National Government at the last election were devoid entirely of foresight and common sense. But while it is stupid not to recognise what has already been done, it is equally dangerous not to recognise what still remains to be done. The hon. Member referred to the fact that we are supposed to be living in a boom period and it is on that matter that I want to say a few words.

"There is no real sense of security in the present prosperity boom. I have the good fortune to represent one of the most prosperous areas in the world to-day, but even there there is a questioning as to how long it is going to last; is it just another boom, or is it really a foundation upon which we can build permanent prosperity, and will there be no setback? People are asking whether the Government have in mind a level between prosperity on the one hand and depression on the other. If they have such a level in mind would it not be well to take the country into their confidence and tell them how they propose to raise the level itself as prosperity increases. The question is one also of the standard of living.

Many people are concerned that the Government seem to regard the employment and unemployment figures as the only standard by which to judge the prosperity of the country, and when they say that the standard of living has gone up it seems to me that, taking the employment and unemployment figures, their conclusions are based on somewhat unstable ground. People are asking whether it is not possible to have a definite standard of living, and to come to some unanimous conclusion as to how we will judge that particular standard, and whether or not we are in fact making an advance. Employment is only a very small factor in the standard of living. I would say that security of employment and rates of wages are just as important."

After saying the Government had undoubtedly done great things with regard to unemployment, he continued:

"There is the question of wages, in connection with which my right hon. Friend, the Minister of Health, on Friday last, gave us a number of figures, and said, quite rightly, that wages have begun to go up during the last two years. That is true, but they fell continuously from 1924 to 1934, and during that period of 10 years food prices were falling equally. The position now is that wages are going up and food prices are increasing too. It is no use disguising the fact that the cost of living is increasing more than the rates of wages. I put forward these facts not in any spirit of hostility to the Government, but because they are questions that are being asked all over the country, just as much in the prosperous areas as in the depressed areas. I am putting them because the people would like a lead from the Government on these long-range questions."

He finished by saying he anticipated a falling off in the building boom. If so, what was going to take the place of it? The armament programme could not; it was much too small. People were beginning to say—"What is going to happen?"

"They are asking the Government, not in any spirit of hostility, but because they realise that unless they have an answer to these questions they cannot give the answer which they wish to give in their hearts and in their homes to the totalitarian States and to the danger which surrounds us."

Mr. Barnes rose to say:

"I feel that I am voicing the opinion of the whole House when I express the hope that the hon. Member for King's Norton will intervene in our Debates on many future occasions. He began by admitting that there was widespread uneasiness in all circles, even in prosperous areas, concerning the character of the present improvement in trade, and he proceeded to level what I considered to be a very effective indictment against the Government's ineptitude, inaction, and incapacity in grappling with our modern problems."

November 14th was the first anniversary of Ronald's life as a Member of Parliament. The thrill was still with him—he loved the House itself, which he called "the best club in the world," and he was happy in the knowledge that he was at last beginning to move towards his goal of being in a position to help, to lead, to inspire. He knew that he had a long way to go but he never lost sight of this final objective, it was a part of his being; never a day, hardly an hour passed when the idea of his ultimate service to the community was not in his thoughts.

He wrote to his mother from Birmingham:

"Really no news—my life seems very full—very hectic. There is so much to tell you when I see you about the House and so on.

Fancy a year gone by! Well, I'm content. I've enjoyed every second of it, and tried to be grateful. I didn't go to Church this morning which I meant to—but the car was out of action for one thing and another I felt dead tired. Haven't been out to-day—five minutes round the garden! I become more and more like Joe Chamberlain!"

In London a Special Areas Committee had been formed under the leadership of Lord Wolmer who, in his own words—"attracted by Ronald's ability, integrity and idealism"—had asked him to be secretary of the Committee. Ronald had admired Lord Wolmer for many years before he knew him. He felt he was fighting a continual battle to "uphold the ideas of Toryism before the British Democracy." And he had applauded his words some years previously when, tilting at the Government, Lord Wolmer had said—"The post-War world is not looking for sloppy Liberalism; what it wants is good government."

Ronald accepted the post as secretary to this new group with keen interest. The Committee had a maximum of about forty members, although only half a dozen could be relied on to take a really strong line.

News Review, commenting on the Group later, said:

"Viscount Wolmer set out a few weeks ago to press for vigorous action in the gloomy areas. First to enlist was his House of Commons neighbour, Winston Churchill. Others in the Wolmer Group include young, progressive Conservatives Ronald Cartland, Duncan Sandys, round-faced Robert Boothby, and Lennox-Boyd. Object of this 'Poverty Ginger Group' is to make Stanley Baldwin 'build Jerusalem in England's green and pleasant land.'

"Secretary of the movement is thirty-year-old Ronald Cartland. 'Handsome Ronald,' say the prophets, is destined one day to be Prime Minister; for the present the dark, slim, well-groomed M.P. for King's Norton, Birmingham, is concentrating all his energies on social problems, with the Distressed Areas taking first place."

When the second reading of the Expiring Laws Continuance Bill was scheduled to be heard the Special Areas Committee were determined to bring every pressure on the Government to take action on behalf of the Special Areas. They tried to see Mr. Chamberlain—the Chancellor of the Exchequer—before the Bill came before the House, but he was laid up by an attack of gout. Publicity, the Committee's action, and the rising feeling in the House had, however, an effect.

When Mr. Chamberlain spoke on November 17th he admitted

"that in South Wales, South-West Durham, and West Cumberland there has been no appreciable improvement and, indeed, if one takes the special case of Merthyr things are actually worse than they were." But he promised that the Government were going to introduce a Bill in the spring to extend the powers of Special Area Commissioners.

Lord Wolmer suggested it was "high time" the Government did make up their minds to do something. Mr. Ridley showed that infantile mortality figures between the Special Areas and other parts of the country had an "appalling disparity." Following Mr. Hardie—who said that "the Chancellor was simply rehashing the same old stuff"—Ronald rose to speak early in the debate and expressed his views on the statement made by Mr. Chamberlain. He began:

"I am afraid that I, for one, am seriously disappointed with the statement made by the Chancellor of the Exchequer. I welcome the very small advance which he has made to meet the point of view put forward from these benches, but it is a very small advance and I cannot help feeling, as I have listened to this Debate ever since six o'clock, that we might really be discussing the distressed areas for the first time, and that the statement made by the Chancellor of the Exchequer was a statement made on a consideration of this problem for the first time."

Later on he said:

"Once again we have had from the Front Bench the cry: 'We have not the time,' and once again it is the back benchers who take up the cry: 'Too late, Too late.' It is disastrous that, time after time, the Government have to come forward and tell us that it is impossible to deal with these urgent, vital, and necessary problems because they have not looked sufficiently far ahead. What did the Chancellor of the Exchequer say? He said that he intended to give open-minded examination to the problem. Once again I would point out that this is not the first report that we have had."

After speaking of expenditure, he went on:

"We have heard my right hon. Friend refer to the work of the National Council of Social Service, but I want to put before the Government one point which I feel is important. The whole expenditure on social service from the very start has been suspect because it has been Government money, and I believe it does no good to shut our eyes to the fact that half the effect of social service is ruined when the expenditure comes from Government grants and Government money. Social service, if it is to have any value, must be voluntary social service, which comes out of the hearts of individuals, and not out of the cashboxes of Ministerial departments. Finally, on that point, the Commissioner offers what I really must refer to as an almost deliberate insult to the Welsh people. I really cannot understand how Mr. Stewart was able to write, in paragraph 119 of his report:

"'Whatever the efforts put forward to make South Wales attractive to industrialists, they will fail unless the Welsh people make a determined effort themselves to show that spirit of co-operation within their borders which will give assurance to those without.'

"Then he goes on to deal with the whole thing. Naturally, I cannot set myself up as in any way an expert on the Welsh people. I know them very little. I would only say that I believe there is not one Member of this House, wherever he sits, who, going to South Wales in a spirit of enquiry, is not received with friendliness and absolute co-operation. I believe there is complete co-operation on their part to try and get something done, and I cannot understand how any statement that they do not realise their difficulties, or are not prepared to pull together, was allowed to appear in the report at all. It is not generosity that the Welsh people want. I only speak for them because theirs is the only distressed area that I know. It is not generosity that they want, it is justice; and the social service which has been carried out, and which virtually is all that the Commissioner has done as Commissioner which could not have been done by Government Departments, has simply been, to use the phrase of the Chancellor of the Exchequer, to turn the district into a gigantic soup kitchen."

He ended his speech with the challenge:

"We may be asked what we suggest. I suggest that the Government make up their mind on this problem. You can either do nothing or you can do something. If you are going to do something you have got to spend money. If you are going to do nothing, I beg the Government to say so with complete and appalling frankness, because then at least we who support them will know where we stand."

One of the more sensational morning papers reported:

PARLIAMENT WAS IN A STATE OF UPROAR OVER THE DISTRESSED AREAS.
All-Night Sitting.

And added that: "Mr. Cartland burned his boats."

The Birmingham papers spoke of "an almost ferocious attack on the Government by Mr. R. Cartland, speaking amid Labour cheers."

The *Evening Standard* carried the story that four Conservatives had voted against the Government—Mr. Ronald Cartland, Capt. J. R. Macnamara, Mr. Harold MacMillan, and Mr. S. Storey.

In the House itself Mr. Maxton had said to Ronald—"The only trouble with you, Ronnie, is that you are on the wrong side of the House."

The Whips passed him by with stern, unsmiling faces, and he was to be sent for by Captain David Margesson. This was not the first time and now he was warned in no uncertain terms that rebels were not tolerated in the Conservative Party.

Ronald wrote to his mother on the night of Wednesday 18th.

"House of Commons,
3.20 a.m.

"Dear Darling,

"Well, here we are—another all-night sitting, and this time due principally to our own side and to our little Special Areas Group in particular. Really it is difficult to know where to begin to tell you all the news. You will have seen in *The Times* how a group was formed of about forty of us to deal with this problem. Wolmer is Chairman and I am Secretary. Monday was hectic—meetings—a deputation to Margesson—interviews with the Press and so on. We were all determined to force the Government's hands—but even the group needed a certain amount of 'ginger.' This came from Jack Macnamara, Duncan and I.

"Yesterday (Tuesday) the debate came on and it is still continuing. We had a deputation to Neville which in my view was most unsatisfactory. I spoke at 10 o'clock. A good house and I'm told many members came in to hear me—including Austen Chamberlain. I made a very violent attack on the Government but every one has been most kind and congratulatory. We shall see later from the Press exactly how I have gone down, but I think the House (tho' naturally many disapprove of my views) agree I have *arrived*! The debate has continued ever since—one long attack on the

Government—and it is generally accepted that the initiation of the attack is chiefly due to me!

"Well, darling, look after yourself. I'll see you, I hope, in ten days' time. I've just had 'breakfast' with Megan Lloyd-George—now I'll go and see the House and what's happening.

"Dear love to you,

"R."

"I can't tell you the number of people who say—'You won't *get on* if you attack the Government like that, and so on'—as though one doesn't feel one's *cause*."

CHAPTER SIXTEEN

1936-1937

"*No Government can change men's souls; the souls of men change Governments.*"

In the December issue of *Modern Psychology*, a magazine which had only a short life, Ronald wrote an article on Christianity and Politics. In it he said:

"What do we want? What do we expect? What is our idea of the Christian State, and is it possible? Is Christianity too expensive for any Government?

"Let me say that I do not believe that in Christianity there is any static standard at which, having reached, one can repose, confident one can go no further, ambition realised. It is obviously ludicrous—such an idea—put down like that. But neither is there any static standard for a nation. As each individual Christian raises his standard for himself, so must he, living in a society, raise it for that society. Ask any collection of friends to sketch the future, material and spiritual, of the country. There will be agreement on much, but there will be disagreement too. Each man is a judge of his own progress, and condemning the state of society in which he lives he convicts himself.

"But principles are static. The fundamentals of Christianity do not change. They are the rule by which one can measure the achievements or failures of the age. It is easy to have ideals and excuse oneself from allowing them to have any influence on one's life by complaining they are too high, too splendid for this world. Ideals must be related, closely related, to the world in which we live. We live in this world. We strive to better ourselves. We strive to better the conditions of the world around us, as a development of ourselves. No Government can change men's souls; the souls of men change Governments.

"The problems which arise in 'the daily round, the common task' fall into their proper perspective when we have clearly before us a view of past and present and, though hazily, a vision of the future. The task is laid on each one of us. In the House of Commons each day we pray that 'all private interests, prejudices, and partial affections' may be submerged as we conduct the nation's business. Democracy has a hard course ahead, hindered by foes, hampered by sceptics. In the hearts of men and women going about their ordinary business rests the hope of the civilised world. Through the Church, through Parliament, through the Press, through every activity of the land will they, consciously and unconsciously, direct their destiny."

All through that autumn the hearts of the men and women of Britain had been disturbed by rumours and speculations regarding the affection of King Edward VIII for Mrs. Simpson. The country waited apprehensively, for the deepest and most fundamental traditions were effected. On December 11th His Majesty's Abdication Bill was read in the House. Ronald obtained for Barbara a seat in the Strangers' Gallery. They had known Mrs. Simpson since she first came to London, for the latter's sister-in-law, Mrs. Kerr Smiley, was an old friend of their mother.

Christmas was spent at Littlewood, then on Sunday, December 27th, Ronald travelled up to London with Barbara. She was married early on Monday morning to Hugh McCorquodale, a cousin of her first husband. No one outside the family knew about the wedding until Barbara and Hugh had left for Paris. Ronald and Mr. Theobald Mathew were the only witnesses of the legal ceremony at Guildhall and of the service at St. Ethelburgh's, Bishopsgate.

Before he saw her on Monday morning Ronald sent his sister a letter.

"Darling,

"I must send you this morning all my love and thoughts and good wishes for the future. You know what you have meant to me these last five years—much more than I can ever hope to tell you—support, inspiration, courage, faith and love—I've sought them from you often, never in vain. Now, after to-day, it can't be quite the same—our relationship. But I'm not unhappy about it. I'm glad. Because I *know* you are doing the right thing, the wise thing, and the thing that is going to make you happier and even more lovable to all of us in the future.

"Darling, I'd hate you to marry any one but Hugh. I am genuinely delighted that after all this long time you are going to marry him. I can't think of any one I've met who will look after you and care for you as he will.

"Don't ever lose the memory of these last few years; the struggles as well as the victories—and don't forget, darling, all the happy hours we've spent together. I don't think they're finished. There are many more for us in the future. But I want you to know that after them all and because of them I can say you've earned all the love and happiness there is for ever; I know by marrying Hugh that love and happiness will be yours more and more.

"Bless you both—always.

"R."

Ronald wrote to Barbara the day after her wedding from Trent Park where he had joined Sir Philip Sassoon's Christmas house-party. He liked Sir Philip whose culture and wit were legendary, but his reactions to the almost exotic luxuty of Trent were what might have been expected. The contrast between the "fantastically beautiful and comfortable" and the squalid horrors of the extreme poverty that he had seen was too poignant. The way every detail had been thought out—such as the arrangement for each guest to be called with a copy of every morning newspaper that was published amused him. But he finished his description with the words—"The whole thing in 1936 is unreal and I don't think I approve."

Sir Philip was Under Secretary of State for Air and it was suggested to Ronald that he might be offered the post of his Parliamentary Private Secretary. Ronald guessed that this idea came from the Whips' Office, and was in effect an attempt to "close his lips"—for a P.P.S. is not allowed to speak in the House. He refused, despite a personal appeal from Sir Philip for him to reconsider his decision.

The New Year, 1937, opened with another wedding. Lord Carlow was married on January 7th to Miss Peggy Combie, and Ronald was best man. The place of the ceremony was kept a secret until the actual day of the wedding and only about forty friends were invited. Carlow had been a staunch friend to Ronald these past years and had given him, his first Christmas at King's Norton, two tons of beef to distribute among the poorest families. He was to continue his gifts every year.

A symposium broadcast the second week in January was on "Fair Wages." Ronald made two main points. His first was:

"Quite frankly, when I look at the immense complexity of the situation, I do not see how you could possibly fix any wage which would satisfy all the people as being fair. But I do believe firmly that wages could be, and should be, fixed; fixed, not for the country as a whole, but separately for each industry. They will not, of course, remain the same for ever: they must be kept continually under revision and moved up and down according to the state of the industry. The figure would be arrived at by agreement between the organizations of the employers and the employees; if there were no unions in a particular industry, I think they would have to be formed, and once fixed, it would be obligatory on all employers in the industry to pay that wage or higher. The agreement would have to take into account every category and grade of work, and I should like to see the wages for women and men the same for the same work."

His second point was revolutionary:

"There is one more point I wish to make which is bound up with the whole problem, not of wages in the direct sense, but of the payment for work. It is the proper distribution of profit. My own view is that a certain level of profit should be fixed from time to time by Government, in relation to Government securities and Bank rate, and subject to revision accordingly. Say, at the moment, round about 6 per cent or even ten per cent if you like. When, at the end of a year, a company made up its accounts, any profit that remained after the dividend had been paid at the Government-fixed figure would be equally divided, fifty-fifty, between the wage-earners and capital-lenders. Don't tell me this is impossible, because I know at least one flourishing firm that actually does something on these lines.

"These two schemes, as I suggest—the agreement of wages industry by industry, and the sharing of profit over and above a certain amount—would go further, in my opinion, than anything else towards settling this question of a fair wage."

Needless to say a great many people did not agree with him—especially those making large profits.

In February, speaking to the Junior Imperial League at Stoke-on-Trent, Ronald said—"Abstract ideas must cease. People should be shown that it is possible for an idealist to govern the country sensibly and properly. It's no use us talking vaguely about freedom and peace unless you can show people how it is possible for you to carry out those ideals."

He was to put one of his own idealistic ideas into action the next day. He had long tried to think out a way of persuading unemployed boys in one area to move to another where they could obtain work. The best method, he thought, was to let them choose their own job, and as an experiment Sir Herbert Austin agreed to his suggestion that a hundred youths who had been attending the Pontypridd Industrial Centre should tour the Austin Works. The boys were brought to Longbridge in motor coaches, and after they had seen everything each boy marked on his programme the section of the works in which he would most like to be employed. Ronald, who spent the day with them, gave them a short address, and while no promises of future employment could be given the visitors went away full of hope. The Austin Motor Company paid the full cost of the outing and gave the boys luncheon.

One of Ronald's criticisms regarding the Special Areas was the "indifferent manner" in which these areas had been defined. He emphasised on many occasions that outside the areas scheduled as "depressed" the same industries existed and were just as badly hit. He often told people how in one town he had visited in South Wales one half of the hill on which the town was situated was a "Special Area," while the other half—which was in an equally bad condition—was not scheduled as such.

One of the suggested solutions to the problems of the areas was the transference of the population to new centres. He believed the easiest way to start this was to work up keenness among the young people who had not yet been disillusioned by frustration and neglect. He also wished to forge a link between the prosperous areas and the distressed areas.

Starting in King's Norton, he arranged for Mr. A. Lush, agent to Mr. Aneurin Bevan M.P., for Ebbw Vale, to speak to the members of the Junior Imperial League and members of the central political branch from Erdington.

That month it was announced that Ronald had joined the Territorials at the end of the previous year. He told his mother that he thought he would hate the Army but he was sure that sooner or later we would be at war and he couldn't ask other young men to go and fight for him. He had joined the Worcestershire and Oxfordshire Yeomanry and had been gazetted just after his 30th birthday. Thirty being the age limit of acceptance.

Ronald had for some time been preparing a speech on the decrease of population, at which he was seriously concerned. He gathered together statistics—wrote and rewrote his speech a dozen times—and finally, on February 10th, moved the resolution for a debate on "The Trend of Population."

For 37 years the House of Commons had never directly discussed the question of population. An enquiry was promised and the newspapers gave Ronald's speech great prominence.

One remarked: "His brief speech, packed with stimulating ideas, was a great note of interrogation, so succinctly phrased and agreeably presented that an undeservedly thin House cheered him heartily."

The *Daily Express*, however, turned the whole debate into a joke. Their headlines read:

"BABIES—BY YOUNG M.P.s"
Tax Single Men.

Members announced they would rather be taxed than marry the wrong wife. Others said the modern woman compared badly with their mothers.

Ronald received a telegram from the *Express*, asking why he was still a bachelor and replied in Parliamentary fashion: "Regret have no statement to make as to future intentions."

He was, however, to receive five proposals of marriage from complete strangers, but also over 300 serious letters—the majority agreeing with him in his concern, a few indignant and abusive.

CHAPTER SEVENTEEN

1937

"The answer to any nation which assails Great Britain would come from the ordinary people."

In April, 1937, a storm began to rise on the Special Areas Bill, when it was discovered that the Government were presenting it in such a form that the proposals could not be altered. As one M.P. said, the choice was "take it as it stands or vote against it—ideas and suggestions are not wanted!"

The Special Areas Committee under Lord Wolmer came into prominence and considerable activity was expected of them, but at the last moment, when the Socialists tried to obstruct the Bill, to waste time and make party capital out of the debate, Lord Wolmer's group sat silent, and were taunted by the Labour benches who accused them of having "been muzzled."

Late in the evening Ronald broke the silence.

"This is not a problem," he said, "which has arisen in the last five years but one which has been going on ever since the War. Suppose we had said 10 years ago—'This is a special industrial problem, it is not a Special Areas problem.' If we had taken steps 10 years ago, or even 7 years ago, to deal with these special problems of industry on an industrial basis, I believe that we should have made a considerable improvement on what the position is to-day, and that we should have taken steps which we shall be forced to take in the future in order to deal with these problems."

Further on in this speech, he suggested, "by this Bill we offer inducement for new industries to start in competition," and warned the Government that they might be faced with a series of cut price wars. "It is no good," he said, "putting a man in work at Treforest if you put a man out of work in Slough or King's Norton." He suggested as a precaution against this that the Royal Commission who consider the question of location should also consider the actual licensing of light trades starting afresh.

He went on to draw attention to the serious position of juvenile labour, saying there were many thousands of boys and girls out of work and four thousand in each group were registered in the distributive trades.

"My point is," he said, "that if we take these figures and also the long-term unemployment we find that the third worst trade for men and the second worst trade for women is the distributive trade. We are allowing our boys and girls to go into the distributive trades and doing nothing about it, in spite of the fact that we are going to be faced in a short time with a very considerable falling off in the number of juveniles available for employment.

"Is it not possible for the Commissioner or the Minister of Labour to take some steps to prevent the distributive trades from being filled with boys and girls for whom virtually there is no possibility of lasting work? As long as such a large proportion of boys and girls are going into the distributive trades you are going to have aggravated unemployment, and, indeed, you are not starting them in life as they deserve to be started."

He begged that the Coal Bill should be given early attention as he believed that "in dealing drastically with the heavy trades of the country shall we find a solution for the problem of the Special Areas."

Later still in the evening, after Mr. Sexton (Labour) had quoted "I am half sick of shadows" and suggested that hon. Members opposite were satisfied with the Bill, Ronald rose to protest—"We are not satisfied, but it is better to welcome some kind of activity from the Front Bench (Labour cheers) than to block any attempt that is made."

The Debate ended at 4.3 a.m. in a heated controversy after which Mr. Aneurin Bevan was directed by the Speaker to withdraw from the House.

Four years later, in July, 1941, Mr. Ellis Smith, Labour Member for Stoke, speaking in the House on Production, said: "The Ministry of Supply and the Ministry of Aircraft Production should set up a small corps of young production engineers, trained in large-scale industry, and give them full power and authority to be used with discretion. I want the 'Ronald Cartlands' of industry to be given a chance, as they are in America and in Soviet Russia."

Ronald's comments at the time, however, did not make him any more popular with those in authority. In Birmingham a by-election was taking place for Sir Austen Chamberlain's seat. Ronald was the only Member for the city who was not asked to speak.

There was much comment and the following letter appeared in the *Birmingham Gazette.*

"SIR,

"The writer of your London Letter suggests that Mr. Ronald Cartland, M.P., has not been asked to appear on the Conservative platform during the by-election in West Birmingham because of his outspokenness in the House of Commons.

"Mr. Cartland is, I would venture to say, the best representative the King's Norton Division has had for many years at Westminster, yet, if what your correspondent suggests is correct, it may foreshadow the withdrawal of the official party support from Mr. Cartland at his next election.

"In the event of this happening, it would be as well to know now what will be the attitude of the Divisional Conservative Association. Will it support Mr. Cartland and the right of free speech, or will it back an 'official' candidate and the suppression of honest opinion?

"I am entitled to ask this question because I am a

"KING'S NORTON VOTER."

NORTHFIELD.

Sir Austen Chamberlain had died in March and Ronald mourned the passing of one who had been unceasingly kind and helpful to him. Proposing a vote of thanks to Sir Austen in 1934 he had said:

"When, in the years to come, history is written, I have no doubt that when all has been said about Sir Austen's work as Foreign Secretary, and all that he has done in the other offices he has held, his fame will lie not least in the example of character he gave to the whole Nation; to-day, when the preservation of our national character is vital if civilization as we know it is to last, Sir Austen by his example alone bids us hold on and fight for the traditions we honour. It is up to us—the inheritors and the trustees of those traditions—to follow his lead so that we, too, each in our own way, may keep these traditions alive and, having strengthened them, pass them on."

In Easter week Tony, who had been in hospital in Cairo following a fall from his horse, was brought back to England as a stretcher case and taken to Millbank Hospital. Ronald had a pitched battle with the hospital authorities as he thought Tony had not been properly and quickly examined on arrival. He spoke to the War

Office, and after this there was a noticeable acceleration in medical attention.

At the end of April Ronald, who had become Chairman of the West Midland Federation, arranged a political house-party at Malvern and over a hundred members of the Junior Imperial League gathered at the Royal Foley Hotel.

It was the most ambitious function of its kind which had been attempted by the West Midland Federation. Ronald organized the whole thing himself, even to the final allotting of bedrooms. Mrs. Cartland gave a sherry party at Littlewood and the Hon. Charles Lyttelton, Beverley Baxter, M.P., Noel Kerr Lindsay, M.P., and Jim came down to speak. The delegates paid 19/6 inclusive of everything, and that the party was an unqualified success repaid Ronald for the immense amount of trouble he took over the arrangements.

He was at this time oppressed by the clouds looming over Europe, and at a meeting of the Droitwich Conservative Association in Mr. de la Bere's division, spoke of war. He said it was the duty of every M.P. to go to his constituents and tell them that the country faced grave dangers.

The entire British Empire depended upon the strength of this island for protection and security.

The present danger was that of dictatorship, the danger of handing over the common rights and freedom to individuals. There was also the danger of direct warfare. To some extent that was being met by re-armament, but behind it they must have a real sense of national unity.

"One thing is necessary," Ronald finished, "that the people of this country should make it known throughout the world that we are completely united, and that whatever the dangers and difficulties we shall stand four square in defence of British liberty, British freedom, British principles of morality which have made us a great nation, and pray God will long continue to do so."

In another speech he referred to propaganda, a subject on which he felt strongly.

"Great Britain cannot stand apart and watch Europe sink into what may be an appalling fate," he said. "Day after day, week after week, anti-British propaganda has been going out on the air from abroad. Unless we take steps to counteract this propaganda it will eventually be disastrous. It is no longer possible to say we can live in this island without realising what is happening throughout the rest of the world. The whole strength and defence of the British Empire rests upon the strength and defence of this country.

"People talk about the policy of isolation and suggest that the Empire should cut itself off from the rest of the world, but that is impossible for two very good reasons—two modern inventions—the aeroplane and the wireless. From the moment we had a wireless we had a man in Moscow talking to people in England, and a man in Italy sending out day after day ideas and thoughts over the air—each trying to convince people about their points of view. From that moment it was impossible to cut ourselves off and to pretend that those things were not happening. For better or worse we have got to regard what is happening overseas and make up our minds in this country as to the method by which the problem is to be faced."

But England was concerned with preparations for the Coronation and events in Europe faded into insignificance for the moment.

On May 12th Ronald saw the Coronation of King George and Queen Elizabeth from the House of Commons stand in Westminster Abbey. He was thrilled with the beauty, the solemnity, and the ancient pageantry of the ceremony.

When it was over Ronald changed his clothes and, travelling by Underground to Euston station, caught the train to Birmingham to join his constituents in celebrating the occasion. Another Birmingham M.P. received much publicity by flying in a special aeroplane to Castle Bromwich and stepping out resplendent in Court dress, having, he assured the Press, no time to change in his anxiety to join his electors. Ronald, by more normal and pedestrian methods, arrived in King's Norton nearly an hour before his more spectacular colleague landed.

He wrote to his mother in his usual vivid, telegraphic style of his activities.

"Travelled alone in an empty carriage in an empty train the whole way to Birmingham. I had 40 winks!!—and a cup of tea about quarter to six. Arrived at New Street—*No* car! I was on the telephone to the garage—livid. Anyway it turned up at the wrong entrance!—about 5 minutes later. I went straight off to King's Norton. The village green a whirl—bands, roundabouts, swings, ox-roasting—and I should think 2000 people. It was trying to rain—but not more than that. I tore into the school where Canon Dunn had just finished giving away the prizes—had a terrific reception—

a speech—cheers for the King—and then on to the Green where I made another speech through the microphone. More cheers for the King and for me—' For he's a jolly good fellow ' and a feeble attempt to chair me. I shook hands with a large number of people—mostly sober!—looked in at the pub—then off to Allen's Cross.

"Visited two little gatherings—one in the street—another in a hall—then I heard the King on the wireless (quite excellent, I thought). I had a terrific reception there—left about 8.15 for Selly Oak. Saw Mr. and Mrs. Hand in the road—picked them up and with them I visited seven different celebrations, finishing up (to make eight) at the Conservative Club at 10.30. At all of them I had receptions—I might have been King George himself; cheers, singing, etc., etc. Nothing to eat at any of them but I was plied with drink—tea—sherry—porter—beer—brandy and soda—American ice cream soda!! Got to the Priory at 11. The old man sitting up for me—thrilled to hear all the news."

Ronald finished his letter with a reference to his Territorial Camp where he was due to spend a fortnight. He had managed in the past months to squeeze in several extra hours of individual tuition with the Regimental Sergeant-Major, as he was determined to master the intricacies of gunnery. He had been nervous when he first joined because he said "gunnery is arithmetic and arithmetic was always my weak point." But with the help of the Sergeant-Major he soon mastered the initial difficulties. He had also, with his usual love of detail, obtained a great deal of information on Army organization, tradition and routine from Tony. He wrote:

"Really no more news. I go to Camp to-morrow. The rest arrive on Sunday morning but I thought I'd go early and the Sgt.-Major was delighted—full marks to me! Tony's help has been invaluable, tell him—I wish he was well enough to come down for a few days—the Sgt.-Major said he'd love him to come but there you are—I'm longing for him to get quite well again—anyway in time for our holiday together."

His next letter on May 24th was headed:

"OFFICERS' MESS
100th FIELD BRIGADE, R.A. (T.A.),
CHISLEDON CAMP, SWINDON.

"DEAR DARLING,

"I was so sorry about Sunday—I had been looking forward to

it and then as I told you the Colonel suddenly decided, having been on his rounds at 11.30, that he would visit Dinners at 1 p.m. However, I can't enjoy the position of Assistant Adjutant (which I do) without sometimes swallowing part of the pill! I must tell you all about this when I see you. I can't begin, of course, in a letter. But I am enjoying myself enormously and really everyone is charming."

Camp was really a holiday in spite of hard tactical training and all night operations; Ronald returned to work. He had, in his new position as Chairman of the West Midland Federation, begun big schemes for reconstruction, organization and acceleration of the league. When speaking to the young people with whom he was in continual touch during the summer he impressed upon them the seriousness of events in Europe.

At Kinver he said:

"The answer to any Nation which assails Great Britain would come from the ordinary people. When the Spanish Armada was sighted off our coast it was the ordinary people who prepared themselves. A chain of bonfires were lighted throughout the country but bonfires were also lighted in the hearts of the people. I believe that in any emergency the young people of to-day will rally round, but first they must prepare themselves by taking an understanding interest in what is going on in other parts of the world. I think we have ignored things too much."

He spoke of the struggle in Germany between the Church and the State, of the War in Spain, and added—

"I do not think we can stand aside in this country and see these battles going on without saying "Is it going to be our turn next?"

CHAPTER EIGHTEEN

1937

"The freedom of thought, of action, of faith—surely that is our goal?"

IN PARLIAMENT, Mr. Neville Chamberlain had taken up his duties as Prime Minister following the retirement of Mr. Stanley Baldwin. The country had hopes of a new and prosperous era, with a young King and Queen setting an example of domestic happiness and a Prime Minister who represented the vast middle class business interests of Great Britain. As Ronald put it—"to the majority Mr. Chamberlain with his bowler hat and umbrella is the personification of 'Strube's little man.'"

Speaking of Mr. Chamberlain's task in the apportioning of political "jobs," Mr. Fife Clarke wrote in an article in the *Birmingham Gazette*—"Then there is Ronald Cartland. Just 30 with old-fashioned ideas. He believes that an M.P. should speak fearlessly, criticise his own party if need be, and even vote against it; that something really should be done about the Special Areas, and that there is an obvious need for a census of distribution and long-term social planning.

"Since Governments think that their followers require Whips but not scorpions, Mr. Cartland is not likely to be even made a P.P.S. at present. But some people are grateful to him and his friends for infusing into this Old Man's Parliament, sere and mellow, the eager fire of youth."

Before the House rose for the Summer Recess Ronald spoke on the Consolidated Fund (Appropriation) Bill. After contending that this was one of the most important debates they had had for some time, because the cost of living touched every aspect of home life, he referred to the difficulties of computing and misinterpreting real wages as against money wages, agreeing with Mr. Grenfell that wages must be raised to much higher levels and the purchasing power of workers substantially increased. He continued:

"I would ask the House to consider two general propositions with regard to the question of the cost of living. The first is this: there must be some fluctuations, some rising and falling in the cost of living and wages over any length of time. How far is it possible to iron out these fluctuations within the borders of our own land? A subsidiary question to that is, how far is the cost of living actually affected by indirect factors in the production and the marketing of goods and services?"

He considered it essential that the cost of living should be kept at a minimum and suggested it was time for the setting up of a permanent committee to survey this problem. He deprecated the filling up of complicated forms by individual householders, and finished:

"My second proposition is this. Surely the time has come when we should look beyond the bare minimum of the cost of living in all our discussion of the relations between wages and prices. We should look beyond the mere fact of what my hon. Friend the Member for Hitchin called the irreducible and elementary needs of man. Surely in 1937 we have to make some allowance for the necessary refreshment of the mind and for recreation; I would beg my right hon. and gallant Friend who is to wind up the Debate to convey to the Minister of Labour the desire, which I am convinced is in every industrial centre, particularly among the young people, that they should have the opportunity for a fuller life and all that it means. In any calculation in statistics dealing with the cost of living, we should make provision for that fuller life which is the demand of all people in this country."

When the House adjourned Ronald went to Paris for three days with an old and politically-minded friend, Peter Chapman Walker, to see the Exhibition. On his return he had several country meetings which he went to from Littlewood and then he went to stay at Pevensey Bay on the Sussex Coast with Barbara. The latter was having a baby and could not go abroad, so had taken a house right on the beach, and Ronald had a fortnight alone with her while Hugh McCorquodale went to Scotland.

He arrived in a poor state of health, for one of his "cheap" meals had poisoned him. To save money he had bought a ham sandwich at the station on his way down to Littlewood and eaten it in the carriage instead of going to the dining-car for a more expensive lunch. He had been seized later with the most excruciating pains and a partial paralysing of his legs. He couldn't go to bed on arrival because he had promised to speak to the Tewkesbury branch of the Junior Imperial League. His mother motored there with him and he made an excellent speech in spite of increasing pain.

He was ill for over a week after this, but the sea air finally cured him.

From Pevensey he wrote to Miss Ruth Leonard, who had become his secretary in the previous April. Overwhelmed with work and finding it increasingly difficult to do everything himself but unable to afford a Secretary, Ronald had been fortunate in meeting Miss Leonard through one of those lucky coincidences which so often happened to him

He had been introduced to her casually in the Conservative Central Office in 1934 when she was secretary to the Young Conservatives' Union. Three years later in Madeira recovering from an illness she read with interest Ronald's speech on the Trend of Population. On returning to England she decided to get some political work and going to the House of Commons sent in a green card to Ronald. He had no idea who she was, but promised to see if he could find someone who wanted a secretary.

"What about you? Don't you want one?" Miss Leonard asked.

"I'm afraid I can't afford such luxuries," Ronald replied.

Five minutes later, slightly surprised at herself, Miss Leonard was on a bus going home, having arranged to start work almost immediately for Ronald with no salary.

It was not the first time or the last that people found themselves wanting to work for and with him regardless of material remuneration. Miss Leonard was, however, exceptional in her generosity, and her loyalty, devotion and efficiency could never have been calculated in terms of cash. She had a small private income and one of her reasons for wanting employment was because she had just passed through a very unhappy time. Later she told Ronald of her troubles and in reply to one of her letters he wrote:

"THE TOWERS,
PEVENSEY BAY, SUSSEX,

"DEAR RUTH LEONARD,

"It *is* such a big subject. You've not only asked many questions. You've asked all the important ones, and all those to which there are *no* answer—or rather no answer from any one but yourself.

"You can't buy or pick up a ready-made handbook to living—Life isn't like that—certainly not for any serious-minded person who wants an intellectual basis to what, after all, is in itself emotional living.

"Nor must you imagine a Master is necessarily a person. It

may be a job—or Art—or Music. It's only because we're simple people, or perhaps even more because sex plays so large a part in our make-up, that we personate the impersonal—i.e. we make Toscanini or Duncan Grant or the Prime Minister our Master just as others fascinate themselves with dreams of Robert Taylor or Greta Garbo. In other words—go back to the Starting Line. What *do* you know! Only this—that Ruth Leonard is Ruth Leonard. If you build honestly on that foundation most of the questions which trouble other people and some which are troubling you just won't arise. Religion for example—living a 'good' life, and so on. What do *you* mean by 'good'? What do *you* mean by Religion?

"All the categories of High Church, Low, etc., can mean nothing to you, as you go seeking in Religion (or not seeking in Religion) some addition to the foundation we started with—Ruth Leonard.

"And when you ask—what do we want out of Life?—that question *should* only be asked by you of yourself—and *can* be answered only by you. In other words—or written in a word—*Faith.*

"Is this all very inconsequential and no answer to your letter? I am sorry, but living is such a personal thing I wonder if any one can ever answer our thoughts completely, because do we—can we—ever absolutely give them expression?

"Perhaps when I see you you'll tell me Salzburg gave you the key to the whole problem—it may well have—but it might just as easily come on a cross-channel boat or even in the sea at Pevensey Bay!"

In another letter some months later, written from the House of Commons, he gave her further advice on the same subject.

"I have taken a long time to answer your letter, but you know what my life is—and yours wasn't a letter that could or ought to be answered without thought. At last I can get a few minutes.

"Of course all these things—prayer, worship, contemplation, are individual both in method and purpose. One must discover one's best way of praying for whatever purpose you desire. Is it gratitude? Prayer isn't only supplication. Is it worship? It can be the first step to exaltation. Is it confession and remorse? In other words what do you *mean* by prayer—what do you want from it at any moment when you do pray?

"I may be wrong; it seems to me moreover from your letter that you are trying to put prayer into a strait-jacket. It must be elastic and dynamic. Remember *you* make your own prayer and its form. It must meet your needs, but you determine the prayer itself as you determine the needs for which you pray.

"Regular prayer? If by that you mean the physical and mental effect of spiritual striving—as Jesus in Gethsemane Garden—of course you can't pray night and morning (as you wash your face). The kneeling down which most people are taught to do and develops into a purely formal habit is no more than taking off your boots before getting between the sheets.

"But contemplation—a quiet time—five or ten minutes in a church—putting the mind to rest—thinking, perhaps, of higher things—nobility of character and so on is surely to be encouraged. My own view is that solitude is essential to man's development. Solitude is certainly essential to real prayer. But what is real prayer?—do you feel the overwhelming desire to pray, to abandon everything for some earnest seeking after you-know-not-what Truth? Occasionally yes—but not regularly. This is what I mean by real prayer. So near to exaltation, but different in that I think it is less emotional.

"For the rest—give thanks, give praise: fashion the mind on higher thoughts—yes, certainly a daily (it ought to be hourly) occupation.

"How? What does it matter? Most people find kneeling and shutting the eyes easier; but a quiet countryside, or in the sombre shadows of some Church—sitting maybe will be just as potent. Lying in bed? Why not? The body matters little in such things; it is because it is a hindrance to man's freedom of thought that men turn from it in anger or disgust—or as you say neglect it—wrongly again, I think. Avoid compulsion—the freedom of thought, of action, of *faith*—surely that is our goal? Isn't that really Christ's message; that man can only be Free in God's image and through his faith in God—Christ showing the way?

"Then you say to whom should I pray? To God? Well, why not? You believe in a Godhead. It is perhaps easier to think of something personal than abstract—but pray outwards rather than inwards—lift the mind up rather than bring your God down.

"How easy it is to write like this. It is so terribly difficult, of course. One *knows* what one is aiming for, the sort of direction one hopes to move in. You see the danger of life in cities, modern rush existence, not time to think; prayer after all, whether it be worship or contemplation or supplication is only thought.

"I end this as I've ended other letters to you. Only you can decide. 'Think on these things.' St. Paul knew what he was about."

Ronald would always take endless and inexhaustible trouble to help people, whether their problems were spiritual or physical. He believed firmly in "Do unto others . . ." and he himself had been helped so continuously by the kindness of others that whatever was asked of him he would do his best to supply the answer.

People who thought his unending exertions in the constituency were just 'vote-catching' were very much mistaken. Men and women from all over the country appealed to Ronald, and never appealed in vain as far as the effort was concerned. Requests from "a friend of a friend" were attended to just as punctiliously as a cry for help from King's Norton. It was part of the code by which he lived. That code which was being built up, strengthened and disciplined year by year, until the Rev. Gilbert Molesworth could say of him in 1941—

"Nothing was ever forgotten, nothing was too much trouble—always that Christian duty to give of his personal qualities to the uttermost. A personal dedication of his gifts—both small and great—available for every one of his people. The vocation of a faithful Parish Priest."

Rested and refreshed by his holiday by the sea, in September Ronald started his autumn campaign in the constituency. This was proving itself more and more successful every year. He could now say that since he started his mass canvas in 1934 he had visited every road in the Division. The open air meetings were also well attended. He held 34 of them this year.

In his Message to the Electors he wrote:

"I am convinced that many of the social reforms we all desire can be brought about—but only if we do not upset the foundations of our national wealth and prosperity.

"Take away the right of a man to earn by his own work as much as he can, destroy the freedom of a man to save and to live on his savings, put the organization of all industry and commerce under Government control, and you will ruin men and women, not only in cash but in character. Men desire expression in many ways, and in this country we live on our trade which is the result of some men's expression.

"I believe we should not curb some to help others, but we should help all to give full expression to the best which is in them (in trade, finance, art or science) and thus shall we attain a fully developed nation.

"Men want freedom and it is our task to-day, particularly when we see what is happening abroad, to do whatever we can to protect our freedom, in every aspect of our National life."

From the Priory where he was staying with Uncle Howard, Ronald wrote to his mother.

"The campaign going well—I've no complaints—my constituents are a bit smug, though, in the 'eminently desirable residences.' Tony, I take it, will be with you now. Any chance of seeing him before he sails? I seem up to my eyes—but really that suits me."

Tony had recovered after extensive treatment and a long convalescence, and that month he returned to Egypt to continue his duties as A.D.C. In October the First Lord of the Admiralty, Mr. Duff Cooper, visited Cairo during his tour of the Mediterranean. Tony was, of course kept busy looking after him and his party. In a letter to his mother in October Ronald wrote:

"Duff Cooper told me in the House to-night Tony was the best A.D.C. he'd ever met—he was charmed by him."

Other family news that autumn was that Barbara had a son in October. Ronald was delighted with his nephew and godson. He was to have three god-children—Julian, son of Duncan Sandys, Carlow's son, George, and Ian Hamilton McCorquodale. He took his responsibilities very seriously, warning the parents that he had every intention of inquiring into the religious instruction of his godchildren.

Two other friends asked him to stand sponsor for their children and he refused. "I know little of their religious beliefs," he said, "and I don't believe in letting what I consider the important office of godparent be nothing but a sinecure."

CHAPTER NINETEEN

1937

". . . though we may turn human beings into machines we shall not in that way bring them happiness."

THAT autumn a cry arose regarding the progressive devastation of the Malvern Hills by quarrying. Mr. Francis Brett Young wrote to *The Times* and Ronald supported his protest. The latter started his letter:

"HOUSE OF COMMONS,
October 16*th*, 1937.

"SIR,—Not 24 hours before I read Major Brett Young's letter in to-day's issue I was seeking on the Malvern Hills that spiritual and bodily refreshment which he so rightly says is sought there by thousands of my fellow-citizens from Birmingham and the neighbouring districts. Last Friday was a superb autumn day, but its glory was rudely shattered by the working of a quarry, the filthy black smoke belching forth from some engine, and the rumble of the lorries taking the stone away. Those who know Welland and the road leading through the woods to the Eastnor Monument will have shuddered as I did on Friday, and have done so often before, that a few men are permitted to defile the beauty enjoyed by many for personal gain."

It was during these walks that Ronald, thinking of the future, found a solution to his problems and an inspiration to go ahead in his unceasing desire to improve the conditions of his fellow-men. In October at the Scala Theatre, Birmingham, his fellow-speakers were the Headmaster of Westminster School, the Bishop of London, the Vicar of St. Mary the Less, Cambridge, and the President of the Seven Years Association.

At this gathering Ronald, in the course of his speech, spoke of the problem of the new housing estates on the outskirts of Birmingham.

"Old people have been uprooted from their homes," he said, "the old ties with their Church and their friends have been broken, they feel lonely and neglected. Young men and women, expecially in the Midland districts, want a job of Christian work they can do—work for which they can be individually responsible. . . ."

This was the first public expression of what had been concerning him for some time.

During his years at King's Norton he had been appealed to by thousands of people over pension difficulties, unemployment, cases of hardship, repairs to houses, etc. Those he had been able to help were pathetically grateful but Ronald knew he had only been able to touch the mere fringe of what was really a universal need where all great cities were concerned.

When England had been an agricultural nation the villages and hamlets had been built round the Church and the "big house." Later, in the towns there had been Churches, organizations, and philanthropists to whom the people could turn in their difficulties. But with modern industrial development this assistance broke down. To begin with, new housing estates were erected rapidly without the inclusion in their plans of Churches or the representation of any religious body.

In Allen's Cross, for instance, five years elapsed before the foundation was laid for the first church. Also, with up-to-date travelling facilities people who made money in the cities were inclined to move out into the country and organizations which depended on voluntary subscriptions were hampered through lack of funds and often by lack of workers.

Ronald felt that something must be done to assure the people that they were not forgotten, to minister to their needs, and to dispel that feeling of loneliness which was most prevalent in those transferred to the Housing Estates.

After much thought he evolved the idea of an organization to be called "Service." It was to be non-party and membership was open to anyone with a genuine desire and the ability to pledge themselves to the service of their fellow-men. Ronald divided the organization into three groups and applicants for enrolment could ally themselves to any of the following.

1. SERVICE INVESTIGATION and SOCIAL SERVICE. The first involves making enquiries into the various requests, complaints, etc., which are constantly received by Mr. Cartland. Sometimes this implies direct contact with individuals to verify their statements or obtain further details. At other times a member will be asked to report on local conditions—e.g., housing, transport, labour conditions at his or her place of business, street lighting, etc. Again the organization

may ask for help in obtaining a cross-section of public opinion on topical matters by calling for reports of members living in different areas or employed in various works or industries. *Social Service* calls for active help in assisting people or organizations. The bulk of the work in this section is of a personal nature and considerable tact and skill is called for. It is intended that this section should be able to provide help for other organizations by providing them with skilled assistance in times of difficulty, such as sending leaders to help in forming Boys' Clubs, in reviving social or educational schemes that are failing, providing workers for flag days, etc.

2. Political Service, which is definitely connected with the political side of Mr. Cartland's activities, and consists generally in attendance of various political meetings, canvassing, and distribution of leaflets.

3. Service Reserve. It consists of members who do not wish to participate consistently in either of the first two branches, but who are willing, at short notice, to undertake any special job or work in the two categories.

Once a Member had been allotted a certain case of complaint he (or she) never rested until the job was completed. If there was delay they would call frequently on the applicant, reassuring those who were anxious and keeping hope alive. In the case of an unemployed constituent—of whatever political persuasion—the Service member was to visit the three big factories in the neighbourhood and not rest until employment was secured.

Obviously, apart from the active personal assistance this rendered to the local population, Service would also be an excellent means of introduction to active citizenship, and an admirable training for the young men of the Division. The diversity of interest and opinions among the members and their personal high standing soon resulted in the organization being represented indirectly on most of the local social and political committees. It also had among its members representatives of the majority of the trades and professions.

Ronald was the sole judge of what should be done, but was assisted by two very able directors—F. G. Thomas and Clement Sweet—the latter to be a staunch friend, helper and supporter through the many difficult times ahead.

From Political Service there rose a Central Political Group—a collection of people who met monthly to hear talks by representatives of all political parties. The talks were followed by open discussion. Outside speakers were invited on the understanding that they expressed their genuine personal convictions, unhindered by party policy. "Service" in return undertook to respect the confidence of its guests by not repeating any statement they made and by not admitting the Press to the meetings. The list of speakers was amazing in its variety and also somewhat horrifying to the local "die-hards." Among them were—Viscount Corvedale, Richard Crossman (then a Labour Candidate in Birmingham), the prospective Liberal Candidate for King's Norton, Mr. Lush (Aneurin Bevan's Agent for Ebbw Vale), Norman Tiptaft (A Birmingham City Councillor) and a Social Credit candidate. There was also a fair number of accepted Conservatives.

The discussions would last late into the night. Ronald deliberately did not attend all these meetings unless specially urged to do so, in order that his presence might not restrict the expression of opinion or comment. Once a year all members attended an informal dinner at which Ronald was present, and afterwards there was a still more informal talk when he was "peppered" with questions.

Although Service was intended primarily to assist the Member of Parliament in dealing with his constituents, the members also offered their services to the City Councillors and anyone else who needed them. After a few months' activity it was possible to find among those enlisted someone with the special qualifications required by any problem. An accountant could be produced to handle a financial problem, an architect would attend to a housing complaint, a nurse would help with sickness or maternity, etc., etc.

All reports were sent to Ronald direct, and only the Service member concerned knew the private details of an individual case.

All this, of course, took some months to develop, and Ronald at the start planned to begin quietly in a small way; then, when the foundations were laid, to affiliate the service with the West Midland Federation of the Junior Imperial League and get the scheme working in at least three constituencies where the Members of Parliament were live and energetic.

He had wanted for some time to have a great youth demonstration of the Junior Imperial League; he wanted to rouse and invigorate them; and he thought that after this meeting would be the right and suitable time to introduce them to "Service."

As usual there was the need of funds. Ronald raised a little from his personal friends, but it was a very little. Then Barbara thought of the one person she knew who would have the vision and understanding to realise what Ronald was attempting. She asked Lady Waddilove to meet Ronald at luncheon.

Mary Cartland was in India, where she had gone to stay with her brother, General John Scobell, who was G.O.C., Bombay. Ronald wrote to her in December:

"My Youth Demonstration goes very well. I've raised £50 from our list of friends you and I drew up, and Barbara's friend, Lady Waddilove, gave me £500 for that and Service! Wasn't it wonderful—so finally we're on clover. I shall feel happier about it all, though, on February 13th."

Ronald could now go ahead with his plans—he was full of enthusiasm, believing that at last he had something vital and sound to offer the young people both in his Division and in the West Midland Federation. Also in this letter to his mother he said:

"I spoke at Folkestone with Philip Sassoon on Wednesday and in the House on Tuesday. The latter went quite well but my triumph (if it may be called such) was the meeting with Neville Chamberlain. Everyone very complimentary on my speech. We had 3,000 there."

The meeting with the Prime Minister to which Ronald referred was a demonstration of the Empire Unity Campaign held at the Central Hall, Westminster. Two of the speakers were old friends—Sir Henry Page Croft, and Mr. Leo Amery who was Chairman. Ronald was Hon. Secretary. A number of people from King's Norton came to the meeting and he had a big reception when he seconded the vote of thanks to the Prime Minister.

The latter, replying, said that Ronald's eloquence showed that the younger generation was still as full of enthusiasm for those great ideals as the generation which preceded it, and could be trusted to carry on the banner when the old generation laid it down.

On December 16th, as he had told his mother, Ronald had spoken in the House. Once again on the Special Areas and Unemployment. The problems he was trying in a small way to solve by "Service" were in his mind, for in this speech he brought forward the human element very strongly, saying:

"We could solve the problem of unemployment in this country as it has been attempted to be solved in other countries, but at a loss of liberty and freedom. When we talk about the foundations of the present I believe that the real foundation is the human individual and the human individual's desire for freedom to express his personality. Whatever you do with your economic system, and whatever you do to produce a superb economic state, if you are going to do that at a loss of human personality, then you will destroy civilization which is the very thing you want to preserve. Judged by these standards the capitalist system is the best system—although it is not perfect—that can be designed or has been devised up to the present time."

He went on to say:

"The problems of the Special Areas are exactly the same problems which we are facing in other parts of the country, even in the most prosperous parts. Those problems are three in number—a social problem, a problem of capital, and a problem of labour." After taking these points one by one he suggested the solution lay not "by blowing up the existing foundations of society," but in re-creating "a new form of structure on the existing capitalist foundation."

He ended with the words:

"I will only say, in conclusion, that in considering all these economic problems and the solutions for them we must never forget the human factor. Sometimes I cannot help feeling, when listening to Debates, that one is apt to forget that in the end it is the man and the woman in industry with whom one is concerned. When we see what has happened in some of the Totalitarian countries I am frightened lest, in the desire for greater production and cheaper goods, we may forget that though we may turn human beings into machines we shall not in that way bring them happiness, nor give them any of those things which make life really worth living.

It is tremendously difficult to keep the balance between super-efficiency in industry and the preservation of the human personality. It is a tremendous problem, but I believe we can solve it; but only if we remember that it is the human desire for freedom which is at the basis of the capitalist system and which at all costs we must preserve."

CHAPTER TWENTY

1938

"It is the closed mind we must battle against."

ON JANUARY 3RD, 1938, Ronald celebrated his thirty-first birthday. He had altered during the past two years, which had been such happy and busy ones. He had matured, but it had made him more clear cut. Courage was the keynote to his character, a courage clear and unflinching, a courage which never faltered, never prevaricated whatever sacrifice was demanded of him.

It was sometimes hard to challenge not only convention, tradition, and the dignity of old age, but also friendship, affection and trust. But the courage of his convictions meant more than life itself—it was his life—a crusade of moral bravery. To those who knew him the fire of truth, vision and strength of purpose burned more brightly; at times it shone almost too brilliantly; stupid people who got a glimpse of it were afraid because it was something they did not understand.

His speaking, always exceptional, had improved until he was undoubtedly beginning to be an orator. He had the faculty of letting the force and power which guided him pour forth towards his audience. He had always believed he was but a transmitter—a channel through which that which was Spirit could function—but in the past this force, untrammelled and uncontrolled, had sometimes been overpowering.

Barbara told him she had seen an audience listening "open-mouthed like mesmerised rabbits, while those in the front row were almost blasted out of their seats." Now they were charmed into listening attentively, often breathlessly.

Someone wrote—"His keen handsome face, his dancing eyes, his gay, gallant spirit endeared him to all," but it was more than the charm of his personal qualities which attracted people. It was their instinctive, if often unconscious, appreciation of his astonishing integrity and fidelity to principle.

No one could be indifferent to Ronald. When he joined a party the whole tempo was accelerated, voices and spirits rose because he was there. Jim said once that one could feel in the depths of despair, everything wrong and then one would meet Ronald and everything would be different—there was something about him which dispelled difficulties or rather they sank in his presence into their rightful perspective.

It was inevitable that he could, too, arouse anger to a desperate pitch, even from those who loved him, but at a smile and a few words they would be ready, if not to die, at least to work their fingers to the bone for him. However annoyed he might be with a person it was soon forgotten. There would be what the family called "a blood row," but like a thunderstorm it would pass and the sun would come out. Ronald never bore malice.

Once he said to Barbara—"Never pay your enemies the compliment of thinking about them..it's giving them an undue importance."

The quality of him was inescapable—he was so unlike any one else. He was easily touched by little things—easily moved by all that was fine. He would tell a story of individual courage and the tears would gather in his eyes, but he despised more than anything else a parade of personal emotion in public.

"You mustn't cry, Mummy—I couldn't bear you to cry in front of people," he had said to his mother in 1919 when a memorial to his father had been unveiled.

But if he asked restraint from others the standard of discipline he set himself was a high one. He never drank or smoked while he was in the House of Commons; he generally went without dinner altogether before making a speech, or drank only a glass of milk. But he was no asthetic—he admired the Georgian ideal of a "full man"—one that appreciated all that was best in life, in food, in art, in literature, in conversation, in family life.

Ronald took an interest in good food, he appreciated claret and vintage port if he was on holiday, and a really good cigar. He liked to talk over a dinner-table until after midnight; and he loved children—he always said he would like a dozen of his own.

He enjoyed seeing his friends, but mostly in his own home; never having been social minded he had grown to dislike parties of any sort. For relaxation he was happiest at Littlewood in the garden—and he took a personal interest in the arrangements of the house. His fastidiousness had become intensified, it was a form of sensitiveness. He could not bear untidiness, slovenliness, and dirt. This was applicable mentally as well as physically.

However busy, Ronald always had time to read; he was appalled at the ignorance of those M.P.s who had no concrete knowledge on which to build their theories. To him books were a never-ending delight, as well as a source of stimulation. He liked writing and took tremendous pains over it, but his personality was not easily translated on to paper. It was revealed in his living contacts and in his spoken word, supported by his energy, his inner fire and inescapable charm.

His religion had become more and more important to him in the passing years. He believed fervently in the power of prayer, in being able, through meditation, to draw on a great Spirit force for inspiration. To him the Communion service was always a mystical experience of beauty and wonder, a source of spiritual strength which never failed him.

His health was better than ever before—although he was working increasingly hard. In the New Year plans for his big Youth Meeting occupied him almost exclusively. He was determined that it should not only be a success but a sensational success. He felt so many of his future plans for the youth of the country rested on the crusade he visualised for them being presented in the right way.

In the programme for the Meeting Ronald wrote these words:

"This Demonstration was originally conceived after the experience of the great Empire Youth Rally held in the Albert Hall, London, at the time of the Coronation last year. The occasion was moving and momentous; moving because the sight of a vast concourse of young British men and women called to one's mind the triumph of our race and the hopes we cherish for its future: momentous because Lord Baldwin, making his last speech as Prime Minister, spoke words which will never fail, whatever the passage of time, to summon the Youth of our Nation to lives of Service and Nobility.

"Now the heart of England lies in the Midlands. Through the grey-walled country of Gloucestershire, through the red soil of Herefordshire and Langland's meadowland where the Severn flows, through Shropshire's woods and Arden Forest and Cannock Chase into Burslem and Stoke, Birmingham and Smethwick, Wolverhampton and Walsall, there moves some spirit which gives to the people of our seven counties faith in the common man, belief in his ideals, conviction in their ultimate success.

"Words are but symbols and feeble when it is the spirit that needs expression. We cannot say what we want to: maybe we can show. In this Demonstration we, young men and young women from Gloucestershire, Herefordshire, Shropshire, Staffordshire, Warwickshire, Worcestershire and Birmingham attempt to reveal the faith that is in each one of us—faith in our land, our Empire and its destiny."

In 1937 Jim had become P.P.S. to the Rt. Hon. Anthony Eden, Secretary of State for Foreign Affairs. Through him Ronald asked Mr. Eden to be the guest of the evening and when the latter had accepted the great task of organization began. Ronald's only disappointment was that his mother was still in India and that Barbara had gone to the Sudan with her husband—neither could be back in time for the Meeting.

He had taken the Town Hall, Birmingham, which had caused a good deal of comment, especially from Empire House, which had for some time been raising its conventional eyebrows at the youngest and certainly to them the most unsatisfactory member of the Caucus. Mr. Edwards pointed out to Ronald that he was most unlikely to fill the hall. Junior Imperial League response to meetings in the past had not been up to expectations. The opportunity of arranging a Town Hall Rally had been given to the Birmingham Junior Imperial League Council but they had refused it on the advice of Mr. Edwards. A Birmingham Unionist Association Rally a few months previously had, in fact, been a complete failure.

Ronald went ahead with his plans. He arranged special trains for members of the Junior Imperial League from 43 constituencies. Vouchers and free travel on these trains from any authorised stopping place was included in the price of tickets for the Meeting (3/6). This small sum also entitled them to tea and hot refreshments before they left for home. He asked Reginald Foort of the B.B.C. to give an organ recital. He dealt personally with the applications for seats, working at the office until 3.30 a.m. the night the tickets were allocated; he "staggered" the arrival of trains, arranged that each Branch was allotted a separate cloakroom, wrote the programme, chose, collected and instructed the stewards.

On January 13th he wrote to his mother from the Priory.

"Since Christmas except for two days in London—one was yesterday—I've been here all the time, madly busy with the Demonstration. Such a lot to do, but my dear, Closing Day was Wednesday 12th—a whole month before the Meeting. Everyone said the Juniors never make up their minds until the last minute, etc. We are full—every seat sold! I've never known such enthusiasm. It does really repay me. We start sending out tickets next week. The Central Office have turned up trumps, Hacking, Topping, Gower all coming.

I wish you were here—it's the only thing that spoils it. And Barbara won't be here either. However, there's always something, I suppose. I toured the Area last week—500 miles—Rugby, Coventry, Sutton Coldfield, Wolverhampton, Shrewsbury, Forest of Dean, agents and branch offices—but it's obviously repaid me.

"Really no news. I've simply become an office boy again—working like a black 10-5, then meetings in the evenings."

The three people referred to in his letter were the Rt. Hon. Sir Douglas Hacking, Chairman of the Conservative Party, Sir Robert Topping, General Director of the Conservative Central Office, and Sir Patrick Gower, Chief Publicity Officer.

Ronald's secretary, Miss Leonard, said afterwards—"I shall never forget the look on Mr. Edwards' face when he asked Ronald if the Hall was getting fairly full, if applications were beginning to come in—and Ronald replied that the Hall could have been sold twice over!"

On February 1st Ronald wrote to his mother from London.

"The House started again to-day so I've at last left the Priory. But really I've enjoyed being there. I get on so well with the old man and I think he likes my living there. I've spent all this month organising the Eden Meeting on the 12th. And I think it's going to be a huge success. But, my word, I've had to work. The most marvellous thing has been selling the Hall right out a month before the day and collecting £250 in donations. Of course I've made a few speeches in the Division and elsewhere as well, but every day since January 1st I've been in the West Midlands office. You know I do enjoy a good bit of organisation."

"Service" had been busy about the Meeting, and over Christmas 150 joints of meat sent by the ever generous Carlow had been delivered to really poor householders, together with soup and other foods Ronald had collected himself. In his letter to his mother he said:

"I mentioned the meat—Uncle Howard behaved awfully well about that—the whole lot was brought here, unpacked in the yard by Watson and Mrs. Sweet, and he asked them in to tea. Then 25 Service young men and women came in their cars at 6.15. Uncle Howard had them all in the hall for sherry, port, and whisky—gave them cigars, etc., and was thanked by them and they by him. The distribution went off well and I've had such a lot of letters of thanks."

"Uncle Howard" was now 89 but he seemed to enjoy the even tenor of his ways being altered by Ronald. He was in good health, his only disability being that he was very deaf. Ronald was genuinely devoted to the old man and delightful with him, keeping him informed as to all that was happening, which was the one thing he really enjoyed.

Service was growing in strength and effect. Mr. Sweet said later—"Ronald's power to attract young people was a never failing source of wonder. Many of those who became his supporters were originally his critics. He seemed to inspire everyone with whom he came in contact with his own enthusiasm and vitality. My wife frequently recalls that we never remember feeling tired when he was with us, even when we came home after an exhausting meeting and sat talking until the small hours of the morning. I know he gave us, and all members of Service, a new and wider conception of public service and made our wildest and most distant ideals into practical possibilities."

That was Ronald's great power—he gave people faith in their own capabilities; anything became possible; no goal was unattainable.

The Day of the Demonstration arrived. Ronald was working up to the last minute; he had not only arranged the meeting, and collected together 2500 Juniors, sent out the tickets personally, anticipated every difficulty or hitch which might occur in the handling of such a crowd; he had also "staged" the show.

The platform at the Town Hall was decorated with Disraeli primrose yellow and massed with red, white and blue flowers. Behind the speakers was a gigantic Junior Imperial League badge and the names of the six counties in the area. Above them in the gallery leading to the great organ, were the standard bearers of the 155 branches, who marched to their places as Ronald called out their names through a loud-speaker.

Every arrival was cheered and there was a big reception when Ronald led in Lord Plymouth, Chairman of the Midland Union, and Lady Plymouth, President of the West Midland Federation. Then, while young voices sang "Land of Hope and Glory," Ronald walked slowly through the audience towards the Hall's main door. As the singing ended the door opened and he led back Mr. Eden, Lord Dunglass, Chairman of the Junior Imperial League, Mrs. Eden, and Jim, accompanied by cheers that swept out wave upon wave, until Ronald commenced a roll call of the 43 Divisions—each answering "Aye."

Mr. Eden made a fine speech, summed up in the sentence "The heart of the country is sound." The young men and women who listened were stirred. They took away from that meeting both inspiration and a desire for achievement. Ronald's words in the programme of what the Junior Imperial League means can portray briefly the spirit which moved that vast assembly.

"They recognise that Imperial Democracy can survive only if each citizen accepts willingly the responsibilities which Empire and Democracy, separately and together, entail, if sacrifices are ready to be made and knowledge relentlessly to be pursued. By precept and example, they set out to make men thrill again with love of Country, once more to give them pride in their dearest possessions, to give them faith in Britain's destiny."

In the West Midlands Review of the following month in a series, I BELIEVE Ronald said:

"It is seldom that great occasions arise when the Federation can show its strength. It is normally by steady, often pedestrian, activities that the Federation progresses.

"There is no merit in being young. There is immense opportunity. Where Physical youth is combined with idealism, initiative, and the inquiring mind, what worlds cannot be conquered! It is the closed mind we must battle against to-day. What are its symptoms? Defeatism—('Peace at *any* price'). We must fight cynicism—('You can't change human nature'—'Ideals are all right, but they aren't practicable').

"Above all we must avoid the quack recipes that advertise short-cuts and quick results, false standards for men or Nations, and the belief that we can find Salvation and Success through the efforts of others.

"Individual responsibility—Individual duty—should be our watchword, with the betterment of all as our goal and the traditions of the people as our guide."

CHAPTER TWENTY-ONE

1938

"Can anyone believe that the whole of civilization does not rest in the end upon the British people."

A POLITICAL CRISIS arose over Italy ten days after the Junior Imperial League Demonstration, following which Mr. Eden was to resign his post as Foreign Secretary. In the Debate which followed on February 22nd a motion was brought by the Opposition to deplore the circumstances in which Mr. Eden had been obliged to resign.

Ronald interrupted Sir I. Anderson to challenge the rumour and the suggestion that Mr. Eden "took the action which he did on account of ill health." He went on to speak of the difference between the Prime Minister and Mr. Eden as a method and outlook not confined to the House of Commons, but something which seemed to run right through the country.

"It may be that sometimes the difference is a matter of age. Perhaps those who scan the horizon and have many years ahead of them look with rather different eyes at all the problems of to-day from those who have not so many years ahead. I know there are many people who sincerely say that to maintain a certain conduct in international relations at the present time is foolhardy, in face of the existing dangers, but expediency in foreign politics has never been a tenet of the Tory faith. I say frankly as a Tory that I believe that in all questions of foreign policy—or indeed of any policy, but particularly foreign policy—right should always come before expediency, whether it be dangerous, difficult or foolhardy."

The next day the *Birmingham Mail* remarked:

"Few M.P.s believed that the Government stood in any serious danger from the attack of the Opposition yesterday. Before the Debate was properly under way, it was evident that Mr. Chamberlain could count on the support of all but a few back-benchers.

"He had the backing of all his fellow Birmingham members except Mr. Ronald Cartland, who, as M.P. for King's Norton, has more than once taken an individualistic course. He was an abstentionist, and indicated his inability to accept the Premier's handling of the Italian problem."

The Spectator two days later said:

"The last and most important question of all is what effect the events of the past week will have on Mr. Eden's future. That, certainly, never entered for a moment into his calculations, but there is little doubt that in the country, and probably in the end in the Conservative Party, he will gain more than he loses. Only one thing can undo him—and of that there are signs already—excessive zeal in the Opposition in their endeavour to make party capital out of his resignation. This is no party matter and much the most important speeches in support of the late Foreign Secretary came from Conservatives like Mr. Churchill, Major Hills, General Spears, and Mr. Cartland."

On March 1st Anthony Eden wrote to Ronald:

"17, FITZHARDINGE STREET, W.1.
March 1st, 1938.

"MY DEAR CARTLAND,

"These few lines are to try to thank you for your speech last week. It must have required great courage to make it, for nothing is more difficult than to disagree with one's political associates at a critical time.

"I am naturally deeply grateful for the spirit which prompted you to speak as you did.

"Yours sincerely,
"ANTHONY EDEN."

It was not without humour that in King's Norton a public challenge was made by Mrs. Pakenham, the Socialist Candidate, to Ronald to reconcile the present policy of the Government he was supporting with the statements he made in his Election Address in regard to the League of Nations.

Mrs. Pakenham had recently been adopted by the Labour Party in King's Norton. Ronald, in a letter to his mother at the beginning of January, had said:

"We're getting a Woman Organiser for six months in King's Norton because Mrs. Pakenham is working hard and I'm worried about the new districts. I told the Association at our meeting last night I thought they were living in a fool's paradise."

Ronald replied to Mrs. Pakenham's challenge at Bournville,

speaking to an audience of intellectuals, labourers, Communists, Fascists, Socialists, Liberals and Conservatives. He was in a fighting mood.

"I take exception to the Foreign Policy of the Government," he said, "and I take equal exception to the Foreign Policy of the Labour Party. Since when was Mr. Eden the Labour Party's blue-eyed boy? For two and a half years I have held meetings in this Division, and ninety per cent of the questions were about foreign affairs—attacking Mr. Eden. "A little more support when he was there would have been better than so many kisses when he was gone. I say quite frankly that the sloppy sentimentality they are pouring on Mr. Eden makes me— and I have little doubt, him—sick."

At this meeting, as was often his custom, Ronald dispensed with a Chairman. As soon as he rose to address the hall he was interrupted. A little man jumped up and asked—

"Why don't you do the thing properly and have a Chairman like everyone else?"

Ronald replied: "I see no reason to have any one between me and my constituents, and a Chairman is not necessary."

There were cries of "sit down," but the interrupter was not satisfied and pressed the point.

Quickly Ronald suggested—"Very well—you be my Chairman."

The little man's courage failed him.

"No—No!"

"Yes, indeed," Ronald insisted, and the audience cheered as, still protesting under his breath, the little man was obliged to climb nervously on to the platform—where he sat an awkward, silent cipher for the rest of the evening.

The audience were delighted, and even those who habitually scoffed and opposed Ronald's unorthodox methods seemed to take him to their hearts on this occasion.

Later in his speech dealing with the possible creation of a great German Empire in Central Europe, Ronald said prophetically:

"It is possible to envisage Britain isolated, faced with a colossal Germany asking 'Now what are you going to do about it?' We, turning anxious, distraught eyes towards the Nations who would help us, would suddenly realise they had been gobbled up."

The idea of war permeated all his speeches this month. At Erdington—to a branch of the League of Nations Union—he stated:

"I do not believe you will ever again get the British people to march on some purely materialist enterprise, but I do believe they will respond, as they have always responded, to an appeal which they believe to be truthful and right. Nothing appeals to the British people more than a resistance to a challenge against freedom. There is no part of Europe which does not concern this country."

Again, on March 26th, at the Annual Meeting of the Divisional Unionist Association in King's Norton, he warned his audience:

"Our immediate aims are peace and prosperity. We want the two together: but it is no good purchasing either peace or prosperity, or the two together, if the price we have to pay is too high.

"In many quarters of the world to-day we have whole nations accepting compulsion, and accepting a regulation of their whole lives. I tell you quite frankly that we are faced to-day with forces in the world which, if they go unchecked, must threaten peace, if not in the immediate present, certainly in the eventual future. There are in this country some who hold the view that dictatorships and democracies can exist side by side. That might be so—although personally I doubt it—but what might be the cost to democracy? Might it be at such a cost that in the end the very essentials of democracy had to be thrown overboard?

"Can anyone believe that the whole of civilization does not rest in the end upon the British people? I believe that the next few years are going to be vital years so far as this country is concerned. There are still some people who shut their eyes to what is happening in the world. It is no good meeting positive action with negative emotion. One of the chief tasks for each one of us is to try and make others aware that democracy has its responsibility. The main purpose of Government at the present must be the defence of the country, and there must be no slackening of re-armament. I hope the Government will not hesitate to call upon all sections of the community for sacrifice during the next few years in order to make this country safe."

In July, 1941, Mr. Ellis Smith, Labour Member for Stoke, speaking in the House of Commons, said—

"Some of us long ago saw the danger of the growing expansion of German armaments, and our consciences stimulated us to work. Ronald Cartland was an example of what I mean, with his clear-sightedness, his great energy, his far-seeing qualities. his courage —and it took some courage in those days—drive and dynamic personality, all those qualities that find avenues of service."

In April Ronald seconded a clause introduced by Mr. Salt, Member for Yardley, to the Rent and Mortgage Interest (Restrictions) Bill. The Clause asked the House to limit the evil effects of the decontrol. In Birmingham the demand for houses had been so great that tenants would put up with deplorable conditions for fear of being asked to leave. There were cases where rents were increased from 6/6 a week to 25/- as a result of decontrol. Ronald regretted that these houses could not be put back under control, saying:

"All the letters that one gets from industrial constituencies deal with housing conditions and the difficulties of finding alternative accommodation in face of the tremendous shortage and of having to pay these big rents. It is fantastic to expect tenants to pay 50 per cent of their wages in rent.

"What I would really like to see is the re-control of all these houses, but what we suggest is—and it seems to me a most reasonable and sensible suggestion—that the tenant who is faced with what he believes to be an excessive rent should be able to go to the local authority—that is an added safeguard—and explain, and that the local authority should then be able to take action against that sort of thing. All of us know that it is not an easy thing for a tenant to take action against his landlord, but if he is able to go to court with the whole force of the corporation behind him, I believe it will be found that we can deal effectively with some of these excessive rent charges."

Mr. Tom Johnson described Labour's vain efforts to secure the right of appeal to a county court and promised support for the Clause.

But, as one paper said briefly next day—"Sir Kingsley Wood did not like the Birmingham group."

The Clause was defeated by 47 votes. Three Members voted against the Government, each representing Birmingham constituencies. They were Mr. E. W. Salt, Wing-Commander Wright, and Ronald.

Ever since Ronald first began to work in King's Norton he had been dealing with housing complaints. The City Council had investigated case after case which he had brought before them and he had managed to get a lot done in the way of repairs, additional sanitation, etc. He had been horrified at the condition in which some families were forced to live and said frequently that in his experience women were the worst landlords. "Service" was to be an ever-increasing help in getting abuses remedied and in reporting unsatisfactory and often insanitary accommodation.

Ronald was also concerned with another local problem, one for which he had tried to find a solution when he was still a candidate. Foreseeing encroaching danger to private traders through chain and multiple stores, Ronald had started the King's Norton Division Traders' Association with three main objects—

1. To assist traders in continuing their business profitably without unfair conditions among themselves or with the large combines.

2. To enable the community to have the advantages that comes from private trade—i.e. individual attention, variety of goods, easy access, reasonable prices, contributions to the rates.

3. To influence the tradespeople politically, and incidentally to exert indirect influence on their customers.

It was a big undertaking and Ronald was not satisfied with the effort which had been made in the first three years of its foundation, so he reorganised the Association, elected a new Committee, made Clement Sweet the Honorary Organiser, and started an extensive campaign to which there was a big response.

Social facilities were provided—outings, concerts, dances. Local complaints were taken up with the authorities. Competitions and a large Exhibition were organised.

Not only in a united front could the traders combat the dangers to their existence and livelihood, but Ronald was also able to gain and to maintain excellent relations with a very useful section of the electorate who would not have been reached through normal channels.

That April the B.B.C. moved the weekly Parliamentary talks, "The Week in Westminster," into the National evening programme. Ronald was asked to be the Conservative commentator. The B.B.C. said later that he was the best speaker they ever had in these talks, and he was so successful that when he reached the usual limit of six months there were so many requests for him to continue that he was to remain in the same series for over a year and a half. He received £10 a broadcast.

In May there was a debate on Air re-armament. Mr. Winston Churchill headed a group of Ministerialists who called for an independent committee of enquiry, and the Socialist motion on the debate was tantamount to a motion of censure. Those who supported Mr. Churchill of course included Ronald; he was becoming more and more alarmed by the situation in Europe, especially as, during a private conversation with a very important Foreign Office official he was told:

"The Diplomatic reports from the Continent are extremely serious—but speaking frankly I believe that the Prime Minister puts them straight into the waste-paper basket—unread."

But the battle at home was still over unemployment. Ronald spoke on a Motion of the Unemployment Assistance Board on the 18th July. One paper next morning remarked:

"Unhappily for the Opposition Mr. Amery, Mr. Cartland, and Sir Smedley Crooke—three of 'those Birmingham Tories'—insisted on speaking in terms that would have seemed faultless in any genuine representative of Labour."

Ronald began by saying:

"I think we are in very grave danger of coming to accept unemployment assistance as a permanent relief of the unemployment problem. I will go further, and say that the problems we have so frequently raised in these Debates; the relation between wages and relief, the relation between wages and insurance, and so on, are all minor problems. The major problem which this House must face seems to be—is it possible for us to create in this country conditions under which employment ceases to be a curse and becomes a boon?

"That is what to me constitutes the difference in definition between leisure and unemployment. I cannot believe that there is anyone in this House who is going to say that permanent ceaseless work must always be the cure for unemployment, in all circumstances and at all times. If that is the suggestion, then the entire policy of this country is wrong.

"Most people will agree that there is a time in every man's life when it is not work which is wanted but leisure—but leisure implies saving and security."

He then went on to speak of the Pilgrim Trust report, saying: the theme which ran through every chapter was the theme of low wages. He quoted a boy of 21 working 12 hours a day for 10 - a week. A girl of 18 employed in a tea shop at 6 - a week. There were many such examples which made the real problem—"Are you going to let your allowances and assistance go beyond your actual wage rates?"

He went on:

"I cannot help feeling that the case is overwhelming, that the longer you keep your wages at a low level the more permanent you are making your employment problem, and that you will never really begin to solve the problem until you go right back and tackle it from the wages end and not the assistance end."

He spoke of elderly men, saying that if a man of 50 dropped out of work it was exceedingly difficult for him to get back. One-third of the unemployed who were over 55 were actually in the prosperous part of the country—the South and Midlands.

He asked:

"What can be done? I believe everything should be done. The first thing surely is for everybody in the country to put himself into a frame of mind in which he will be prepared to accept any suggestion from whatever source it comes. One fatal frame of mind is to believe that something can or cannot be done by any one system, whether it is Capitalism or Socialism.

"If one reads these reports and the extra-Parliamentary reports, what must strike one all the time in all of them is, that the position of the unemployed is not just a challenge to the Capitalist system. If it was I do not think it would be of very great consequence. What is far more important is, that it is a challenge to the whole democratic system. You cannot go on talking to people about the defence of liberty and of freedom. It is absolute cant and humbug to talk about that as long as you have economic insecurity deadening the majority of our people.

The hon. Gentleman said that we all now used nice words for unpleasant facts. We all talk about economic insecurity. What we mean is industrial slavery. We must be able to overcome that in the minds of the people. They know it every day. They go to draw their wages each Friday, and have not the slightest idea that, perhaps after 25 years' service, they will not be wanted back on the following Monday. What is the use of defending democracy until you are able to convince them that democracy can work and does work and provides them with the sort of livelihood they want and cannot get under any other system.

"I cannot see why the Government cannot really come forward and give our people the psychological aims for which this report on unemployment asks. Why not? Our people want it. They believe in this democratic system. How much longer are they going to go on believing in it, I sometimes wonder? I would ask my right hon. Friend not to neglect the psychological side of the problem. I cannot see anything to be said for modern methods of industry; there is nothing to be said for mass production unless the surplus energy which is released can find its outlet in other ways.

Driven all the time into the background by this ghastly machinery is the real fundamental idea of work—that it gives man an opportunity to create things and to express his own individuality I cannot believe that it passes our comprehension and our wit in 1938, with all our inventive power and with this tremendous production and out-pouring of wealth, somehow to assure and give to our people a fairer and fuller life, which all deserve but which so few enjoy."

CHAPTER TWENTY-TWO

1938

"*Democracy can only survive if men believe in it more strongly than in Dictatorship.*"

IN AUGUST Ronald went into camp with the Worcestershire and Oxfordshire Yeomanry on Salisbury Plain. Two former Hussar units had been converted under the Mechanisation Scheme, and consolidated into the 53rd Anti-Tank Regiment R.A. with the strength of two batteries. There were all-night operations over difficult country, firing on the ranges, lectures by Regular Army Officers, and a great deal of light-hearted ragging.

Ronald enjoyed himself, he forgot to be a "statesman" and became for two short weeks a carefree young man of thirty-one. They were a very cheery crowd. The Colonel—"Tony" Muirhead—was also a Member of Parliament and a personal friend of Ronald. Other friends in the Regiment at that time were the Hon. Charles Lyttelton, Captain Jack Christopher, and the Earl of Birkenhead.

At the end of the month Ronald and Barbara set off for Switzerland while their mother looked after Barbara's children at Pevensey Bay, where the latter had taken a house.

As usual Ronald wrote a long descriptive letter to his mother of the journey, their change of plans, and his impressions of the country.

"GRESSBACK,
BRIENZENSEE, SWITZERLAND.

"DEAR DARLING,

"A rough crossing. B. felt ill—tho' managed to survive—I slept three-quarters of the way. Calais and into our sleepers for the long trek. Not a bad night and got to Interlaken at 8. A lovely half-hour through quite unbelievably beautiful country before we got here. Then half an hour's motor ride to Briez. Not a bad little village. but we knew the hotel was 'not us'—single rooms, no creature comforts. B. made up her mind at once. We went after breakfast, still in our travelling clothes, down the village street, saw a postcard of this hotel, inquired about it, hired a car, drove out in twenty minutes, saw the rooms we are now in—back and gave notice to quit—shook hands all round, and we're here unpacking at 11.30!

"This place is too lovely to describe. The lake itself a thousand feet below—huge mountains either side a thousand feet high—to the side of them a series of gigantic waterfalls—'les cascades'—quite one of the sights of the neighbourhood. The walks through the pine forests are beautiful *and* deserted. Beds superb, food first-class. In fact so far we can find no snag.

"Switzerland is packed with middle class English. The difficulty to find the Swiss. Every one talks English, even the old woman high up on the mountains where we got a cup of tea yesterday. To-day we went across the lake to Briez—nothing much to see—a Calvanistic Church—pretty old village."

In his next letter he wrote:

"We went for an immense walk on Tuesday. It's a three and a half hours' walk and we did it in two and a half, B. protesting—and I'm not surprised—up hill the whole way, a most tiring climb. But the thought of tea spurred us both on. It was well worth it, a lovely view from the top!

"Switzerland is the most expensive place, everything in the shops far far more expensive than England. Never have we been to a place so expensive in *Everything*. We've yet to discover one single item of luxury or necessity in which Switzerland is cheaper than our native land. Hence expect no souvenirs. I said we read. B. has just informed me she has read 21 books since she has been here. I have devoured 10. So you see our lives are not idle. The difference in the above figures is chiefly due to our difference in taste!"

On these walks Ronald talked a great deal of Winston Churchill—he had for him a great admiration and also a growing affection. In the summer Mr. Churchill had gone to Birmingham to speak at a big meeting of the League of Nations Union at the Town Hall. The next morning he visited the Austin aeroplane factory, at that time the largest works operating under the Government's shadow factory scheme. Ronald had accompanied him on his tour.

"The men were thrilled to see him," Ronald told Barbara. "I've never seen such enthusiasm. It's not surprising—he has such presence—such personality—also the man in the street realises that he has been right in everything he has said since 1933. Those in high places say he's finished—I don't believe it. He has a following in the country far bigger than those in Westminster think."

Just before the House rose one of the older M.P.s had said to Ronald—"Let me give you a word of advice, Ronnie. Winston's no good to a young man—keep away from him."

Ronald replied in that icy voice that those who antagonised him knew so well—"Thank you. I must be allowed to choose my own friends."

Ronald returned to England to start his annual campaign in the constituency. This year his Message to his Electors was written to convey very clearly that he meant to "follow his conscience" wherever it might lead him. He wrote:

"The number of letters I have received in the past year has been enormous. Often, I fear, I have not been able to do all that I have been asked or tried to do. All of us are bound by laws and regulations, and though new laws and fresh regulations are continually being made, no one will suppose that everybody, by Acts of Parliament or otherwise, can be entirely satisfied. The most that we can do at any moment is to express in the law the desires of the majority of the people. It is the duty of Parliament to see that the wishes of the people are voiced and put into effect. If Parliament fails to do that sooner or later Parliament will be destroyed, and some form of dictatorship will take its place. Parliament must neither rush ahead nor lag behind the general opinion of the country. And it is for the forming of that general opinion and seeing that the House of Commons is aware of it that every elector is responsible.

"A Member of Parliament, apart from his purely local duties, has a double task: to see that the views of his constituents so far as they affect the interests of all, are taken into account by Government and Parliament, and to use his influence in support of those aims which he believes should be the aims of the nation.

"Parties, Unionist, Liberal and Labour, have come into being because men found that they could further their aims best in association with others. But the obligation of a Member of Parliament to express his own opinion or his constituents' must always be superior to his obligation as a Member of a party. It will be fatal to Parliament if any other view than this ever comes to be accepted.

"At the present time men of all three parties are supporting a National Government. I believe myself that the idea of a National Government is sound. It seems to me to be the answer of Democracy to Dictatorship, and the challenge to Democracy is surely our greatest danger to-day. The challenge to Democracy comes from those who do not understand how deep is our belief in freedom, and the value we set on the right of each individual to live his own life with minimum interference and maximum opportunity. What I fear is that our domestic differences here in England may be misunderstood abroad, as they have been before, and it may be thought that we are not a united nation.

"We are not at war but men go about their business with fear as to what may happen. We can only have peace if men are convinced that peace is the best policy. Democracy can only survive if men believe in it more strongly than in Dictatorship. What must we do? We must make it plain that though we hate war we shall fight with all our strength to preserve our freedom; we must never in any way compromise our belief in democratic principles; we must strive still for the international acceptance of the League Covenant; we must always remember that the British Empire can be the greatest force for good in the world.

"If we can give our people a higher standard of life, more security in employment and in old age, better conditions of living, greater opportunities for seeking happiness than elsewhere, we shall provide Democracy with its most powerful weapons, and Peace with its surest foundation.

"It is this belief which has urged me particularly in the last few months to stress the importance of our using the marvels of modern invention and the wealth of modern industry to provide a fuller, freer life for every one.

"There is no short-cut to the solution of our modern problems—no ready-made easy answer. We have to rid ourselves of all prejudice and preconceived notions. We have to do some hard thinking and, I believe, take drastic action. But it is worth it. Because the security of our land and the future of our people depend on the success of our efforts."

From Birmingham he wrote to his secretary: "The campaign continues most successfully and we're having glorious weather. The largest crowds I've ever had—but Mr. Hitler is to thank for that—not me."

The Czechoslovakian crisis rose suddenly like a tempest. Parliament was recalled on September 28th. Ronald was an early arrival as were a great many other Members. Mr. Chamberlain's broadcast the night before had left an impression that if war was not inevitable it would need a miracle to avert catastrophe.

There was an atmosphere of tense anticipation in the Chamber.

Queen Mary and the Duchess of Kent were in the Speaker's Gallery; the Duke of Kent, Earl Baldwin, and the Archbishop of Canterbury were in the crowded Peers Gallery.

Mr. Chamberlain started his speech and before it ended made his sensational announcement that he would go to Munich. The scene which followed was dramatic and un-English. One Member yelled "Thank God for Neville," others wept with relief. Ronald was calm, silent and aloof in the midst of what was to him undignified emotionalism.

All Britain waited breathlessly while the British Prime Minister, representing his Majesty's Government, flew to Germany for a second meeting with an upstart dictator, representing the insatiable bloodlust of the German people.

Ronald, talking to Barbara on September 29th, asked—"Do you think the Prime Minister is praying as he goes? No man needs more help from God."

Mr. Chamberlain returned to receive the plaudits of the crowds at Croydon, the hysterical cheers of M.P.s shouting and waving from the windows and pavements of Downing Street. The Prime Minister's reception in the House seems in retrospect unreal, exaggerated. Ronald said afterwards—"I rose very slowly to my feet. I did not cheer."

On October 3rd Mr. Duff Cooper resigned. Mr. Vyvyan Adams described him as "the pioneer along the nation's way back from hysteria to reason." The words of the former First Lord of the Admiralty to his friends expressed the feelings of a few—a very few—others.

"It was 'peace with honour' that I couldn't stomach. If he'd come back from Munich saying 'peace with terrible, unmitigated, unparelleled dishonour' perhaps I would have stayed. But 'peace with *honour*'!"

It was the 'peace with honour' which stuck in Ronald's throat. He said to Barbara—"Of course, Neville couldn't do anything else, once he had got to Munich. He had been warned, but he wouldn't see it coming. But what one hates is the terrible ghastly farce of that 'victory drive'—that 'triumphant' appearance on the balcony of Buckingham Palace when in the streets of Prague the people wept openly at being forsaken."

Commenting on this Noel Coward said bitterly to Ronald: "Neville Chamberlain has just discovered what every chorus boy discovers his first year on the stage—the heady quality of applause."

Feeling ran high over the whole country. People who were

ordinarily calm and unpolitically-minded lost their tempers, were furious with those who disagreed with them, rude and offensive at the slightest provocation.

In King's Norton Ronald had the support of the majority of his young people and the violent disapproval of many of the older ones. The latter's feelings were adequately expressed by a resident in the Division who rose at a public meeting and announced that in his opinion "with the possible exception of Our Lord no greater man than Mr. Chamberlain has ever trod this earth." In London Barbara was told at a luncheon party that "those traitors—Winston Churchill, your brother, and his like should be shot."

In the House there was talk of an Election; there were cheers for the Prime Minister whenever he appeared but it was not unanimous. One paper stated "the position is that outside the Conservative Party there remains a formidable bloc of opinion led by Mr. Winston Churchill, Mr. Eden, Mr. Duff Cooper, Mr. Amery, Mr. Cartland, and others which is hostile to the Government's present policy."

Ronald was unable to catch the Speaker's eye in the Debate that followed and on October 7th he set forth his views in a letter to the Birmingham papers.

"SIR,—I should not have troubled you with a letter had I been fortunate enough to catch Mr. Speaker's eye during the debates in the House of Commons.

"No one has challenged the sincerity of the Prime Minister's efforts for peace. It is the effect of his policy, both immediately and in the future, that some of us question.

"It is now obvious that, having counted the cost, we gave in to Herr Hitler's ultimatum. It may well be that our people do not regard the price paid for peace as too high. But many of them, I am sure, could not understand what the Prime Minister meant when he talked of 'peace with honour.' Surely no one can regard the Munich agreement as a triumph for peaceful negotiations, while the circumstances in which the Anglo-German declaration was signed appear to many in the light of presenting a testimonial to a gangster.

"It seems to me essential that we should have a foreign policy which is understood not only abroad but by our people at home. Will any one deny that in the present state of the world it is also essential that we should have a foreign policy in support of which we are a united nation?

"If it is accepted that civilization is built on the practice of keeping promises, and maintained by making that practice work, it follows that we must have a system of collective defence against the enemies of civilization.

"Is war the worst that can happen to mankind? Loss of freedom would undermine our national character and destroy the British race. We are suspicious of all Dictatorships. But it is the policy pursued by the Dictators of Germany and Italy, and the philosophy which inspires their regimes, which alarms and horrifies our countrymen.

"It cannot be denied that the means whereby foreign affairs are conducted are symptomatic of the end in view. Herr Hitler and Signor Mussolini think in terms of militarism, and we in terms of commerce. They regard foreign affairs in terms of strategy, and we in terms of a bargain. The effect of the recent crisis has been to confirm the rulers of Germany and Italy in the belief that the threat of force is the most successful method of negotiation.

"No one, be it noted, has suggested that now is the time for disarmament. Indeed there have been pleas for the acceleration of our rearmament programme. One effect of the crisis has been to reveal the gross inadequacy of our air raid precautions, and people all over the country have seen for themselves the state of our defences.

"We cannot, I believe, save our country from the disasters which threaten us without real and inspired national unity. We must not only have a foreign policy on which we can all agree, but a conception of the social and economic conditions which we wish to create in this country.

"What makes co-operation almost impossible is the present rigid party system. We must find a way by which men of all parties can work together if a positive, virile democracy is to stand the strain of Nazi and Fascist tactics. In the last few years the Democracies have been forced to show that these tactics are irresistible. Quite recently the Prime Minister said that "Democracy can afford to make mistakes.' Every responsible citizen must ask himself now, if we are to survive, whether we can afford to make any more.

"RONALD CARTLAND,
(M.P. for King's Norton)."

This letter produced a spate of correspondence, both in the newspapers and to Ronald personally. Ronald was naturally in disgrace as far as the Whips' Office was concerned, and in October, speaking at a luncheon of the Birmingham Jewellers Association, he attacked the Party system saying:

"It is nonsense to pretend that it isn't possible to have some change in Parliamentary machinery and method without destroying the character of Parliament or the high place it holds in the minds of the people.

"If you are going always to have every scheme assailed—and in many cases, destroyed—just because it comes from one side of the House, we have no hope in this country of meeting the competition of those countries where no opposition is allowed at all.

"I believe implicitly in criticism but much more implicitly in co-operation. And one of the hindrances both to co-operation and to free criticism is this hard and fast, hide-bound party system. It is, I believe, much more hide-bound at Westminster than in the country as a whole."

In November Ronald wrote in *Headway*:

"This is not the time for post-mortems. There will doubtless be some decent burials and indecent exhumations in Parliament. But I'm convinced that it is of the future that the British people are anxious. The recent speeches of Mr. Churchill and Mr. Eden have been devoured because they have been expressing (so it seems to me) the views of the time and the desires of the people.

"What is needed at once is a clear, positive declaration of aim to which men of all parties with good will in their hearts and good sense in their heads can subscribe. Shall we get such a declaration? And if so from whom?"

CHAPTER TWENTY-THREE

1938

"I do not care who does it, so long as it gets done."

PARLIAMENT met on November 8th with its usual pageantry of ceremony, robes, tiaras, and so on. But to Ronald there was a drabness, not in the scene but in the scenario. In his own words—"So much is happening these days off stage that the Chamber has taken on the appearance of a backcloth against which the old favourites do their turns while the audience wait for the grand transformation scene."

But whatever happened in Europe the unemployed in traditional manner "were always with us." Their numbers increasing instead of diminishing. Ronald had said several years previously—"the Unemployment Bill reminds me of the Paris tumbril grinding and creaking its way on to the guillotine, with Captain Margesson in the role of Defarge counting heads."

Now he felt that it had almost stopped creaking, that the Government were doing little and had no plan for the future. Mr. Ernest Brown gave him personally the unfortunate impression that if progress was made by a small decrease in numbers he was prepared to take the credit for it, but that in the many debates he had never shown any anxiety as to the future. A future which would produce an acute situation if the international outlook lightened or re-armament ceased.

"Like most of the Government supporters on this subject," Ronald said to his friends, "Mr. Brown preaches 'faith, hope and charity' and when we ask for something more definite, deplores our ingratitude with raised hands."

On November 14th, Ronald, in the Debate on the Address, said: "One thing at least is clear now, and it is that the Government have no unemployment policy as such."

He went on to state that there was a big drop in exports, there was a falling off in the building trade, there was concern about the future of shipbuilding.

"It is no use talking about markets," he said, "unless we do something about men. Frankly, I think we must face the fact that, in order to solve our special unemployment problem, we shall have to recognise that, at one end of the scale, work is no solution for unemployment. The only solution at one end of the scale is savings. The old age problem is not one of unemployment and work, but one of savings and the ability to retire. At the other end it is a problem of the recruitment and training of labour."

Again he asked for central direction, a "thinking staff," over the economic life of the country—so that the Government could harness industry, and finance the development of markets abroad, and exploit to better purpose the inventive genius of the country.

He referred to Mr. Eden's speech—a survey of the country's needs and the need for a supreme effort—as the sort of speech we ought to have from the Front Bench and stressed that to rebuild our whole social and industrial life would involve immense sacrifices, and in order to get sacrifices we must have Leadership.

"When you get leadership," he ended, "you will get the country responding to sacrifices, but unless you face up to your difficulties and make an appeal, and the right one, and unless people know what you are aiming for, you will go down to disaster and destruction."

Mr. Ernest Brown thundered that Ronald's speech amounted to "words—words—words," and continued: "We are a little tired of being lectured by people like the Hon. Member."

A few days later an article by Ronald appeared in the *Birmingham Mail.* He started it with the question:

"What is the purpose of Democracy but to give men complete freedom for self-expression and self-development? Any limitation in aim at once undermines the strength and prostitutes the meaning of democracy. But this is not to say that the aim will be attained, either at once or hereafter, without voluntary control, in itself a restriction of freedom, but only, of course, where such control is in fact restrictive.

"To-day fear prevents the realisation of democracy as much as the lust for power prevents world peace. Yet against lust for power only the love of freedom can finally be certain of victory. Power cannot be shared by all; freedom can. Surely, therefore, it behoves the countries which call themselves democracies to urge, side by side with their measures for defence, the spiritual invigoration of their people and progress towards their ultimate goal. The people must know what they are being asked to fight for; otherwise they will not fight."

Ronald's ideas had a great deal of support from the young

people in his Division; he received a large number of letters not only criticising the Government but the Parliamentary system.

In an issue of *Headway*, Ronald wrote:

"Just how much does Parliament mean to the twenty million men and women in this country who work for their livelihood? There is no doubt in my mind that to very many the House of Commons appears as a cross between Madame Tussaud's and a marionette show. The machinery of Parliament is chiefly to blame. The infrequency of a vote on a 'straight' issue, the rules of order and debate, amaze and then aggravate. Is it all a game, or is this the method—not the best, but the only method—by which England can solve her problems of poverty, ill-health, malnutrition, above all, of defence?

"But if those who are not members feel frustrated and exasperated, no less so do those who are. Anxiety and unrest have increased since Munich and the crisis. The ghastly horrors in Germany have rudely torn the scales from the eyes of all. Appeasement is put into cold storage. But what of our rearmament, which concerns much more than guns and aeroplanes? The virility of the whole nation must be nurtured. The condition of the people, especially of the young people, is a vital part of defence; so is our trade and finance—the list truly is unending. And the common denominator is the human individual."

Ronald was justified at the end of the month in asking how much Parliament cared for the problem of the "ordinary man and woman." The Expiring Laws Continuance Bill was considered in Committee on November 28th. During this important Debate there was rarely a quorum—40 Members—in the House. At almost any time it looked as though the House might have been "counted out." At one period there were only 15 Labour representatives present and 4 Conservatives.

After an opening Speech by Mr. George Hall who laid all the reasons why the distressed areas existed at the charge of the Government, and another by Major Lloyd George who suggested it was a much more historical problem, Ronald said:

"It seems to me that the outstanding conclusion is that this is not an area problem. It is really an industrial problem. We cannot envisualise employment or the solution of unemployment only from the area point of view."

Speaking of the problems of evacuation and saying that they were in a trinity with the location of industry and transport,

Ronald asked why our evacuation had not been better managed, saying:

"In war-time your evacuation will be orderly—or at least we hope it will be—and on certain definite lines to certain definite areas. Let us remember that evacuation has been going on in this country for the last 10 years though principally on the part of a certain section of the population which hon. Members who represent distressed areas do not like to see leaving their homes. That kind of evacuation is uncontrolled. It means people going anywhere, and very often where they are not really required. Is it not possible in some way to have something approaching the orderly and controlled evacuation of war-time when you are dealing in peace-time with evacuation which is the result of industrial war?"

Ronald went on to say that in his opinion problems could only be solved if capital and labour were prepared to "give and take." It was the task of the Government to bring the two together and he believed that Labour would be asked to accept the principle of compulsory training for young men and in return "industry should be asked to give up some of its rights and to see that workers are properly provided for in their old age."

He finished: "I should like the Rt. Hon. Gentleman (Sir Denis Herbert) to say—" Nothing is ruled out. True, we have put in this Special Areas act, but it is only temporary. We have not given up and are still open to suggestion.' If he could say something like that I think we should have still greater confidence than we have at the present time that the Government can and will solve the problem."

One of the lobby correspondents, Mr. Harold ffoulkes, wrote of Ronald:

"To say that he was more a Socialist than the Socialists in his keen sense of desire to help the country's needy communities would not be to express quite accurately his outlook. He was as much impatient of what he called the "stick-in-the-muds" on the Labour Bench as he was of the die-hards in his own party. His motto was "I do not care who does it so long as it gets done."

CHAPTER TWENTY-FOUR

1938-1939

"Only through freedom can man find salvation."

THAT autumn Ronald experienced what he regarded as one of the spiritual highlights of his life. Rom Landau invited him to a Conference at the Bishop's Palace at Chichester.

It was a small conference of about twelve people and included educationalists, theologians, business men and writers. Sir Francis Younghusband and Sir Frank Beane, the Vice Chairman of Lloyds Bank, were two eminent men representative of their own spheres of life, while Ronald was easily the youngest present.

Christianity and Public Life was the theme to be discussed and, in particular, the all-important question of the relevance of the Christian faith to social and political action.

Ronald stayed with Rom Landau at Stoughton, where the latter had a charming old Manor House, and every morning they would drive into Chichester and spend the day at the Palace.

Rom Landau wrote:

"Ronald enjoyed every moment of the Conference. The sincerity, the deep faith of those present, struck a sympathetic note in him; the realistic and businesslike atmosphere throughout the Conference appealed to his well-ordered mind; and he enjoyed both the actual experience and the surroundings with a zest which had a most infectious quality. He loved the silver grey of the old Palace walls, he enjoyed the walk through the Bishop's lovely garden and would always find time to notice a rare plant or the way a border had been planned; he revelled in the "official" and informal conversations which filled our days.

As for the others, there was no one who did not fall under his spell. Though he spoke with a reserve and a modesty, no one could remain indifferent to his burning sincerity, to a sparkle which enlivened everything he said, and last but not least to the soundness of his views. To see a young politician whose faith and personal integrity simply radiated from him must have been a new experience for most of our fellow-members.

"We had our meals at a very long table but Ronald would invariably become the centre of interest: not because he tried to monopolise the conversation or to impose his views upon others, but because he could speak so much more interestingly, more vividly than did most, and because the essential seriousness of his nature never interfered with his *joie de vivre*, nor with his sense of humour. The Bishop asked him why he was opposed to Mr. Chamberlain's policy at Munich. "Because you cannot compromise with the devil," came his answer like an arrow from the bow.

"The Conference was certainly the richer for his presence. His zest and integrity had an inspiring influence upon men who, perhaps, had had longer years of disappointment, more reason to feel disillusioned. Brought to a simple formula, Ronald's belief in the spirit was nothing else but his Christian faith, and his realisation that that faith was a living force in England."

On the Bishop of Chichester Ronald made "a singularly vivid impression." The former wrote—

"He was so conspicuously a man of principles, who was resolved to go wherever his principles led him, cost what it might. This did not at all mean that he felt he knew already in what particular direction the Christian faith ought to be applied. He wanted to know, he wanted to learn, and to get at the truth. He took his full part in the discussions and, while ardent, was always extraordinarily modest and friendly and sympathetic, as well as sincere. In discussions outside the conference, in which his own strong opposition to the policy of Neville Chamberlain was clear, I remember being much struck by what I might call his incorruptible character. He would do nothing, even though Neville Chamberlain was the leader of his party, and, like himself, Member for a Birmingham constituency, to compromise his own integrity by taking part in what others might consider perfectly harmless social functions. He would infinitely rather be an exile, than a courtier in a court which he condemned.

"Yet he was the least selfish or self-opinionated of men. He put principles first, because he was devoted to his country and inspired by a passion for truth and justice. He was, with it all, a most delightful companion, the most natural of human beings, and with a great zest for life, a most attractive gaiety and lightness of touch, possessed of a deep religious faith, and with a rare spiritual quality which shone through everything he did."

Ronald was deeply impressed by the Conference. What he learnt was to permeate many of his future writings and speeches.

In the ensuing months he was to help Rom Landau with a book he was writing. This was called *Love For A Country*, due for publication the following August. Ronald corrected a great deal of the book and contributed a few pages to it.

In the first chapter Rom Landau gave a brief résumé of conversations with famous personalities on faith and politics. Finally, under the heading "The New Society," he came to "one of the younger and more independent Conservative Members of Parliament," of whom he remarked: "It is young men like him who seem to be the main hope for our political future. Rooted in what is best in National tradition, they nevertheless are trying to visualise the future on its own new terms."

Ronald insisted on Rom leaving him anonymous, but in the conversation that followed he mentioned many points which had appeared in his speeches, especially regarding inter-Party co-operation and his idea that unemployment and leisure should be synonymous.

Rom Landau gave Ronald a copy of his book when it was published, writing in it:

"Because our love for this Country is so great, let us remember, Ronald, that the final salvation of our country depends upon our love of our ideals. In affectionate friendship and in complete faith in your loyalty to your ideals.—Rom."

Ronald was to make an important contribution to another book. Mr. Richard Acland, Liberal Member for the Barnstaple Division of Devon, was compiling a symposium to be called "Why I am a Democrat." He asked Ronald for his views and other contributors, ten in number, included Mr. Atlee, the Duchess of Atholl, Sir Stafford Cripps, and the Bishop of Liverpool. The Conference at Chichester undoubtedly helped Ronald in this by no means easy task. He wrote:

"Now, in the face of brutal aggression and manifest intention of domination, no one is left in doubt that England is faced with a conflict in which her whole being is involved, in which there can be no compromise and in which the future of the Christian world is at stake.

"The most serious aspect of the conflict only gradually came to be appraised. National Socialism issued a challenge to our existence, not merely through force of arms, but through the force of ideas. The fundamental beliefs on which our national character rests, the ideals so deeply rooted in our people that they are unconsciously accepted, were called to account. Our people found themselves almost inarticulate in their own defence. They could not express their faith, they fumbled for words, and they watched with dismay the pathetically feeble attempts of their leaders to meet the new forces in Europe with appropriate language and action.

"The boys and girls in Germany, Italy and Russia were being daily instructed in their own nation's philosophy of life and purpose. The spirit of their nation meant something to them. Our adults, let alone our children, were quite unable to formulate in their minds their position as citizens of an Empire or the part that the Empire should play in the world's development.

"The battle to-day, however, is in fact between Totalitarianism and Christianity. It is because we have refused to recognise this that we have attempted to compromise. There can be no compromise. The Christian world is the world of the spirit. In so far as man is concerned, Christianity demands respect for each human personality. Totalitarianism can have no respect for individuals; its very ideal is the subordination of the individual to the common will.

"What is commonly called 'democracy' is no more than the first steps to the attainment of Christian principles in the practice of living in society."

He went on to speak of Leadership, saying:

"Leadership does normally imply the surrender of free will. To the Christian there can be only one absolute allegiance—to God. This should be openly avowed and generally accepted, for it is the foundation of the whole structure of democracy. Leadership must be judged from the standard of what demands it makes upon the common man. There is no better definition of leadership than the business of preventing the abandonment of the long aim for the sake of the short view. Many a statesman prides himself on being a realist when in fact he is a rationalist. To deny the spiritual basis of democracy is to destroy at once the only argument in its favour."

After speaking of the problem of existence and more about the conflict between Christianity and Totalitarianism, Ronald continued:

"What we must settle at once is whether we rate freedom above equality. For divisions of opinion on beliefs which are fundamental must weaken our defence against those who would destroy us. Why are we assailed? Our material possessions naturally attract those whose materialist philosophy is openly asserted. Our place in the world is due to those possessions. But, shorn of them, should we make no contribution to the development of mankind?

"To me, there is only one explanation of man's existence: that with God's help and through His mercy men and nations may add their quota to the stream of life. Can it be seriously contemplated that all men's contributions are the same? It is the variety and assortment in the qualities of men and nations that make the sum total of life. Respect and acknowledgment of each man's opportunity to add his quota entail that tolerance and equal justice which are possible only in a democracy.

"Only through freedom will man find salvation. Only in freedom can a man add to his natural wealth."

After regretting that in England the party system had grown increasingly rigid, that men who held views contrary to their party leaders were termed rebels and subservience held of more account than originally, Ronald said, speaking from bitter experience:

"Members who are not in step with their party Whips are threatened with expulsion and attempts are made to undermine their position in their constituencies. Measures are taken to prevent their voicing their opinions, both inside and outside the House of Commons."

He then spoke of the future of Parliament—as a safeguard for our liberties, as a suitable instrument through which we could develop a capitalist society into a complete democratic state. He went on to say:

"Yet if Parliament has declined in public esteem, the various voluntary societies are probably to-day more virile than ever. Freedom as an ideal does not run counter to personal service; and there can seldom have been an age when personal service was more encouraged and catered for. But there seems to be little faith behind it, and the circumstances of the age make it necessary for government to give expression to it.

"People seem almost desperate for leadership. They would, given the opportunity, respond to any call for sacrifice. Any government in a democracy would be foolhardy indeed to ignore this.

"It is belief in the ultimate destiny of man which must drive us forward. We must propound our programmes and strive for what we believe to be progress; in the end it will be the Christian spirit which will uphold us and maybe give to our efforts in the cause of democracy the noble character of a crusade."

The Duchess of Atholl said a year later, "I am so glad he wrote that article for that 'symposium' about Democracy. I thought what he said about the party system most true and most beautiful—and all the more remarkable because he had done so much work at Party headquarters."

Ronald himself was to write in the last week of September, 1939—"It may be too early yet to picture the Party system at the close of the war. But that the unhealthy supremacy of the Whips' Office will be destroyed already seems assured. That, and growing evidence of the desire on the part of the more progressive Members in all Parties for all-party collaboration are at least pointers in the direction whither the House is travelling. The Government is likely to find, should the occasion arise, a very strong body of informed opinion not afraid to speak and to act."

As 1938 drew to a close Ronald was asked for a New Year's Message to the *Birmingham Gazette*. He said:

"I feel that the old wish—'A Happy New Year'—must be of deeper significance at the start of 1939 than it has been for years past. It would be idle to deny that the New Year, whatever our hopes and aspirations, opens in any but grim circumstances. One does not have to be an alarmist to feel a sense of foreboding as one views the international situation.

"We can but trust that the New Year will bring a new spirit into the hearts of men. With this new spirit, how quickly would the world change, how soon would we be able to tackle confidently the task of providing all peoples with the opportunity of living their lives to the full.

"At the present time, we must face the New Year determined not to shut our eyes to the dangers and needs of our age, and ready, whatever the sacrifice, to keep Great Britain Great."

But he felt despairingly that the majority would follow the Government and close their eyes. And he wrote in the *Fortnightly Review*:

"The next election is at the back of the Government's mind all the time; 'always put off till to-morrow what may cause trouble to-day' is accepted as good sense and sound morality. A nation of sleeping dogs has come to be regarded as the highest tribute to a democratic Government."

Christmas had been spent at Littlewood, the whole family gathered together, Tony back from Egypt, Barbara, her husband and two children. It was a very happy time, days of laughter and childish excitement both for children and grown-ups over presents, crackers, and a Christmas-tree. Ronald was amusing in his own inimitable way, keeping every one talking, laughing, arguing until the early hours of the morning—galvanising the party with his limitless vitality and inexhaustible spirits.

He returned quickly, however, to the world of affairs. There was now a definite group of members who met at various times and in each other's houses to discuss the situation, to wonder how soon—if ever—the Government would see the abyss which lay ahead. The most distinguished members of this group were Anthony Eden, Leo Amery, Lord Cranborne, Lord Wolmer, and Duff Cooper; the younger ones included Jim, Paul Emrys-Evans, "Dick" Law, Harold Macmillan, Harold Nicholson, Anthony Crossley, "Ronnie" Tree, Mark Patrick and Ronald.

Winston Churchill was still the prophetic voice crying in the wilderness unheeded save by this handful of men who believed that the nation and, indeed, the whole world was being misled by the ignorance, apathy, and crass stupidity of a Government who was content, in spite of every warning, to wrap itself in a rosy cloud of "wishful thinking."

Leo Amery had made a series of speeches since Munich, both in Birmingham and the House of Commons, seeing and foretelling the dangers to peace and freedom. But he, too, spoke to those who would not listen, and Ronald in exasperation cried out: "If the present dangers are the herald to eventual disaster, it will be of our own making: we blind our eyes and shut our ears: so it will be written."

In *Headway* he wrote:

"More and more one hears the statement—'Well, at least we've gained time.' Munich is now generally justified on that score. The 'peace with honour' line is demodé. But time can seldom have been purchased more dearly, and never have been more wantonly wasted afterwards."

In the *Fortnightly Review*, writing on "The Machinery of Government," he said:

"A reorganisation of Government Departments, and their co-ordination with the Statutory Bodies and the various extra-

Parliamentary Boards, involves little more than replanning according to function.

"The key to the situation is the Cabinet. Much more depends on its reform than the creation of an efficient machine to expound and execute national policy. That is very necessary. But it is the inefficiency and lack of national effort which is regarded as a symptom of the democracies' decadence. Tired, over-worked men, employing outworn machinery, can never give to a country the leadership it requires. By overhauling the machinery of the State we may at last give leadership a chance. And without leadership Democracy is doomed."

CHAPTER TWENTY-FIVE

1939

"Our job is to do all we can to keep England great in a difficult world."

RONALD had for some time known that he must have more space in which to work. His two rooms in Petty France were minute and Miss Leonard was forced to take a great deal of the typing home. This was unsatisfactory and at the beginning of 1939 Barbara persuaded him to move into a larger flat in the same building. She could help him with the rent and Ronald himself was better off than he had ever been before due to an increase in Parliamentary salaries and to being well paid for his frequent broadcasts and articles.

But because he looked well turned out, he had got the most erroneous reputation of being wealthy. This was difficult to contradict or refute and had unpleasant repercussions—for instance, the Editor of one of the Birmingham newspapers was annoyed because he did not make a substantial donation to their Christmas-Tree Fund.

Big subscriptions were an impossibility. He still had to be careful and consider the pence. His car, although an absolute necessity, was also an expensive item, and there were always unexpected and unbudgeted-for extras.

He could not help, too, being generous to those who worked for or with him and he would go to a great deal of trouble and expense to select a suitable gift, being as delighted as a child if the recipient was pleased and grateful, and equally hurt and disappointed if it was not received enthusiastically.

His taste was impeccable, and he made his new flat charming without spending more than a few pounds on the move. His sitting-room had three windows, so the remaining wall was covered from floor to ceiling by his beloved books. His ornaments of Disraeli, his prints, his big mahogany writing-desk and the photographs of the family were all arranged with loving care. He had, too, a tiny dining-room, an office for Miss Leonard, and to his great joy a bathroom of his own.

Ronald was almost fanatically clean. Tidiness, neatness and cleanliness were an outward and visible sign of the discipline and order which permeated his whole character.

His delight in the new flat made him more reluctant than ever to accept invitations. Always anti-social, he preferred now to eat at his own table or in the House of Commons. Yet he lived every minute vividly, vivaciously, sure in his heart that the clouds of war could not be ignored for long—that no umbrella of appeasement could ward off the holocaust.

Early in the New Year Ronald went to stay with Paul Emrys-Evans at Peatswood—his home near Market Drayton. They drove early next morning to some forest country four miles away and walked through the Bishop's Wood and back by the village of Hales. In the distance across the northern part of Shropshire they could see the Welsh mountains, blue against the grey of a winter sky.

Paul Emrys-Evans said:

"Ronnie talked with his usual vivacity of current politics and personalities, of the Munich controversy and the lengthening shadows. He was certain that war was coming and that all the well-meant endeavours to prevent it would fail for it was too late. He feared we were ill prepared, but he never doubted either the spirit of the people or the eventual victory. These things he had said before but on this morning he seemed to look towards a Promised Land into which he knew he would never enter. Against the background of the hills and woods he appeared to see in his mind's eye the long pageant of English history and to look forward to even greater adventures, struggles and triumphs for the English people. He confessed quite naturally and simply the faith within him. He felt with almost uncanny certainty that his time was short, that every minute was precious and that all the rest of his life must be lived intensely in the few remaining months that were left to him. He told me his days were numbered. It did not appear to make any difference to his keen interest and belief in that sterner England which he saw emerging from the struggle, not so easy-going, more Christian perhaps, more Puritan, and conscious of her responsibilities."

Ronald's anxiety for the immediate future seemed to be justified by the end of the month.

January went out in a storm of rumour and apprehension. The Prime Minister's visit to Rome did nothing to lessen the oppressive atmosphere. Ronald thought Mr. Chamberlain's statement on his visit was extraordinary—most of it in his opinion being in the nature of "a bread and butter letter." He wrote—"The feeling now is of the inevitability of Fate and the impotence of ordinary men and women to direct their destiny."

On February 16th there was another debate on Unemployment. Mr. Arthur Greenwood's motion began with the words: "That this House deplores the fact that over two million persons are workless, views with grave concern the evidence of widespread and serious malnutrition. . . ."

After saying that in his opinion Mr. Maxton's speech did not offer one iota of contribution as to how to solve the unemployment problem, not in 10 years time, not when he had brought about a revolution, but next week or to-morrow when the answer to the problem had to be found, Ronald said:

"I would put a question to my right hon. Friend, the President of the Board of Trade (Mr. Stanley). Does he seriously think that we can continue to try to solve the problem on the present lines? I do not believe you can make much impression on the real problem unless you start off with a complete re-thinking out of the problem itself, and what we are doing to solve it."

Further on he suggested:

"My right hon. Friend the Member for Warwick and Leamington (Mr. Eden) said we should have a four-year plan. Why cannot we have such a plan? There is the arms programme. We had about three years ago a White Paper which laid down a particular programme. It was elastic and designed to suit the needs of the time, but the point was that you knew what the position would be at the end of the first year, at the end of the second year, and at the end of the third year, and you knew more or less the sort of provision at which you were aiming. I believe that we have to begin at once, by laying down a definite programme which could be started to-morrow. Who can work and who cannot work? Who is immediately available for work and who requires training?

We have to face the fact that there are some people whom we should have to pension off for life, but to do so would be cheaper and far more honest and far more appealing to those whom you want to bring into your scheme than the present method. It would be far more appealing to those whom you want to get to your training centres if it were felt that you were dealing with them on a definite programme and that each category of people would be cared for properly."

After dealing with the industrial side of the picture, asking for a committee of economic defence and for the encouragement of new inventions, Ronald ended:

"Anybody who has taken part in Debates on unemployment knows how ideas are shovelled up to the Treasury Bench, and sometimes I feel that from there they are shovelled into pigeon-holes and there are allowed to remain. I am sure that the Front Bench realises that everybody in the country is ready for any sacrifice, any effort, to help cure once and for all, not the normal fluctuations of unemployment, but the real unemployment problem. I urge the Government to think it out again, from the leisure not the unemployment angle, from the production not the work angle. If they can do that and can give us a new inspiration, they will find a new solution."

Speaking to the officials of No. 7 Area of the Bank Officers Guild at King's Norton the next night, Ronald said: ". . . one of the greatest solutions of unemployment, that would turn it into a blessing, was an adequate pension scheme. One could not draw up such a scheme without the assistance of the banks and insurance societies, and that raised the question of recognition. Civil and political liberty did not exist if they could not obtain recognition.

"I wonder how much longer you can allow a situation in which associations, trade unions, recognised as such by the Ministry of Labour—recognised as it were by the Government—are not recognised by the industry in which they work. I look ahead twenty-five years and see every man a member of a trade union in the widest sense of the word—an association of employees or employers. I don't see how you are going to manage industry unless you have it organised on a basis that brings in every man."

At Bournbrook Ronald said that he felt deeply and increasingly concerned at the position of the unemployed and of the old age pensioners. For the older unemployed work was not required, but the means for decent retirement. He also stated in the same speech that if public opinion failed to bring forward recruits for National Service compulsion would have to be applied.

"There is nothing undemocratic in compulsion," he said. "Indeed, service to the State is the basis of Democracy."

At this meeting, speaking of the concern felt regarding Germany and Italy, he asserted:

"This is certainly no time for hesitancy, either in our re-armament or in the strengthening of those ties which bind us to our friends. We must use every means in our power to maintain our friends and potential allies, against political and economic domination, and on every account Russia should be included amongst our friends. That, I believe, is the intention of the Government. Let us never forget, too, that those principles which England has always upheld, it is at once her interest and her duty to continue to foster."

Ronald spoke of Russia again a week later in a speech at Erdington, saying:

"Russia is the key to many situations which might arise. Everything that can be done to put our relations with Russia on a firm and friendly basis should be done, and we should give every encouragement, if necessary by economic concessions, to those smaller Powers who would more willingly be brought into our orbit than into that of Germany."

On March 1st Ronald was bidden to a luncheon party at the Council House in Birmingham to meet the King and Queen. It was not a large gathering, and the Lord Mayor presented his guests to their Majesties. Ronald had met the Queen informally a short time before when Lady Maureen Stanley had invited six of the more progressive-minded younger Members of Parliament to her house in Tufnell Street. The Queen had been there and all the young men had a short talk with her.

A great many people were now beginning to believe that Ronald had a big future ahead of him, but most of them added "if he will be less aggressive, more inclined to accept unquestioningly the leadership of his party." Ronald's invariable reply was—"I must follow my conscience"—but once, after a long harangue from some well-meaning friend, he burst out to Barbara:

"They say I'm making mistakes—if I can't make mistakes at 32 when can I make them? And remember, when I am 45, the average age to start a political career, most of those in power will be dead or gone."

The Parliamentary correspondent of the *North-Eastern Gazette*, Mr. Harold ffoulkes, in March published an article headed:

"ONE DAY THEY WILL BE FAMOUS.

"First among the eight I place tall, slim, handsome, bachelor Mr. Ronald Cartland, Government representative for the Norton Division of Birmingham. His finely-chiselled classical features and jet black hair brushed well back make him a striking figure.

"When he stands up to address the House one can visualise him in a future administration at the Treasury Box as Home Secretary or Foreign Secretary, and possibly as Prime Minister. His progressive views are part of his young manhood.

"Mr. Neville Chamberlain always displays the liveliest interest when Mr. Cartland is speaking on behalf of what might be described as the younger generation."

Writing to Barbara Mr. ffoulkes said of Ronald:

"His zeal for the cause he espoused was born of intense sincerity and belief in its righteousness. It was his flaming intense conviction that made him so attractive and lovable a character in an assembly where those qualities among the younger men of our time seem to be lamentably lacking."

In March came the State visit of the President of the French Republic with Madam Lebrun. Ronald took Barbara to the memorable occasion in Westminster Hall when the President was welcomed by the Houses of Parliament. That evening he broadcast his impressions of this ceremony in the Empire Programme.

At the end of the month Ronald gave up his Chairmanship of the West Midland Federation of the Junior Imperial League and became President. In two years he had carried the Federation to a premier place in the League; his enthusiasm and practical organization had made vast changes, and had brought a new vitality to members and Federation. He felt now there was little more he could do, and his place was taken by a friend of his—Jack Profumo, who was to become M.P. for Kettering in 1940.

Ronald's final word to the Juniors was that he attached more importance to the ideals of the Federation than to its work as a political organization to win electors.

"Our job is to do all we can to keep England great in a difficult world," he said.

It was certainly a difficult world for those who were desperately apprehensive about the future. The House was interested only in defence questions, and it was understood that a Ministry of Supply was to be set up. There was growing opinion that nothing less than a full-scale Department was needed and that Mr. Churchill was the obvious man for the job. When, after many rumours and speculations, the announcement was made that Mr. Leslie Burgin had been appointed Minister of Supply it was received by the House in uncomfortable silence.

Ronald, needless to say, expressed his opinion freely that "not to make use of Winston's great qualities is scandalous—but to jeopardise the Nation in what will be her dire need is criminal."

CHAPTER TWENTY-SIX

1939

"Arm and unite should be our cry."

ON MARCH 15TH Hitler walked into Prague. Ronald's article in *Headway* struck both a bitter and a warning note.

"Ever since the days of Munich the apostles of appeasement have asserted their belief that all was for the best in the nearly best of all possible worlds. They never questioned Herr Hitler's good faith, for the Prime Minister himself had declared his belief in it. Sir Samuel Hoare had told the jitterbugs off; another Cabinet Minister had said the barometer was set fair. Why worry? Germany's internal policy, of course, was to be regretted; most of all, perhaps, because of the reflections it cast upon Mr. Chamberlain's appeasement efforts. Dr. Goebbels, too, was unfortunate in some of his utterances. Dr. Ley's contempt for Christianity, expressed on his return to Germany after his cordial interview with the Prime Minister, was really deplorable. And things were going on in Sudetenland and Austria that it didn't do to think too much about. But confidence was returning; appeasement was succeeding. The Golden Age was nigh.

"Though the Munich critics made no attempt to hide their feelings, the fault with them maybe is that they did not voice them sufficiently loudly or often enough. They cultivated their own constituencies. They omitted to gather up the tares of ignorance and fear which nearly smothered the faithful all over England. For a time it looked as though their forebodings would be proved to be wrong. But there were no recantations. Justification, when it came, came swiftly and terribly. Would that such justification had not come! When the House met on the 15th—the Ides of March—they were in the presence of disaster, too late to do more than sorrowfully regret the past, and shudder at the present.

"Members confronted with Nazi morality were surprised, shocked, indignant; for how long would that temper last? Within twenty-four hours, in some circles, it had come to be considered of the first importance to restore approval for Munich and the policy of appeasement. However, this is not the general opinion. Nothing is to be gained by regret. The future alone matters.

"Is it possible even now to get agreement on policy, and on the immediate steps which must be taken for our own security and Europe's salvation? Arm and unite should be our cry. No personal prestige must be considered if by the sacrifice of individuals national unity can be obtained and made effective. If after this writing on the wall the nation is allowed to sink into lethargy and is misled into a false security, every member will stand arraigned."

Towards the end of the month Anthony Eden put down on the House of Commons Order paper a resolution for a demand for the vigorous prosecution of the foreign policy—which had recently been outlined by Lord Halifax—coupled with the suggestion that for this task a National Government should be formed on the widest possible basis. A further demand being that the Government should be entrusted with full powers over the nation's industries, wealth, and man power as a means of enabling this country to put forward its maximum military effort in the shortest possible time.

This meant a call for Conscription and Anthony Eden's motion was signed by the 35 members of their particular little group, headed by Winston Churchill.

This Motion was at once taken up as a challenge to the Prime Minister's personal prestige.

Ronald remarked privately—"It is a sad—and I suggest bad—commentary on the change that Parliament has undergone in the last five years when policy is so closely bound up with personality."

But the appeasement policy was considered the personal policy of Mr. Chamberlain and any criticisms of the Government based on that were regarded as personal attacks. Yet as Ronald had said "the writing on the wall" was there. And speaking to the National Federation of Sub-postmasters at Birmingham he added:

"I would far rather be a 'jitterbug' than the opposite thing. We are up against something in this country, and the other democratic nations are up against something that we have never been faced with in quite the same way—something not to be battled with just with cannon, guns and people, but something that strikes right to the structure of our national life."

He went from this meeting for a three days course with the Worcestershire and Oxfordshire Yeomanry at Aldershot, returning to speak at the Annual Association Meeting at King's Norton.

"I am convinced," he said there, "that we should make a profound mistake if we were to fall into party politics. I can imagine no occasion on which party politics has been less desirable. It seems to me that the one thing we have to strive for in these days is to present a united front at home and abroad, and to leave unsaid any words which might counteract that national unity."

In April he was invited to speak at a luncheon-time service at St. Martin's-in-the-Fields. He was very pleased at being asked and took a great deal of trouble over preparing his talk.

When the day came there were under a hundred people to hear him, but from the pulpit he spoke stirring words. He showed the danger of Nazi-ism to the Church; he pointed out that faith was the only criterion by which one could judge good and evil. He stressed the dangers of propaganda—its growth from a commercial asset into a new and deadly weapon. He asked if we were ignoring the effect of this weapon on the rising generation. Were we insuring that their faith was as deeply grounded as our own had been by the indefatigable efforts and by the high standards of our forebears? Without faith they would be left defenceless against an insidious and real danger. He wanted those who loved England of a gigantic battle ahead—a battle both physical and spiritual.

"He had the look of a crusader!" one stranger remarked to another as they left the church. Barbara overheard; she wanted to answer that Ronald's whole life was a crusade but left the words unsaid.

During the month of April the international and political scene altered as rapidly as any kaleidoscope, and there were sombre facts to be faced. Guarantees and agreements were given, made, and signed with breath-taking speed, but as Ronald wrote—"The slogan that ' Guarantees every day keep the Führer away,' like all slogans, leaves the operative factors unsaid."

When the Easter recess came he wrote of his feelings in *Headway*:

"No one, I think, went away for the Easter recess in an entirely happy frame of mind. The Polish guarantee had been universally approved of. I have never seen Parliament, at any rate superficially, so united in support of His Majesty's Government.

"But we all recognised in face of the reports—far stronger than mere rumour—that nothing less than a guarantee was called for. No one, again, imagined that this guarantee to one threatened country was any more than a stop-gap. But most people felt that this declaration would at least carry us peacefully over the holidays.

The tradition that our holidays, and our religious festivals in particular, are ' close seasons ' for international alarms dies hard.

"I heard over and over again before we separated such expressions as ' I am only going to Le Touquet,' or ' I shan't go farther than Paris.' They reveal the conventionality which even now many members attribute to Herr Hitler and Signor Mussolini. It is still thought, apparently, that we shall receive an ultimatum, giving us time to mobilise and to prepare our minds as well as our guns for the opening bombardment. When the Dictators' plans for our destruction are mature, the blow will fall as suddenly as the landing at Durazzo.

"The fact that the honourable member is on holiday is likely to prove no more than an incentive to our foes to venture a quick decision. Just because we were all scattered for Easter, and because only a few hours before the House dispersed the Prime Minister declared that he had nothing to report in regard to the Albanian rumours, most people were more than usually horrified when the news came through that Mussolini had added Albania to his Abyssinian triumph.

"Mr. Churchill alone in the House of Commons, in the debate for which we were specially recalled, laid emphasis on the time factor in the Dictators' plans. But again—how came the Government to be so misinformed? How was it possible for Mr. Chamberlain to catch the midnight train to Scotland not twenty-four hours before the Italian naval guns released their first salvo? The Commons should continue to press for an explanation, though I fear they will not. They seem to me to underestimate its importance. Mr. Churchill used grave words when he suggested that the proper information was being withheld or doctored before it reached the Cabinet.

"Finally, and most serious, there are many people, and especially young people, who ask what positively shall we be fighting for? What does England mean to us? What should it mean to the world? I have heard more talk of the two million unemployed in this connection than ever before, and of extremes of wealth and poverty, luxury and starvation existing side by side. I am appalled by the number of people, particularly those who should know better, who imagine that wish-fulfilment will meet the situation: that ' something ' will prevent war, and that we therefore can continue the same round of existence."

One of the things Ronald criticised very strongly in the Prime

Minister was what he called his "pre-1914" attitude towards the Socialist party. Mr. Chamberlain was continually levelling personal criticism, sniping at the members in his speeches, scoring off them in debate with a joyous derision decidedly reminiscent of the days of "high party politics."

"It's unfair and it's undignified," Ronald complained to Barbara. "To begin with, the Socialists are a very small body. Neville can afford to be generous. Secondly, such behaviour is not becoming in a Prime Minister. The latter's job is to be the Father of the House—to be in a position, should the need arise, to call for unity and to get it. Neville is continually rubbing salt in the wound, he infuriates the Opposition—they would never follow him—he would never have their support even if the Germans were landing in Dover! Now Baldwin's method was so different—I've often heard him speaking soothingly to Atlee or Maxton during some bitter debate, saying in parenthesis—'I know, I know, but when the hon. Gentleman is in my place—as I have no doubt he will be at no far distant date—then I feel certain he will follow the same course that I am obliged to follow to-day.' You see the difference? And the long years of Lord Baldwin's leadership have taught people to expect a different attitude from a Prime Minister than that of party champion."

Ronald joined Anthony Eden, Winston Churchill, and five others of their little Group in abstaining from voting in the Foreign Affairs debate when the question of Russia was raised. The Government was strongly urged to do more to meet the Russian point of view and to concede an alliance with the Soviet, but the Prime Minister defended the British Government's attitude after the debate had been opened by Mr. Lloyd George.

Ronald, with a touch of prophetic insight into the future, wrote:

"Mr. Atlee was at the top of his form. He was quieter than Mr. Lloyd George, both in gesture and in expression, but for that reason, perhaps, the two of them made a fine team which, completed by Mr. Churchill, Mr. Eden, and Sir Archibald Sinclair must surely, when they all bat on the same wicket, prove invincible. Mr. Chamberlain looked tired, and made, I must confess, a tired speech. Mr. Churchill gave the impression that he was inspired."

Speaking at the League of Nations Union at Malvern a few days previously, Ronald said:

"The only foreign policy for Great Britain is one of collective defence against potential aggressors. We cannot hope to have an adequate system unless it includes Russia."

He went on to say that he could not understand people who, faced with the situation as it was at the moment, believed they could build up collective defence against an aggressor and yet leave out that great European power. The next twelve months was bound to be a defensive year, and the only defence of law and order was collective action, in which all must be prepared to play their part. He, Duncan Sandys, and "Bob" Boothby had this in mind when, at the beginning of the month, they had tabled a motion for the immediate completion of a National Service Register "in order to avoid dangerous confusion and delay in the first critical stages of a war, and in order to ensure from the very outset the most prompt and effective allocation of the nation's man power."

Mr. Chamberlain refused the request on behalf of the Government and the motion was not debated, remaining on the Order Paper as a forlorn gesture.

CHAPTER TWENTY-SEVEN

1939

"But are we awake? Worse, have the gods sent us mad before destruction falls?"

THE Government Whips were busy persuading their cohorts that the mere appointment of Mr. Churchill to the Cabinet would bring a declaration of war, and that those who wanted Churchill in more truthfully desired Chamberlain out.

Ronald wrote in a newspaper—"a very large body of Tories still distrust Mr. Churchill and dislike his friends."

No one knew this better than he, for he was becoming more and more devoted to the one man in Parliament whose personality, vigour and vision were to him an unfailing source of inspiration. But with his personal allegiance was the conviction that Mr. Churchill's following was growing day by day.

"It is my experience," he said to one critic, "that you can divide the country into two halves. Every one over forty is for Chamberlain —fanatically so—because he saves them not only from war but also from the 'bold, bad Russians' whom they are convinced, in Douglas Reed's words, 'want to steal their two-seater cars.' Those under forty believe in Mr. Churchill, he has the vitality, the enthusiasm, and the progressive mind of youth. He is the personification, not only of youth itself but of all that youth wants—ideals, a high standard to live up to—leadership—and above all a vision of the future."

Few people in London would listen to him, but Ronald was not entirely concerned either with Westminster or Mayfair.

"London opinion!—Government opinion!" he said more than once. "That's not England's opinion. Go into the provinces, to the great industrial cities, to the country villages, into the fields and lanes, and then tell me what the people are thinking."

He finished an article in *Headway* with the paragraph:

"One would hesitate to say that the Government is out of touch with opinion in the country; but they do seem to suffer either from underestimating the courage and virility of our people, or from a habit of creating bogies which are nothing but bogies, and which are inclined to frighten them. Ministers are still insistent that they must not alarm our people by revealing to them in full the dangers of the international situation. The Prime Minister's father made one of his more famous speeches on the theme of "Trust the People," and nothing is so alarming as to discover for oneself that one has been kept deliberately in ignorance.

"But what we lack above all is inspiration and a measured design to which the whole nation can bend its efforts, so that our democracy may not merely be safe but better."

Ronald wrote in May to Miss Leonard who had gone to Scotland for the Whitsun holiday. She had asked if it was lack of guidance and leadership which emptied the Churches, and raised the age-old question of why a "kind, just God" should permit so much suffering?

"I too went to church on Sunday—about 30 people there, average age 193! and only three of us males. Is the answer to be found in your question to me? It may be.

"Surely Evil and Good both exist, because of the other. If Evil disappeared Good too would cease to be. God did not create Good and Evil. He created Spirit or freedom. Man has created Good and Evil because of his inability to realise the Spirit—or full freedom. Physical suffering—indeed any suffering—is a road to salvation, i.e., to the attainment of Spirit. There is a purpose in suffering—that we should try and spiritualise it—and ourselves through it. We should equally attempt to overcome it.

"Suffering is part of the freedom of life—as is Good and Evil, and Joy and Misery. Justice and Injustice cease to have any meaning if you disregard their human implications.

"Is this an answer to you? To pray for 'physical things' is merely to show yourself bound by things of the earth rather than of the Spirit."

Ronald's thoughts must continually soar far from the earth. The Christian life as he saw it was a living, working philosophy, controlled and guided by that Great Creative Force of which he was always acutely conscious. Other people were seeking a formula for living; he knew that for him personally—"self-control, high endeavour and the sense of initiative which comes from freedom, with faith in the destiny of oneself and one's race, remain the immemorial prescription for a happy life."

Ronald went into camp in July with his Yeomanry. He found that foreign eggs were supplied to the Officers' Mess and there was no fresh milk available for the Sergeants' Mess, and immediately on his return he asked a question in the House on these matters.

He wrote to his mother from London.

"The House very flat I thought. Winston, they tell me, will never get into Neville's Cabinet unless there is war—which seems too high a price to pay. The Danzig statement was good. I'm up to my eyes in arrears of work. Letters galore!"

Ronald was not unduly disturbed by being frowned on continually by the Whips and the ardent Chamberlainites. He was in good company and the friendship of those in their special "Group" meant a lot to him. They were gathering strength both in numbers and in spirit, and they were determined—if go down they must—to go down fighting. Ronald was a fighter, he had said so often—"I am at my best in Opposition."

The majority of his constituents were with him, too, despite the open and continual criticism of Empire House. But one could not pretend things were running entirely smoothly at King's Norton. With a small section of the community there had been a growing feeling of strain since Munich. Mr. Edwards, the Head Agent at the Birmingham Unionist Association, made little effort to disguise his personal disagreement with all Ronald did or said, and the blind faith in the Chamberlain tradition was being used consistently against him, especially in the women's organizations.

The local Press, who received much of their copy from Empire House, now emphasised his "misdeeds' and many of his virtues and less controversial speeches and actions were ignored. This tendency to overlook all but the "rebel" aspect was also very obvious in Mr. Edwards' reports to the Birmingham Unionist Association Management Committee. Local M.P.'s were supposed to address the monthly meetings of this Committee, but Ronald's turn never came.

Mr. Edwards also disapproved strongly of the practice of allowing opposition speakers to address the Central Political Group of Service, and had arranged a rival organization to be formed at Headquarters, run on similar lines but with orthodox speakers.

The young people, especially in the poorer districts of the constituency, were wholeheartedly in support of Ronald—just as they believed in the energy and vitality of Winston Churchill rather than in the traditional infallibility of a Chamberlain. But many of the offices and positions of authority were held by the older, more prosaic members of the community who on principle suspected the enthusiasm of youth, and who mistrusted ability which was not entirely conventional.

These looked to Empire House for guidance, and no one will deny that "nothing succeeds like success." As Beverley Baxter wrote to Barbara in July, 1940, when Ronald was "missing"—"I was in his constituency the other day. As you know, his outbreak against Chamberlain caused them great distress and, in fact, Ronnie was in high disfavour. Now, however, since he has been proved right and since his actions in the war have been so brave, he has become a man with a halo. If he is a prisoner and will eventually come back to public life he will have a big position." But in the meantime Mr. Chamberlain was Prime Minister and Ronald had openly allied himself with those "in the wilderness."

There was in the Division an uneasy feeling of what a few months later one would have called "Fifth column" activities. It was difficult to prefer an open charge against anyone with planning Ronald's rejection from the Party, for they never committed themselves. But Ronald knew that individuals were constantly influenced against him, that opponents were encouraged, and if help was ever required from Empire House even in the smallest matters it was not forthcoming.

Yet trouble brought some compensations—loyalties shone the brighter against a background of suspicion and treachery. Service was doing extraordinarily well, and the energy and devotion of Clement Sweet and a small band of workers both to the organization and to himself personally were a continual joy to Ronald. The Election loomed ahead, with its heavy burden of expense, but Ronald knew that would be met somehow. He had many new ideas he wished to put into practice regarding the organization at that time and there was also a substantial sum in the Education Fund which could be used to combat Labour propaganda.

In the House of Commons Ronald and Harold MacMillan put down an amendment on the Pension problem. Their plan was for a comprehensive system of National retirement pensions, embracing and supplementing many voluntary schemes in operation. They went further in their suggestions even than the Labour Party and called for the question to be examined from the broad aspect of security in old age. This had long been a treasured idea of Ronald's.

It was not the first time Harold MacMillan and Ronald had been associated. A year earlier they had worked together on what was called the "planning school" of the Royal Commission on the Distribution of the Industrial Population. They suggested the complete removal of certain "miserable, insanitary blots of towns" in the older industrial areas, and the building of new towns "more pleasantly planned in more healthy surroundings." It should be possible, they averred, for society to deliver its people from the squalor of obsolete towns and transport them into new cities constructed in accordance with modern ideas.

They held that certain industrial drifts should be regulated, and that there should be plans and zones for defence. Flat rates of transport should remove the competitive disadvantage of taking industries out of congested areas.

Ronald had enjoyed his collaboration with Harold MacMillan, he liked him and respected his brain and ability which, like that of many others, did not commend itself to the Government.

By July there was a belief in many quarters that the sky had cleared. The King and Queen had been welcomed home after a triumphant tour in Canada and the U.S.A.; the danger of war was popularly supposed to have been dispelled. Only in the Far East was there a crisis, where indignities were being suffered by His Majesty's subjects in Tientsin.

Ronald wrote in *Headway*:

"The jeers of the Nazi Press-hounds grate on our ears. We must all the time hold ourselves in readiness for the decisive struggle. But to do nothing now or to waste time in unprofitable wordy protests is to court humiliation and disaster. To wait for others, to hang back hoping someone else will come to our aid before we take the first steps in our own defence is a policy based on bad psychology and worse morals.

"'The tempo of international affairs to-day leaves us all breathless.' How often have I heard that said lately! If it be true it is deplorable. Herr Hitler is not out of breath. If lack of stamina, either from inherent weakness or from blind indulgence, is the cause of our misfortunes, let us find sound men to retrieve what we have lost."

After speaking bitterly of the lost Czechoslovak gold, which had been handed over without prior consultation with the Government, he ended:

"And so we go on: playing cricket, waiting for the racing specials, planning summer holidays. If there were any with doubts of the spirit of our people they should have mingled with the crowds who gathered to welcome home the King and Queen. It was at once the most rightly royal and democratic of processions. We are the most civilised race on earth, whatever culturally we may be. But are we awake? Worse, have the gods sent us mad before destruction falls? I feel, even now, the mass of our people are quite unaware of the determination and vigour of the tyrant across the sea who, like the tyrant of ancient days, in Demosthenes' words, ' makes no difference between winter and summer, hath no settled season for repose.'

"Here we have Sir John Anderson. What impressed him most about the Chelsea experimental air raid was that there was no panic. Did he expect it, in broad daylight, without any aeroplanes, and with a great deal of preliminary publicity? I am impressed by the kindliness of our people towards their leaders, by their infinite patience and long suffering."

CHAPTER TWENTY-EIGHT

1939

"Within a month we may be going to fight, and we may be going to die."

AT the end of July Ronald, in a letter to a constituent, wrote:

"I feel at the present time that we should most certainly have a National Government including Mr. Churchill and Mr. Eden and the Opposition Leaders if they would consent to come in. I am bound to tell you that I see little chance of this happening. Personally I also feel it is a great mistake for Parliament to adjourn until October in the present dangerous situation. The matter is being raised in the House on Wednesday: perhaps the Government will at least effect some compromise with those who take this view."

On Wednesday, August 2nd, the Prime Minister moved the Adjournment until October 3rd. Mr. Arthur Greenwood moved an amendment to leave out "Tuesday, 3rd October," and insert "Monday, 21st August."

He quite openly said that his Party distrusted the Government which might, once the House had risen, "take the wrong turning." Sir Archibald Sinclair was more temperate but pursued the same tack. Mr. Churchill in his best form made a strong speech supporting the Opposition. Sir Herbert Williams argued that if the Amendment was carried the dictators would say the British people had "the wind up." He accused Sir Archibald Sinclair of being the longest speaker in the House and suggested he would be happier in his own home—"the House of Tongue than in the House of tongues." He went on to say that the Labour Party resented criticism, that Mr. Shinwell "who is a fairly fierce critic ought not to get too cross" and that the goodwill of approaching holidays should prevail on "his rather caustic mind." He suggested that what was behind the proposal was not that the House should meet on August 21st but "the anger of certain people because they do not sit on the Front Bench."

After a speech from Mr. Adams, Mr. Aneurin Bevan spoke strongly against an Adjournment for two months at the very moment when industry throughout Great Britain was being put on a war basis. It seemed to him that the hon. Members opposite were looking at the matter very frivolously. The suggestion was, that the boys of the pits, steel-works and factories should be ready to give their lives for democracy, the expression of which was the House of Commons, but that the institution itself should be dispersed for two months.

Mr. Victor Raikes, in replying, took the Amendment to amount to a lack of trust in the Prime Minister. Personally he thought "the danger, as far as it is a danger, from the point of view of hon. Members opposite, is that if we trust the Prime Minister, it may well be that there may not be war, and some of them would like war."

He then attacked various members who were opposing the motion in respect of their Division record, referring to Mr. Bracken and Mr. Boothby, "who so eloquently supported the right hon. Member for Epping" (Mr. Churchill), as "the heavenly twins who sit at the right hon. Gentleman's feet." He commended Mr. Vyvyan Adams for his Division record, but reminded him "that one swallow does not make a summer."

Mr. Law and Mr. Amery reinforced the plea for some compromise with the Opposition Amendment, if only in the interests of National unity. Mr. Chamberlain's reply was all the more remarkable, and to many unexpected, when he made the question one of confidence in himself and preferred to debate the issue on Party lines.

He said: ". . . it is the good faith of the Government that is at stake, and whether there be a three-line whip, a two-line whip, or no whip at all, a vote against the Government on this occasion must, after the position taken up by the right hon. Gentleman, be a vote of want of confidence. It must be clear in every quarter of the House that the good faith of the Government is questioned."

In continuing he stressed the personal aspect, saying: "It does not matter whether you mistrust the Government because you mistrust their good faith or because you mistrust their judgment; the question is whether you trust the Government or distrust the Government. If you distrust them and show it by your vote, very well; it is a vote of no confidence in the Government, and no confidence in the Prime Minister in particular. That is all I want to say on that point."

He went on to examine some of the arguments put forward, saying his impression of the critics was that they "were very badly in need of a holiday, that their reasoning faculties wanted a little freshening up at the seaside."

He read a letter from the Leader of the Opposition written the previous year asking that "Parliament should be consulted," when to do so would have made the task of "difficult and delicate negotiations" on which he was engaged impossible.

He ended by saying that the Amendment is "inconsistent with its avowed purpose, that it has no logical foundation" and "it is moved because of the distrust of the party opposite with the Government in general, and with the Prime Minister in particular."

Following the Prime Minister Mr. Mander commenced:

"I venture to say that the Prime Minister in the speech he has just made has missed one of the greatest opportunities of his career. He has made a narrow, bitter, partisan speech, which shows him to be, as my right hon. Friend has said, the greatest single obstacle to unity in this country. It was quite easy for him to ride off in the way he wanted to, but we know quite well that, apart from the speeches made on this side, there have been many speeches from his own supporters, many representing different points of view, appealing to him to make some move, to make some concession to the widespread feeling throughout the country."

Ronald followed at 7.48 p.m.

"I am sorry to detain the House for a few moments, but I would like to say a few words as a back-bencher of the Prime Minister's own party. It seemed to me, listening to-night, that there was a difference of view put forward by those who spoke from the Opposition side and those who spoke from this side, and perhaps the Prime Minister was quite justified in saying that many of the speeches made by the Opposition showed that Members lacked confidence in him. (Interruption.) Hon. Members have every right to say it. They are here so that they can express their opinions. I am sure my right hon. Friend would agree that everybody who spoke from this side put forward quite different arguments. All who have spoken from this side were meticulously careful to say that they did not regard this as a vote of confidence, and they welcomed the fact that the Prime Minister, in his opening speech, had most carefully not said that he regarded it as a vote of confidence. My right hon. Friend the Member for Sparkbrook (Mr. Amery), right at the end of his speech, made an almost passionate appeal to the Prime Minister to view from the angle of national unity the demand that we should come back at an earlier date and not adjourn until 3rd October. If the demand came from Opposition Leaders to the Prime Minister, he should try to look at it, even in spite of the speeches which had been made to-day, in an impartial manner.

"I am profoundly disturbed by the speech of the Prime Minister.

We are going to separate until 3rd October. I suppose the majority of us in this House are going down to our constituencies to make speeches. A fantastic and ludicrous impression, as everybody on both sides of the House, with perhaps one exception, knows, exists in this country that the Prime Minister has ideas of dictatorship. It is a ludicrous impression and everybody here on both sides of the House knows it is ludicrous, but it does exist in the country. (An Hon. Member: 'Nonsense.') The hon. Gentleman says nonsense. I happen to represent the division next to that of the Prime Minister, the largest in Birmingham—(Sir Patrick Hannon: No.). My hon. Friend has more people in his division, I have the largest area. I do not know how many meetings I have addressed in the last year, but over and over again I have had to deny the absurd impression that the Prime Minister in some way has ideas of dictatorship. I happened to speak some time ago on the same platform as the hon. Gentleman the Member for East Wolverhampton (Mr. Mander). I heard him say, on that occasion, what he has just said, that he has never challenged the personal work and the personal desire of the Prime Minister for peace. We have all said that, and yet there is the ludicrous impression in this country that the Prime Minister has these dictatorship ideas. The speech which he has made this afternoon and his absolute refusal to accept any of the proposals put forward by Members on both sides of the House will make it much more difficult for those of us to try and dispel that idea."

Sir Patrick Hannon interrupted. "Has my hon. Friend heard, in his division or anywhere else, when engaged in the prosecution of his political work, any suggestion in any quarter whatever that the Prime Minister is pursuing a policy of dictatorship?"

To this Ronald replied:

"I regret very much to say that I have. That is precisely what I have just said, and if it is of any interest to my hon. Friend, I received a letter this morning from a constituent of mine posted in King's Norton and signed 'Conservative.' She has been a Conservative all her life, and she writes to me now to say that she is very upset because so many people think the Prime Minister is a friend of Hitler. I would not have brought that in if my hon. Friend had not interrupted.

"The right hon. Gentleman is the head of a strong Government. He has an immense vote and he knows that he can carry anything through the Lobby. He has only to consult his right hon. Friend the Patronage Secretary and he can get anything through. How easy it would be for him, when the whole of democracy is trying to stand together to resist aggression, to say that he had tremendous faith in this democratic institution. Personally I cannot see why he could not come down and say, 'We will decide to meet on 21st August, or on a certain date, and if, after consulting with the Opposition Leaders, we are all agreed that there is no reason to meet, then do not let Parliament meet.' Everybody would accept that. We are in the situation that within a month we may be going to fight, and we may be going to die. (Hon. Member: 'Oh!') It is all very well for the hon. Gentleman to say 'Oh.' There are thousands of young men at the moment in training in camps, and giving up their holiday, and the least that we can do here, if we are not going to meet together from time to time and keep Parliament in session, is to show that we have immense faith in this democratic institution.

I cannot imagine why the Prime Minister could not have made a great gesture in the interests of national unity. It is much more important, as my right hon. Friend the Member for Sparkbrook said, to get the whole country behind you rather than make jeering, pettifogging party speeches which divide the nation. Why cannot the Prime Minister ask for real confidence in himself as Prime Minister, and as Leader of the country rather than Leader of a party? I frankly say that I despair when I listen to speeches like that to which I have listened this afternoon."

Mr. Harold MacMillan began:

"The House is always generous to a view which is sincerely put forward, even if it is not universally held in this House, and I crave only a few minutes of the time of the House to make two observations. All those who have listened to the whole of this Debate must be struck with the contrast between the speech with which the Prime Minister opened it and the tone of the speech with which he closed it. I do not think that the Debate, except in a very few speeches, was such as to explain the extraordinary change that came over the character of the speech with which he wound up the Debate. He made a very adroit speech, making the most of accusations of bad faith, which, of course, is just the normal procedure which adroit Parliamentary speakers use to show the mistakes or maladjustments in the speeches of their opponents. The speeches which were made in the course of the Debate did not seem to justify that attitude."

After Mr. MacMillan's speech Ronald left the House.

Mr. Gallacher said:

"I want to raise a point which has not been touched on throughout the Debate, but before dealing with it I want to comment on the very cheap character of the Prime Minister's speech. The earnest, deeply felt speech of the hon. Member for King's Norton (Mr. Cartland) was a thousand times more damning to the Prime Minister than all the cheap jeers of those who sat behind him during that speech, in which he dealt with the arguments for the earlier calling of Parliament."

Sir Patrick Hannon began:

"We have heard this afternoon a very remarkable speech from the hon. Member for King's Norton (Mr. Cartland) and as I was partly responsible for getting him in his present seat I am bound to apologise to you, Mr. Deputy Speaker, and to the House, for the poisonous quality of the speech he delivered this afternoon." He went on to make a bitter attack on Ronald's views, saying that he wished to declare on behalf of the City of Birmingham their profound confidence in the Prime Minister and their devotion to his policy. He was interrupted continuously by Sir Richard Acland, Mr. Foot, Mr. Davidson, and Mr. Bracken.

When Sir Patrick Hannon sat down, Mr. John Morgan rose and said:

"I want to pay my tribute to the courageous speech of the hon. Member for King's Norton (Mr. Cartland). It was a speech such as I do not expect to hear again in this House for some time. It was not the speech of a man who was stabbing his own party in the back, though it might be so interpreted in some quarters. I do not want to go into that aspect of it at all. I regard it as the speech of a man who has consistently in this House—and we have watched him—tried to gather together all the elements in this House that could get the backing of the country, for the purpose of facing the situation which we have to face. It was a speech which indicated what the quality of this Debate ought to have been, but I feel that the last contribution to the Debate showed signs of succumbing to the poison which the hon. Member himself was denouncing."

He continued, after speaking of when Herr Hitler had taken his holidays:

"I believe that the Prime Minister in his second speech to-night was not directing his attack at hon. Members on this side. I believe the right hon. Gentleman sensed a breakaway on his own side and a lack of party loyalty on his own benches and that he issued a kind of ultimatum. His speech was not directed towards reproving our attitude. He was exercising a strict party control over those Members who had attempted to express views different from those in his own mind and those reflected by his decision in this matter. But the right hon. Gentleman's words aroused a speech of a kind that will live long in the memory of this House, in spite of the way in which the hon. Member for Moseley (Sir Patrick Hannon) dealt with it.

"There is no good in attempting to dismiss the speech of the hon. Member for King's Norton as the hon. Member for Moseley sought to do. That speech reflects a very fine spirit. It is the kind of speech which, if responded to in this House, would do more good, would give public opinion more reason to believe in this House as an institution, and would make a better contribution to the national spirit than the Prime Minister's second speech. That, I believe, will be the reflection of most hon. Members to-morrow morning. I think they will realise the anxiety of the public in seeing Parliament break up for such a long period at this time; they will realise that the Prime Minister to-night has behaved in a strictly party sense and that that is not the mood of the moment in this country."

The reaction to Ronald's speech was, to say the least of it, sensational, both in the House and outside. When he had finished speaking Winston Churchill said, "Well done, my boy, well done!" Lady Astor remarked audibly, "The spirit will out." In the smoking-room a Cabinet Minister ejaculated "Ronald Cartland!!" and turned down his thumbs. Many of his friends, while admiring his courage, were afraid that this would ruin him. The personal devotees of Mr. Chamberlain were certain that it would, and there was for them considerable satisfaction in the idea.

Ronald rang up his mother and then Barbara. "I want you to be prepared for a shock in the morning papers," he told each of them.

Telegrams and letters arrived in shoals from all over the country until there were over 500 in number—the large majority of them congratulatory—their senders ranging from a poor illiterate washerwoman in Lancaster, to a distinguished professor of a Scottish University.

The newspapers all spoke of a bitter debate. The *Birmingham Gazette* carried headlines:

"PREMIER ATTACKED BY SUPPORTERS.

"BITTER DEBATE YIELDS ATTACKS BY CHURCHILL AND KING'S NORTON M.P."

The *Evening Standard* wrote:

"*Premier Calls for List of M.P.s Who Did Not Vote Last Night.*
"THEY WILL ALL BE BLACKLISTED.

"Consultations will take place on what action should be taken against the deliberate abstainers.

"They will be black-listed and their action remembered against them, but the indications are that they will not be disciplined beyond being remonstrated with by the Whips.

"I understand, however, that the case of Mr. Ronald Cartland is regarded as being different because of his criticism of the Prime Minister.

"Mr. Cartland is not likely to be treated differently by the Whips, but it is suggested that he may be asked to explain to his local Conservative Association and his constituents."

The *Evening News* remarked:

"Mr. Cartland is a bold young man. He will need to be. He will not recant."

As an epitaph a weekly paper wrote:

"This most amazing debate petered out in desultory political and personal sniping between the Yes-men of all parties."

CHAPTER TWENTY-NINE

1939

"*England through the strength of her people will conquer the tyranny of those who have set out to destroy the supreme values of life.*"

RONALD left London and went to Littlewood, where he had Carlow and his wife coming to stay for the Malvern Festival. He then went to Camp in the New Forest for a week's special course, and had a strenuous time preparing himself for the war he expected within a month.

The morning he left he motored, after all-night manœuvres, to Caister-on-Sea where Barbara had taken a house for the summer. He arrived at ten o'clock at night after a 266 miles journey from Burley Manor. Tired though he was he told her in detail what had happened in the House of Commons on August 2nd, conversation being so much more vivid in person than on the telephone.

"Neville's speech was incredible!" he said. "He made the whole debate personal—you know how I've always deplored his attacks on the Labour Party—said over and over again that it is not for a Prime Minister to sink to personalities! It would have been so easy for him to make a big gesture, to accept the Socialist amendment, but no! And his supporters!—I wish you had heard Herbert Williams and Victor Raikes. I included them when I referred to 'jeering, pettifogging party speeches!' They, too, spoke in the best pre-1914 manner! After Neville's speech our little group drifted disconsolately into the lobby. Winston came out.

"'Well,' I said to him, 'we can do no more.'

"'Do no more, my boy?' he echoed. 'There is a lot more we can do. This is the time to fight—to speak—to attack!'

"I went back into the Chamber and when Geoffrey Mander sat down I was called—I regret nothing—I would say it again tomorrow—I stand by everything I said. And when war comes—and come it will—the Prime Minister will be unable to unite the House, they will never follow him. And without a united Parliament you cannot have a united Nation."

Letters continued to pour in over the whole of August. Ronald spent a good deal of his holiday in answering them. One he had received the morning after the debate was from a young Member of Parliament, which started:

"I write because I occupy a position amongst your admirers and well-wishers who nevertheless did not agree with what you said last night. An attempt will be made, of course, to ruin you because of what you said. You will have seen what Paddy Hannon said. I can assure you there will be an organised attempt by Government supporters to prove their own virtue by assailing yours. We can't afford to lose your courage, your sterling abilities, and your obvious sincerity, but the first part of what you said last night will be widely and maliciously misrepresented."

Ronald showed it to Barbara, remarking—"It's what I expected. I can only wait and see what happens in the Constituency."

The King's Norton Association had already asked for a meeting to discuss the future representation of the Division. Major Pritchett wrote to Ronald and informed him of this and added regretfully that he thought the situation was serious, but by the middle of August the first flush of excitement was subsiding a little. Major Pritchett wisely was in no hurry to call the meeting and fixed it for September 4th. Ronald, writing from Caister-on-Sea to Miss Leonard on August 21st, told her:

"Birmingham is quiet. Pritchett wants me *not* to attend the meeting on the 4th. Sweet, whom I telephoned, says everyone is with me so I feel cheerier. Anyway events will swamp us all. I regard the news as very grave indeed. I cannot see how we can avoid war this time. It's a sad commentary on civilization, and if one comes through I suppose in a way one wouldn't feel inclined to do much more than settle down to cabbage growing.

"You have troubles enough so I won't depress you. This has been a mad year."

Writing the same day to Marcus Stapleton-Martin—a friend with whom he had at different times explored Exmoor, Wales, and Somerset, Ronald said:

"I feel inclined to make one more trip to Swanslake Bay. Perhaps on Friday week? But the foreign news is so bad one feels it's ludicrous to make any plans. Frankly I can't see how we are to avoid war now. Hitler appears so determined. Personally I am ready for anything—immediate mobilisation or whatever occurs."

He bathed, lay on the sands reading a new book by Liddell Hart—who had come down to Burley when he was in Camp—visited Ely and Norwich Cathedrals which he thought magnificent, and played with the children. Barbara was having another baby, which was the reason that they hadn't gone abroad. He talked with her of his future.

His autumn campaign with its usual open-air meetings—thirty of them—and six big indoor meetings was scheduled to start on September 5th. In his message to the Electorate Ronald wrote—"In my Annual Message last year I stressed that the obligation of a Member to express his own opinion or his constituents' must always be superior to his obligation as a member of a party. While he should devote his time and talents to the interests of his constituents, he must never sacrifice his right to form his own judgment on the Nation's needs. The liberty of every citizen in the country depends ultimately on whether we have freedom of speech and independence of judgment in the House of Commons.

"I stress this because as your Member, careful of my responsibility and caring for your interests, I have not hesitated during the past year to say what I felt to be true, and what I felt ought to be said, however strongly others have opposed my saying it. The honour, safety and progress of our country I put before everything."

"If the King's Norton Association refuse to support me I shall stand as an Independent," Ronald said to Barbara. "I'm not certain anyway that I can fight another Election under Chamberlain's leadership."

Barbara suggested caution and patience; he must think of his career.

"I can't act a lie, I can't pretend what I don't feel, I can't ignore what I do feel. Neville's sincere—I've never questioned that, but he is his own worst enemy—he's incapable of the generous gesture, and he represents so much that I know is wrong in modern politics. The world has progressed beyond what he stands for—the people are asking for something 'bigger' in every meaning of the word. You can't hold the Empire without ideals—you can't run this country without vision—you can't lead the people of England without generosity of mind and soul."

He spoke passionately on the subject with a vehemence which burst from him. Later, when people speaking to Barbara of Ronald's speech in the House said—"I was there, it was not what he said but the way he said it,"—she knew so well what had happened. It was the old story of the "loudspeaker" being turned on too loud. This time the Members of Parliament had been "blasted out of their seats."

The fight against two months' adjournment had been unnecessary, because in sheer necessity Parliament was recalled on August 24th. Ronald went up to London from Caister and wrote his impressions of the House in *Headway*. He had already written his article for September and sent it to the Editor; within twenty-four hours the situation made it necessary that he should rewrite every word. He finished the new article at the last moment before joining his regiment.

"And so we gathered, 500 of us; more silent than usual, more serious, but without sign of fear. The Chamber to me was almost unbearably stuffy. Others remarked on it too. Later, the windows were opened; most of us had been for a week or so at least in the open air.

"Mr. Atlee's return after his illness was seized as an obvious opportunity to demonstrate our unity. Cheers for him and, of course, for the Prime Minister. But otherwise the day was singularly free from cheers. Members sat impressively silent throughout the speeches of Mr. Chamberlain, Mr. Greenwood, and Sir Archibald Sinclair. Later, as the debate was rather unnecessarily protracted, the House took on its more usual appearance of ceaseless movement and restlessness. Mr. Eden held it for a few minutes—his intervention was very brief. From no one was absent for long the thought that minutes wasted now might, in the very near future, be paid for in hours or days, the loss of which in turn might be reckoned in human sacrifice.

"Somehow, when one thought of the future, the scene was unreal. The words one listened to did not register, as one's thoughts did, the horrors of war. The speeches seemed out of focus to the picture one's imagination so easily, so terribly conjured up.

"The heightened emotions of last September were absent. The dramatics—the Berchtesgaden flight, the Godesberg ultimatum, the denouement of the Munich invitation—were missing. Mr. Chamberlain looked grey, his voice very quiet. "God knows I have tried my best!' It was a cry from the heart, the cry of a man who sees he can do no more. Was the burden intolerable?

"Neither of the Opposition leaders was at his best. Both were a little too long. Yet there was little to be said. The nation's mind was clear. Germany's intentions were plain."

He ended his article with these words:

"Late that evening I travelled home. In my train were some reservists off to join their stations. If they were aware of the dangers that threatened not one of them apparently gave a thought to them. I have yet to find a man or a woman who would have us shirk the issue or who is not quietly confident that right, whatever our tribulations, will triumph; that England, however violent the course ahead, through the strength of her people, will conquer the tyranny of those who have set out to destroy the supreme values of life."

CHAPTER THIRTY

1939

"I will never surrender. I will fight to the end."

AT DAWN on Friday, September 1st, German troops crossed the Polish frontier, and were later reported to be bombing open towns. After breakfast Ronald, who was with his mother at Littlewood, received the news that Parliament would sit at six o'clock that evening. He rushed up to London and heard the Prime Minister's resolute words:

"It now only remains for us to set our teeth and to enter upon this struggle, which we ourselves earnestly endeavoured to avoid, with determination to see it through to the end."

At 2 a.m. Ronald telephoned his mother and told her that war was inevitable.

He joined his Battery at King's Heath the next morning. On Sunday, September 3rd, exactly one month and one day after his prophetic words in the House of Commons, the United Kingdom was at war with Germany.

After a short time under canvas Ronald went to Hythe for a special course. From there he wrote to his mother.

"THE SMALL ARMS SCHOOL,
HYTHE, KENT
Sept. 12th, 1939.

"DEAR DARLING,

"You are an angel to have sent my clothes so quickly. I did bless you.

"Well here I am. Arrived safely after a very hot drive. It's all most interesting though I'm learning a lot of things quite useless for an Anti-Tank Regiment. We work hard 8.30-4, then free. Free Saturdays one o'clock to Mondays. Plain clothes when not on duty—hence my telegram. Weather when I came terrifically hot, now it's broken here. I've managed to bathe every day. I dine nearly every night in Folkestone. We are in billets here—a whole hotel taken over. Not bad—but it's nice to get away. Expensive, but how can one count the cost these days when so soon we may be in another world? 120 officers—all very nice. I've made some friends—particularly with the man I share my room with who is quite charming. We lunched at Goodwin Bay on Saturday—and went on to tea with Harold Nicholson. I wish Philip Sassoon were still here. Lympne is only 4 miles away.

"I may go to London on Saturday but the trains are so bad I doubt my being able to get to you. What news of Tony? Let me know as soon as you hear if he is anywhere at all near here. Petrol rationing will, I fear, restrict my movements a great deal.

"No news. This really isn't bad, though of course I miss the Battery, but I loathe this beastly war and its restriction on freedom and the ruin of my own life. Still there's no looking back. I'm not really depressed, only at times my whole being revolts.

"I shall go to Parliament if a special occasion arises—but not I think otherwise.

"Send me all your news. And all details about the garden—I'm thrilled the rockery is going so well.

"This is a dull letter—but I suppose war is a dull business.

"Love, darling,

"R."

Ronald made arrangements to deal with all correspondence from the constituency. He wrote to the newspapers asking those who wanted to get in touch with him to write to the House of Commons.

He went to London on September 26th and heard Mr. Churchill make a brilliant speech from the Front Bench as First Lord of the Admiralty. He wrote—"Winston smashed and confounded the critics who had been whispering that the years had taken their toll. He revealed to a delighted House all the weapons of Leadership that his armoury contains. I know that the *Nation* will never let him go now that, at long last, he is back in the Cabinet."

But the feeling in the House disturbed him and he said: "the general atmosphere would strike any stranger as almost Gilbertian for the Parliament of a nation at war—bombs will have to fall before the House appreciates the vast changes which itself and the Nation will have to undergo if we are to win."

In the message he had written to his Electors in August—a message fated never to be delivered, Ronald had ended—

"As I write we stand on the brink of war. . . . I have no doubt of the issue. But let us determine now, if war comes, to make, when it is over, an honourable, just and therefore lasting peace. We must have no feelings of hatred or revenge.

"*At this moment let us put aside all personal animosities and party prejudices.* Only as a united nation can we survive and lead the peoples of the world to peace and prosperity."

In the corridor leading from the Members' lobby Ronald met Mr. Lawton Nixon, Parliamentary correspondent to the *Birmingham Post,* whom he had often consulted on any special line he was taking. Mr. Nixon, having watched Parliamentary life from the Press Gallery for eighteen years, said of Ronald—"I believed he would make a name for himself in Parliament. I think he was happy in the House of Commons except at moments when he was shocked and disgusted by the insincerities of political life. How he detested them, and with them all the 'Yes' men and time servers—detested them with all the impatience of youth." Ronald said good-bye to Mr. Nixon, told him he expected that he would be going to France soon, then added—"I don't suppose I shall ever return here."

He also said good-bye to the policemen; they had always been particular friends of his.

In October he left Hythe and returned to his Battery and they were stationed at Wantage. He had, of course, ideas even in the Army which were different to other people's. He wrote to his mother on October 23rd:

"My troops are grand—already I think with the reputation of being the smartest, keenest and certainly most *original.* We start about 9 a.m., finish at four. But I take a class every night 5.30 to 6.30 teaching them about the guns, etc.—I learnt at Hythe. I have seven officers and six men. It *is* fun—and lasts for three weeks."

His activities were not to stop there; he continued:

"The church here is all I could ask and a very present help—ex-Bishop of Nassau. The troops have a service at 11, Matins to which I went to-day. Not bad but poor organist. I shall have to do something about it, in the same way that I'm gradually reorganising the Officers' Mess and the battery. I'm starting a library now!"

There was also other reorganization taking place apart from Ronald's personal schemes. The Worcestershire Yeomanry had been separated from the Oxfordshire owing to the expansion of the Territorials. Now, with an exchange of some batteries, the Oxfordshire Yeomanry became the 63rd Regiment, the Worcestershire being the 53rd. Colonel Muirhead returned to command the latter and among the manifold changes Ronald became second in command of his Battery. He was then waiting for his Lieutenant's appointment to come through.

Tony was now with the B.E.F. in France. Ronald wrote to his sister:

"OFFICERS' MESS,
CHURCH STREET, WANTAGE,
BERKS.
October 27th.

"MY DARLING,

"So sorry I have been so bad about writing to you but one seems to be on the go all the time. I'm the complete soldier nowadays. One thinks and dreams only of war. Occasionally in one's more sane moments the stupidity and boredom of it all overwhelms one. But so long as I'm busy all goes happily.

"My billet is most comfortable. I am delighted to be on my own. I have a gas fire, writing-table, hot bottle, light over the bed?—tea every morning at 7.15. What more could I ask for? Three charming old ladies and the brother—retired Headmaster. They couldn't be kinder, and I think they are quite satisfied with me as their war service.

"Uncle Howard is ninety next week. He was in great form over the week-end. He'll outlive us all.

"A letter from Tony—boredom seems his worst enemy so far. Really no more news: I can't bore you with details of Mess and men. The soldier's life is *not* a happy one—but I'm all right and I still laugh. I've put my best brain into cold storage. But I ought to get my red tabs or two rows of medals before the war ends in 1946.

"Dear love to you—I've never asked how you are—I *do* think so often of you all.

Bless you,
"R."

Colonel Muirhead was found dead a few days later and Ronald wrote in a letter—

"Tony Muirhead—I can hardly speak of. It was a terrible shock. I'd seen him on the Friday. He seemed the same as always—and then this. Another war victim?—one sighs and passes on, but life is never quite the same afterwards."

In an appreciation he said:

"The House of Commons as a body consistently underrated Colonel Muirhead; he deliberately eschewed any of the artifices which might have enhanced his reputation; while soldiers who acknowledge his military capabilities were blind to the character which underlay them. But those who were privileged to have gradually revealed to them in friendship the quality of his mind and affections realised that his public life and his military duties were the inevitable outcome of the pattern of existence which he fashioned for himself and determined to follow."

Colonel Muirhead's death effected Ronald deeply and intensified the depression from which at times he could not escape.

In his letter to Barbara, Ronald enclosed an extract from a book called *Right Honourable Gentleman* which had just been published under the pseudonym of "Watchman." It was written after his controversial speech on August 2nd.

After speaking of Ronald's youth Watchman wrote:

"You may have heard him broadcasting his comments on 'The Week in Westminster.' The rather formidable task of putting life into the extinct body of questions and debates is performed by him as freshly as it can reasonably be done. He is a vital young man, sharp of feature and acute of mind, so far to the left of the Conservatives that he must find it hard, when electioneering, to disagree with his hecklers or to attack his adversaries.

"He tilts at two vulnerable points in his leader's armour—foreign policy and the Special Areas. One day, when he becomes significant enough for some champion to be deputed to destroy him, he may be thrown and break his lance. But, if his buoyancy is as natural as it seems, he will rebound from the arena and come up smiling. He and Sandys sit alongside. Their modified enthusiasm for various items of Government policy are obvious from the Gallery. In that most public of all places, the Chamber of the House of Commons, a word or a silence, a wink or a grin, has often an ominous meaning. They sit with precocious and preternatural solemnity while the cheering for Neville Chamberlain reverberates all around them. But it would appear that, whereas Sandys has succeeded in stirring antagonisms, Cartland is too engaging to incur them. Are we then to conclude that he is a comparative nonentity, a fragment of thistledown hovering beside a plaguy wasp? I think not. The democratic cheers which hailed his description in the House of a performance by the Prime Minister as a 'jeering, pettifogging, party speech' stands a good chance of drowning the outraged rebukes of the Chairman of the Birmingham Conservative Party, Sir Patrick Hannon, M.P. It is hardly Cartland's fault if he is too pleasant to embitter those who disapprove of his frequent heterodoxies."

"Watchman" hid the identity of Mr. Vyvyan Adams, Conservative Member for West Leeds, and later he wrote to Barbara:

"Ronald was one of the most luminous figures in the House of Commons, perfectly fitted to represent the best in the character and aspiration of his own generation of Englishmen. His interest in his party was wholly secondary to his loyalty to his country. One instance I recall which illustrated Ronald's impatience with the worst manifestations of the party game. Some members of our party were trying to turn the 'Peace Ballot' into an act hostile to themselves, with the natural consequence that it began to recoil upon themselves. Ronald, who had taken the trouble to study the wording and meaning of each of the five questions, saw in them not mischief but value. We were discussing the need to keep this movement clear of the narrower channels of party warfare and I remember him saying impatiently—'What is all this commotion about? Why *shouldn't* they have a ballot?'

"And I have always felt this light-hearted question was a gay but complete justification of democracy."

In his letter of October 15th to his mother Ronald said:

"Wednesday I motored over to Hungerford and dined with the R.A.S.C.—three or four of their officers were old friends of mine working in Austins'. They've about 140 ex-Austin men with them and propose to have an Austin dinner soon in Newbury with Lord Austin there. I am to be invited to make yet one more speech."

The dinner took place on November 10th and nearly 200 former employees of Austins' were entertained. At the last moment, owing to ill-health, Lord Austin could not be present, and Ronald was in the Chair.

He made his last speech. His life was altering completely, all the things he loved were passing day by day. This same week he began to move out of his flat in Petty France. His furniture was stored with the exception of his desk and books and things from the sitting-room which were sent to Littlewood. He hated to leave, it was so symbolic of the happiest years of his life, the years of small but undoubted achievement.

To Barbara he wrote after he returned to Wantage.

"London was a depressing affair saying good-bye to my flat. I've been so very happy there—thanks to you. There seemed so much to do, packing up and everything, that I never had time to write to you. I meant to send you the last letter I wrote from there. Did you think of me last Tuesday, 14th November, my Election day! What a lot has happened since then. Ah well, you never know what still lies ahead."

To his mother he wrote more sadly and less philosophically.

"It was a grim business packing up. I hated it. I have loved that flat—you know how much I have. But there you are. There is no news. You know this life. If one works very hard and thinks very little one survives. But at times I get depressed—my talents run sadly to seed. Do you remember to-day—Nov. 14—four years ago? Election Day. How swiftly do one's hopes die. My love to you. I do hope I get home soon. I wish even more for work more compatible with all I set out to do just four years ago."

To Miss Leonard who had written to wish him many happy returns of November 14th, and who had helped him pack up, he wrote:

"I feel a bit grim. Four years ago—what hopes and aspirations. And now? But there you are. And in the future no doubt this will be seen in the correct light—a grand correction for me and a second stepping-off place for myself. Packing up was a horrible business. Of course I felt it all as you so rightly saw and understood, but it's just the end of a chapter and there's a lot more of the book to come."

He was fighting all the time against the depression that this time of transition brought to him. Courageously, but with an obvious effort, he added:

"Don't think I'm not happy—I am—but my old life is over. I'm a soldier now—it doesn't do to think. That indeed is fatal. So I train and instruct and, I hope, inspire. But the old life is over. But don't moan for that. I am happy and fairly content. It's not *my* life—but I get along. I've been out a good deal, because, as you know, I'm not exactly sociable and even an Officers' Mess makes me long for solitude—or the companionship of a few chosen friends."

He got back to Littlewood for several week-ends which were a tremendous joy to him; all his books and some of his furniture were arranged in a new room and it made him much happier to feel everything connected with the past was not hidden away in closed packing-cases. The windows of his room looked out on the Malvern Hills from which he had drawn so much help and strength in the past.

Alterations in the Regiment were also to bring him comfort and a new interest. Colonel Medley came in command, a man of great ability. Ronald wrote of him on his arrival—"The new Colonel is the man for me—immense energy, resourcefulness, strong and determined, and I think quite brilliant at his job."

Some of his restlessness was due to the old trouble of not enough to do. A year earlier he had said to someone in trouble—"Never give up—work is creative—a stimulus, and a holy thing." Now he longed to be busy, yearned for work to stimulate and use his vast energies. As he wrote in one letter—"You know how frustrated I get—and how a waste of effort infuriates me."

He spent Christmas alone with his mother. Tony was in France, Barbara in Cambridgeshire, and the house was very quiet and peaceful. He knew that he would be shortly going abroad, he set his affairs in order, arranged that Miss Leonard should take over the entire correspondence from King's Norton. He spent most of his time in his new room, writing and reading bits of what he had written to his mother. He told her he had no fear of death, but that if he was taken prisoner he would give a false name, as he thought it would be a mistake for a Member of Parliament to fall into enemy hands.

It was, however, one of his theories that in war a soldier should not surrender, nor be taken prisoner, but should fight to the finish. This may have been instilled deeply in his subconscious mind by the death of his father in 1918 when the formal order given to the 8th Division was to fight where it stood—"not a yard of ground is to be given up." This order was nobly carried out—there was no surrender, all fought to the last.

Ronald to many of his personal friends and to his mother stated more than once—"I will never surrender. I will fight to the end."

He motored into Tewkesbury and went to the Abbey for the midnight service on Christmas Eve, of which he said—"A lovely, joyful, candle-lit service and tho' alone I didn't feel lonely." He read a lot, walked a little, and thought things out in relation to himself. There were some lines of Browning which he was fond of quoting; they were particularly applicable to his need.

"The common problem, yours, mine, everyone's
Is not to fancy what were fair in life,
Provided it could be,—but, finding first
What may be, then find how to make it fair
Up to our means—a very different thing!
No abstract intellectual plan of Life
Quite irrespective of life's plainest laws,
But one a man, who is a man and nothing more,
May lead within a world which (by your leave)
Is Rome or London—not Fool's paradise."

Ronald had written four years earlier—"It is our duty, surely, to harmonise our personal search for God with the necessity of living in the world with other men."

Now, with the strong, stimulating air from the hills on his face, with the beauty of their winter bareness before his eyes, he, passing through the hard shell of personal readjustment, came to the underlying truth. He wrote:

"I've figured out the whole business of living now. This war is a tremendous opportunity. It is a colossal mental jerk for which really we should be deeply grateful. We have just got to think out everything anew. Sort out our ideas on living and life. We must shed the non-essentials, strive for non-attachment. And by example in our daily round in which war has given us added opportunities we must bend men's minds to a new, truly Christian society. It's easier for us. We've soldiers to think of, to work for; a kind of community in which to live. But our roads are all the same. And if we can do it *now* and do it consciously, then we should be able to make something of the Peace."

Christmas had brought Ronald personal peace and he had ceased to "kick against the pricks." He celebrated his thirty-third birthday on January 3rd, and five days afterwards he rang up his mother and then Barbara. He was very guarded on the telephone but they knew it was good-bye. The same night he wrote to his mother.

"Dear, dear love to you, my darling. Look after yourself. It is horrid—this going off—worse, I suppose for you. But how *you'd* hate me to stay at home! We leave at nine but all details are secret. I'll send you word as soon as I can.

"Bless you always,

"R."

CHAPTER THIRTY-ONE

1940

"*There is nothing more to* say. *It remains to pray.*"

RONALD'S first letter from France to his mother is interesting because it was an experience shared by so many in that gallant Expeditionary Force. Ronald had gone out with a very badly inflamed abscess on his heel.

"53RD WORC. YEO. ANTI-TANK REGT., R.A.,
B.E.F.
Thursday 18.1.40.

"DEAR DARLING,

"Your letter arrived to-day—so I don't feel quite so bad as I should about not having written to you before. It must seem incredible to you but it's none the less true that I've not had a moment since we came to France to sit down and write to you the sort of letter I wanted to.

"Let me begin at the beginning. We left Wantage, as you know, on that Monday morning—a lovely day. No crowds, a few friends only. A shopkeeper gave me a St. Christopher—very sweet of her. The Colonel's wife at the station, very brave—otherwise no outsiders at all.

"Quite a good journey by train to the port—then on board. The ship rather crowded, but we managed to get together and found a corner in the saloon. Each had a sofa to sleep on. I produced an excellent lunch, tea, and dinner for my Battery officers but the men didn't fare too well—they were pretty cramped, sitting up on deck all night. I did the best I could for them with rations, chocolate, etc., but it wasn't very satisfactory. We arrived at the port at twelve—didn't leave till nearly five. Quite fantastic standing on deck, watching the troops below—a lovely warm sunny day—one felt outside it all—hardly knowing one was off to war oneself. We went outside the harbour about five—a few miles. Dropped anchor and didn't move again until two or three in the morning, a very smooth and uneventful crossing until about six or seven then a most unpleasant roll. I felt at once most unwell—you know what a bad sailor I am! So I lay down firmly on my sofa until we arrived about 8.30. Most people got through all right, a few like myself, others more sick. Fortunately I had shaved the night before and just managed to wash before the worst started! The washing arrangements, incidentally, were disgraceful.

"Well, at last land. We got off fairly well—and the Colonel motored me about 20 miles to our temporary home as my foot was still bad. The men had food and came on by train. We were in the country, not far from a market town—the men in barns, we in cottages. Sanitation non-existent. The cold pretty bad, tho' I managed to get hot water morning and night to wash. A bath out of the question.

"We got a Battery Officers' Mess going in the back room of a small café-estaminet—not bad, good omelettes and so forth. My Battery Commander and I went to market in the local village—great fun and except for the cold and the lack of sanitation we managed to enjoy ourselves. The men fairly happy, but the cold worried them and barns are not ideal sleeping places.

"Three days there and we moved off to where we are now. Our cars and guns, you'll remember, came over before us. We picked them up on arrival. Now we came by car—170 miles journey which I enjoyed enormously down a great stretch of France—so much of it where our men had fought in 1914-18—past cemeteries and so on. We stayed one night *en route*—again in a village where we weren't too uncomfortable. The men in lofts—we in a sort of annexe to the big house. But again no sanitation! The drive was cold, but I arranged for excellent sandwich lunches—hot thermoses of coffee, etc., and personally I've seldom enjoyed a drive more.

"Our arrival in our new home was pretty grim. We found ourselves in a sort of Black Country mining district—pits and ironworks—poor houses, flat ugly country. The men were billeted in low-down dance halls and when we arrived at 6.30 p.m. no officers' billets had been arranged at all! I tramped round until 9 p.m. and eventually got us all fixed up. I lodged in a sort of villa—electric light, central heating—but no bath and tho' the lavatory *was* inside, no water! The Commander was in the local brewery!—fairly comfortable, the others not too bad, but the men were very uncomfortable. The cookhouse out of doors and they had to eat out of doors too. The cold terrible—22 degrees of frost every night. I can't describe it, and my foot still far from well. Except for my cursed abscess I felt grand, I kept warm—but I loathed not being able to get about. Altogether the place was grim. No washing facilities for the men—

out of door lavatories dug in the ground. Our Mess in a workman's cottage. We did our best, but it was a beastly few days.

"We had a scare—packed all our vehicles again preparatory to moving. I was up all night but it came to nothing. Two days ago, determined to do something, I set off to the local town—about 2 miles away—and to cut a long story short (and a long day) we are all, officers and men, now in superb billets.

"I told you this was a mining district. There is one vast concern, coal and iron. In one of their big garages we have lodged our men—central heating and light—a splendid canteen where the men feed—hot pit-head baths every day and daily washing facilities besides. As for the officers! Every one in a house within 100 yards of the Battery and the Mess, each house with a bathroom and inside water sanitation!

"I am lodged with the chief director of the Company. A magnificent house, superbly furnished. I have a bathroom leading from my bedroom—linen sheets, central heating, etc. The family are charming. The Director himself, his wife and two delightful daughters. He asked me personally to stay with him. The M.P. had something to do with it! I couldn't be more comfortable! It's all very delightful. In the garden they have a winter garden which they have given me for the Officers' Mess—kitchen attached. Lovely flowers, and we get all we want from the house, plate, etc. So at the moment we are on the top of the world. Last night four of us came over and made polite conversation after dinner with champagne. I run the Mess—as you can imagine—and again all are satisfied. It's a funny war!

"The cold *is* bad but I wrap up and my old white sweater has proved invaluable. We've spent most of the time settling in. Training will start seriously next week, but my job, as you know, is administration.

"My Battery Commander is down with 'flu and I am in command. The regiment has it pretty badly as a whole. Personally, I've never felt better tho' my foot has caused me a lot of trouble. The abscess has still not healed and I've been limping about now for nearly a fortnight. But it's much better to-day and in two days should be absolutely all right.

"One of the first things I've done is to arrange with the parson that we have a quarter to eight Holy Communion every Sunday morning for the Battery by themselves—much appreciated, I gather. I hope to see Tony—I've sent him a telegram to meet me on Sunday.

"I can't say I'm bored or unhappy. I'm busy and I don't think about the war. Black-out, by the way, is almost non-existent. It's just struck 11. I must to bed—to my double-linen-sheeted bed!!

"Dear, dear love to you. *When* I think about it I hate the thought of being so far away, but time flies and I shall soon be with you again, darling.

"Bless you always,

"R."

"J. R. H. Cartland,
"*Capt.*"

Ronald was delighted to be in command, even temporarily, it gave him so much to do and so much to organise. He also found it "a most extraordinary war." Changing for dinner and the exchange of sociabilities seemed strange while they waited for Hitler to strike. He saw Tony. In a letter to Barbara at the end of January he said:

"I couldn't be enjoying the war more—but I feel a fraud when I get a letter from home. We are training hard. It's more fun, naturally, being in command. Each Battery is on its own but we dine out. Needless to say, this is by far the best run and fed—in fact our reputation for hospitality is almost embarrassing. I've a small dinner party to-night. I'm writing this 7.30 p.m. in bed after a hot bath! We all change for dinner. The place is well lit up—black-out a huge joke. The last sign of war was the British Destroyer convoying us across the Channel.

"I've seen Tony too. Went up to lunch with him last Sunday—he's about 20 miles from here—and again on Wednesday when I took a party from here to have a look round and see what the infantry had been doing. Tony obviously very well, popular, and frightfully keen. Home seems far away. I may return to make a speech and revive the scandal. Believe me there are some too—the Colonel said to-night it might yet be my best war work—forty-eight hours in the House of Commons!

"Our talk here is almost exclusively of the weather—very English. It doesn't do to think too much of home—one becomes absurdly sentimental."

In another letter he ended: "We've had some starry nights too—but they and children make me stupidly sentimental, and that is the *one* and only thing one mustn't become out here."

Tony wrote home: "Ronald came over yesterday, he's about one hour's drive away. I was so overjoyed to see him. He spent the day, saw round the line, and in the evening I gave him dinner in the big city (Lille). We had an excellent dinner at a new place I have discovered. R. looking very well and in terrific form. We laughed a lot."

Ronald's heel recovered and he escaped the influenza which had taken such a heavy toll of the Regiment. After some weeks he wrote:

"My health? Wonderful—I've never been better. My heel took one month to get well. In the end a French hospital and nuns did the trick. The Army Medical Service defies description. The hospital situation here is a scandal—men in tents and frost about 25 to 30 degrees. My speech in the House will reveal all."

In a letter to Lady Colefax written a month later he said:

"There are innumerable scandals out here; we want another Miss Nightingale, another Lloyd George, and every soldier I've spoken to wants Churchill in place of Chamberlain."

In February the Battery Commander returned from sick leave, and took everything into his own hands once more. Ronald found himself with little to do. Unfortunately, the Commander had no sympathy with any but the most time-honoured Army methods and Ronald soon realised things couldn't go on as they were if only for the sake of the Battery. He decided to get a transfer, if necessary as a Lieutenant, to another unit. He had a long talk with the Adjutant, who went to Colonel Medley.

The latter, as Ronald had discovered on their first meeting, was an eminently able and resourceful person. He sent for Ronald, told him that he wanted "young, flexible minds." They were using a new weapon—the anti-tank gun—for which new methods and new unhidebound ideas were required. He ended by offering Ronald the command of another Battery with the rank of Major.

Ronald's feelings are best expressed in his own words.

"I am highly delighted, and frightfully busy because there is an enormous amount to do here. I don't know 209 Battery so I shall have to learn a lot, but I think in a month I can make a fine thing of it. It will mean a lot of work. I am in my element, complete reorganisation—office, training, men—everything. It's grand and great fun. The more I think about life the more certain I am that its secret is work—and happy and useful work. I hope Tony won't be disappointed that I've got my 'crown' before him. Fantastic, in a way, when you think I started the war as a 2nd Lieutenant."

He then threw himself into training and reorganising his battery with the indefatigable enthusiasm he gave to everything he undertook. He spared neither himself nor others, as he wrote home.

"The Battery improves, tho' I fear regards me as a cross between Hitler and an ogre. I've had to make many changes which I know have upset people, but this soldiering is a grand thing. The Colonel is a first-rate man in every way."

He was original in his methods as might have been expected, but was also prepared to take endless trouble to achieve the desired results. For shooting practice, for instance, his of all the batteries had the most spectacular range, which was a show piece of the Regiment. Ronald sent to Hamleys for miniature tanks which were electrically propelled against—over—and behind scenic effects excellently painted by one of the troops. He had, too, special schemes for night fighting for which they wore black glasses in the day-time and practised long hours at night in the dark.

He had to leave his superb billet and in new and not such exceptional quarters in a small mining town he took endless trouble over the comfort of his men—a recreation-room, a covered wash-house, books and magazines begged from those at home, and great improvements in their food. He wrote of his troop after a month in command as "a grand lot," and in dealing with them individually he had his own methods.

One man was reported to him frequently as "very tough—a difficult, disturbing fellow." Ronald sent for the man, who came before him somewhat defiantly, expecting to be found fault with.

"I hear you're tough," Ronald told him. "Well, I like tough men—we're going to need them in this war. They tell me, too, you've a disturbing influence. I think that's due to your having too little to do—not enough responsibility. Have you ever thought of getting a stripe?"

"No, sir," the man stammered.

"Well, think of it now. I'm going to give you not one stripe but two—you'll be a Bombardier. If you fail you'll be not only letting yourself down but me as well."

The man became one of the best N.C.O.s in the Battery.

Ronald loved his men and in a short while they grew to love him too. He was exceedingly popular with the troop and the N.C.O. s. Only with his fellow officers was he sometimes at variance; they didn't always understand him. He moved the Mess from a dirty, noisy Parsonage and paid for better quarters. He produced new furniture, curtains, glass, flowers, all paid for out of his own pocket because he couldn't bear squalid surroundings. But not every one could appreciate his desire for improvement, the way he must always seek perfection even in little things. Still he was happy. "I devote all my energies to the Battery—I am very happy and very well. But what a war! I do long often to be back again—but as things are thank God I'm out here. I don't dream too much of the old days—they're over. But what a *future*! I'm more revolutionary than ever! and dynamic and (perhaps) more high idealed than ever. Yes—quite incorrigible."

Politics occupied a great deal of his thoughts despite his reiteration that he had put them on one side. In every letter he referred to them. To Paul Emrys-Evans he wrote:

"Incredible as it may sound I'm very busy and when the day's work is done I fall animal-like into sleep. Twice a week we're up all night—my Parliamentary training at last comes in useful! Seriously I think I'm through with political life. I certainly am while the war lasts—I can do no good at Westminster. I am doing some good here. So here I stay. I am quite convinced never to support the Tory *Party* again. And you will never save the soul of England until you *destroy* the party machines. I'm discouraged by all I hear and read.

"And so we train and train for the big offensive which I suppose one day will come—when Germany is ready."

The fuss in King's Norton over Ronald's alleged attack on Mr. Chamberlain had subsided, but at the end of March, to his mother—who had asked him if she should attend a meeting in the constituency—he wrote:

"About King's Norton I'd love you to go to anything you like up there—but *nothing political.* Avoid all political things, please. The more I think about it the more certain I am that I shall not stand as a Unionist again under a Chamberlain Government. Life seems to be slipping away here. I can't imagine myself immersed in home politics again—but I expect I shall think differently when the time comes. If there's a Secret Session I might come home soon but otherwise not until May. I'm more useful out here, I think. Really I'm glad I'm out of the House of Commons for the moment. Nancy Astor wrote a depressed letter to me, also Jim busy with war work and Anthony Eden."

One thing which Ronald spoke of continually was the lack of

spiritual help in France. He told Miss Leonard of his Easter services:

"I stayed the night in the big city over Easter because I wanted to go to Church. I think that's the thing I miss most out here. But my Easter Church was disappointing—I didn't feel very edified. I now rely on one particular Catholic church in the big city which is quite lovely. I visit it each week—sometimes for a service—it is one's only solace. But what terrifies one is the utter paganism of the Army. 'Crusade' is a meaningless word for them. The problem of looking after the men spiritually worries me a good deal.

"You talked to me of prayer. That's the only thing that matters. I know that *now* if I wasn't sure of it before. I'm also sure of this—that buildings and Orthodoxy, or the embodiments of orthodoxy—churches, services, and so on are of immeasurable assistance. When they are cut off one at last realises their value. But how difficult it is to pray as you say. Why? Because we've not learnt to contemplate—we're ignorant of how to meditate—without those two we *can't* pray. I feel it out here more and more. You at home do too because the war has smashed the armour of all our common lives. It is none the less a superb opportunity. Now is our chance to overcome what is probably sloth—our own unwillingness and incapacity to think afresh and *pray* afresh. Difficult? Of course. All real belief is. One has just got to persevere. Not that I can talk. I think I've failed miserably out here. It's a comment on our lack of spiritual stamina. That is what we must strive for; nationally and individually.

"I can't say more on the subject. There's nothing more to *say*. It remains to pray."

Summarising his whole need he wrote to the Rev. Gilbert Molesworth, Vicar of Bournville.

"The one big lesson I've learnt is how much one misses the Church—yes, organised, orthodox religion—when it is cut off from one.

"In all the very difficult circumstances (and I quite agree with you that compulsory church services are not the way to keep religion alive) one feels how important the personality of the priest is, and beautiful buildings are, and how essential to most of us is corporate communion (non-existent, of course, here). I am alarmed at the general paganism of the Army—and the difficulty of the Army clergy in coping with it, and I fear the peace when it comes. If the body of practising Christians can't and don't do something now—

what can they do *then* in immeasurably greater difficulties?

"We want leaders—human ones—everywhere working in harmony with each other. If we don't get them, then I do seriously believe the lamp of Christian civilisation will only be kept alive in Orders removed from the world as in the Middle Ages. Eventually it may come out all right—but in the meantime, what a world for our children!

"I think you who are at home are the only people now who can do anything. We've enlisted for the duration. We can help—but the burden is yours."

But with a flash of his irrepressible buoyancy Ronald finished the letter:

"I am extraordinarily fit and wildly revolutionary. In a word, my dear Gilbert, just exactly as you have always known me."

Two years earlier Gilbert Molesworth had visited Ronald at his flat in Petty France. He had been very impressed not only with the size of Ronald's library but also that there were as many Christian books as political ones. As a parting present Ronald gave him Christopher Dawson's *Beyond Politics*—a volume he considered important and brilliant. The book ended:

"To the Christian the world is always ending, and every historical crisis is, as it were, a rehearsal for the real thing."

It was the keynote to Ronald's faith—his whole philosophy of living. He had with him in France a book which he valued more than any other—"it never fails me," he wrote. After a long day he would open *The Imitation of Christ* before going to sleep, reading those words which had a special message for so many of the men waiting and wondering what the future held—

"Always, therefore, be thou ready, and so live that death may never take thee unprepared."

CHAPTER THIRTY-TWO

1940

"We shall win in the end, but there's horror and tribulation ahead of all of us."

IN MARCH Finland was compelled to make peace by a heavy sacrifice of territory. After six months of war there was no break in the apparent deadlock along the Maginot line. Belgium was strictly neutral, the B.E.F. were massed on its border with only rumours which never materialised to relieve the monotony.

The focus of the war was at Kiruna in Northern Sweden, from where the Germans were drawing their supplies of iron ore, which were shipped at Narvik and brought down the West Coast of Norway within Norwegian territorial waters.

In the House of Commons a Secret Session was called. Ronald obtained special leave to attend it and left France on April 9th. That same morning the Germans invaded Norway and Denmark, occupying many key points.

Ronald arrived in London on Wednesday, April 10th, to find the Secret Session had been abandoned. He was staying with Barbara at her flat in Grosvenor Square and he burst in excitedly, glowing with high spirits and delight at being home. He changed into civilian clothes and hurried off to the House of Commons. He had come back to make an impassioned appeal for more guns, for weapons of every description.

After three months in France he still had not received his full complement of guns, and he knew of many similar cases—of a lack of ammunition, of shortage, slowness and the need for co-ordination. He was also dissatisfied with the National war effort as a whole. As he had prophesied so often, Mr. Chamberlain had not received the support of the Labour Party.

In the House of Commons Ronald had long talks with Jim and Dick Law and many of his friends. On Thursday night he came back to the flat after midnight. Barbara was in bed and he went into her room. He looked tired, sad, and suddenly immeasurably older than he had 24 hours earlier.

"I'm terribly depressed by what I've heard," he told her. "The complacency—apathy—ignorance everywhere is even worse than I feared. Factories working short hours with week-ends off, Ministries in a hopeless muddle—petty jealousy obstructing effort—and among certain members of the Government the conviction that they can 'muddle through' without sacrifice—that things will be all right! Speeches like 'Hitler's missed the bus' coming glibly from their lips—while the world is heading for destruction!"

"Is it really so bad?" Barbara asked.

"Bad!" Ronald replied. "I promise you that with this Government the war will last for at least eight years—while there's every chance of us losing it."

"Oh, darling, that's ridiculous—look at all the men we've got in France—the great French Army. . . ."

"The effort has got to come from England. Hitler will take Norway—this is the beginning—then he will overrun Belgium and Holland. I've seen our trenches in France—1914 model—they won't stop him. When he strikes—as strike he will—there will be destruction such as we have never dreamt of. England has got to wake up—if she is going to save herself—or be annihilated."

"I've never known you so depressed," Barbara protested. "You were so happy when you came back. You've let your friends upset you. Things won't be as bad as you think."

"I've never been wrong in the past over what I've predicted—I've told you so often that one day Britain *alone* would face a colossal Germany. That day is not far distant. But this Government would rather preserve their dividends and their shooting and fishing week-ends than face the facts which stare them in the face. Winston has warned this country since 1933 of the ghastly horrors of the war to come—well, it's here. You won't be calling it a 'phoney' war for long—ahead lies devastation."

He spoke quietly, there was none of the vivid fire and dash which had always been so characteristic of his arguments. His face was sad and tired and there was no spring in his step as he went slowly across the room to bed.

Ronald had planned to stay on leave for one more day and go to Birmingham on the Friday, meet his mother there and see Uncle Howard. The old man was now over 90 and for the past six months had been in bad health; no one expected him to live more than a week or so. Actually he lingered on until June 26th, leaving when he died large legacies to Ronald and Tony and a quarter share each in the Priory estate.

But Ronald was not to see his great-uncle. On Friday, April 12th, the newspapers carried headlines of German troop movement crisis in Belgium—an expected invasion. Ronald decided he must return at once. He had missed the boat-train but he hired a car to motor him to Dover, packed up and left the house in half an hour. He had only time to telephone his mother and regret sadly he would not see her.

He arrived in France "at 4 p.m. rather hungry but otherwise all right. Found no train till 9 p.m. so I picked up with two other officers and we motored to the big city, a lovely drive but horribly expensive. I arrived home at 8 p.m. to find the place deserted!—the worst had happened! Anyway, I got hold of another taxi and after chasing round landed up at 10 o'clock in our new home. The Colonel delighted to see me. But nobody had thought of me as they imagined I couldn't turn up for another 24 hours! Anyway, I discovered eventually an excellent billet with the men underneath. My things were got out and I got to bed at 1 p.m., still hungry. I'd no lunch or dinner—one cup of tea and a cup of Bovril since breakfast."

He wrote of his disappointment at not seeing his mother and in that letter said:

"The future of England is really much more terrible to contemplate than the present. Chamberlain still in office—the House still the same. I felt pretty disgusted but I felt as I always do—that whatever I *say* I shall never be able to keep out of public life. After the war—if Chamberlain *still* reigns—the revolution for me—one last desperate effort to save England."

Ronald settled down for three weeks, renting for the Mess a nice little house called "Balmoral."

He wrote: "There's nothing doing on the Western Front—we've settled in again to a complacently peaceful war existence. The 'Season' is with us! I give 'smart' lunch parties and dine out twice a week with other Batteries! Friday we had Regimental sports—the Battery did extremely well—great enthusiasm and we won or were second in *every* event. I gave them *all* champagne in the evening so there was much jollification and every one in very good humour."

In England the failure of the Norwegian expedition had immediate repercussions in London. For a long time there had been considerable public distrust of Mr. Chamberlain's Government, which had been accused of being half-hearted in its determination to increase industrial production. The substance behind this charge was that the Labour leaders had declined to take office in the National Government under the leadership of Mr. Chamberlain. All the various discontents were brought to a head in a debate in the House of Commons and were given expression by Mr. Leo Amery when he addressed the Prime Minister in the words of Cromwell to the Long Parliament, ending in the cry—"In God's name go!"

Mr. Chamberlain resigned. Mr. Churchill was sent for by the King.

On May 10th, the very day of Mr. Chamberlain's resignation, the Germans invaded Belgium and Holland, and the B.E.F., after waiting nine months on the border, answered a plea for help from the King of the Belgians.

Ronald's Company, 209, and Company 210 were given six hours to move, the plan being for them to help the 2nd Division guard the road. Ronald had the first quarter—75 miles—to guard at 7 a.m. At one o'clock in the afternoon they crossed the Frontier. First stop Waterloo.

Ronald's description to his mother was:

"We came here—where we are now—on Friday and your son was undoubtedly the first M.P. to cross the frontier. The reception was terrific—exactly like after an Election! Of course this Regiment is almost the first on the march—the Colonel and I together in his car—rather like Royalty—cheers, waves, flowers, etc. You probably heard the B.B.C. commentary—very true. Magnificent country, like Worcestershire, and wonderful weather. It was nice to leave our old coal mines, though the people were sorry to see us go; we left a fair amount of stuff behind too. I've a good billet here—a pleasant little country town—but I shan't be here long. Crowds of evacuees—I'm sorry for the Belgians, second time in 25 years—but they're very brave and resolute."

His wireless told him the political news—he was thrilled and delighted.

"A grand new Government, I think. I'm *so* glad—all my friends 'in'—now we are justified! And Winston—our hope—he may yet save civilisation."

The next day they were on the field of Waterloo as a flank guard for the 1st and 2nd Divisions. Ronald had one gun blown up but few casualties. In the night it was learnt that there were no French on the right and the Division withdrew; 209 came into action in support of the Infantry Brigade. On this line again there were no French. On May 12th they withdrew to the Scheldt, but the German break through in the South became so severe that the line had to be shortened to safeguard Channel ports. The Scheldt line was therefore abandoned and they withdrew to the extension of the Maginot Line.

Ronald wrote on Wednesday 15th to his mother:

"DEAR DARLING,

"The Lord knows when I shall be able to write to you again. Great things are happening and I've no doubt greater yet are still to come. This is just to send you my love—and bless you always. Don't be anxious if there is a long silence from me—the fog of war is pretty impenetrable.

"We shall win in the end, but there's horror and tribulation ahead of all of us. We can't avoid it.

"I *can't* send you news. You know that, but it's lovely weather still here. How pretty the garden at home will be. I'm glad you gave your garden party last year—so I thought last night.

"I hope Tony comes through all right. I don't know where his unit is—no chance of course of finding out.

"All love to you, my darling—look after yourself.

"R."

"I am, by the way, never parted from the little medallion you gave me."

And to Barbara he gave instructions "if things don't go right with me," ending his letter: "What a waste it all is—but after months of desolation we shall gain or retain what you and I have always understood the meaning of—freedom."

On Thursday, May 23rd, Ronald was at Orchies and he wrote from there to Anthony Eden, who had been made Secretary of State for War in Mr. Churchill's Government.

"53RD (WORCS. YEO.) A/T REGT., R.A.,
B.E.F.,
Thursday 23rd.

"MY DEAR ANTHONY,

"I must find time in a rather hectic life (just at the moment) to send you all my congratulations on your new appointment, and all good wishes for a most successful term of office.

"I do wish you well. I can't tell you with what joy your appointment was hailed out here.

"You could hardly have become Secretary of State at a harder time but for that reason alone so many of us are glad that you are there.

"You know all my news before I do, so I won't bore you. But I *had* to tell you how pleased I was.

"Yours ever,

"RONALD CARTLAND."

On the same day in a long letter to his mother he said:

"After ten days we're back now in the same place from where we started. It's a rum war! There are occasional aeroplanes going overhead and the sound of guns, otherwise it's most peaceful—flowers and cultivated gardens—furnished houses—but the people all gone, evacuated. The long stream of refugees down the Belgian and French roads are, I think, the most pathetic sight I've ever witnessed. The last week or so while we've been on the move we've been living in these evacuated houses. They must have been left in a great hurry—nothing put away—the most intimate things left as they must always have been. It's been fantastic going into completely furnished homes, living as though one was a guest, using all the things and then clearing off.

"Once I got completely lost for two days. The Regiment almost feared the worst. 'The fog of war' has to be experienced to be comprehended.

"We've had some casualties. I lost a Sergeant and three men from an air bomb and two more wounded—two officers have been slightly wounded. So we've been on the whole very very fortunate.

"The men are all well and I think fairly happy. One gets tired—even I lack sleep—but we've been very hard at it recently and I doubt if we've had an average of 4 hours per night for the last ten days. Still we survive and feel wonderfully well. We live in a state of being ready to move anywhere at any time—bag always packed—one seldom takes the risk of wearing pyjamas, frequently sleeps in one's boots. My dispatch rider is looking after me. We're a very happy band.

"The Colonel has just come up to tea with me—very pleased with everything. The Regiment, I gather, has already a very high reputation in the B.E.F.

"I quite see that war is the most astounding and trying experience which man can undergo. It is not all foul, or boring, or even frightening. It is often all of these things—but seldom for long. The intimacy of one's own men is remarkable. My driver and dispatch rider have a curious relationship with me that can never be explained in the language of peace or translated into peace-time terms."

It was fitting that the last words Ronald wrote should have been of politics and of the man he admired more than any other.

"No letters—no papers. I hardly know who is in the new Cabinet and none of the Ministries and Under Secretaries—which of course I want to know a lot. From all I hear Winston is proving simply first-rate. I am delighted about it—a Government at last which I can *wholeheartedly* support."

The French were to take over the next night, Friday, May 25th, but until they came there was a large gap left in the British left flank. Colonel Medley was told to fill it with any anti-tank guns he could raise. Later that evening came orders to find guns for a rear guard. The Colonel took 212 troops for this, leaving Ronald in the vital gap with his own 209 Battery to support the 145th Infantry Brigade under the command of Brigadier Somerset.

The Germans broke through at St. Omer. Colonel Medley was told to take two Batteries out of action and march as hard as he could to Dunkirk, which he was to defend with the assistance of half a machine-gun Battalion.

The 145th Infantry Brigade with 209 Battery were deputed to occupy the lovely old town of Cassel. Brigadier Somerset decided to establish an advanced post at Hodighen, a small village south of Cassel, and sent 6 Bren gun carriers supported by a troop of 209 Battery with four guns to take possession of it. They were ambushed on the way, suffered several casualties, and the guns were lost.

An S O S was sent to Colonel Medley for more guns and he went to Cassel to see the Brigadier and Ronald. He found them most cheerful and in very good spirits and so persuasive that although he meant to tell them that he could spare them no more guns, he eventually sent a troop with four guns out of his reserve and the Battery Commander of 211, Major Mercer—a friend of Ronald's—to help him.

The Colonel knew that they were in a tight corner; he returned to Wormholt and spent a most unpleasant night expecting an attack. Next morning he heard there had been a good deal of bombardment at Cassel and he returned there—a hair-raising journey of seven miles—hearing continual rumours that it was in German hands.

However, he got there comparatively easily and found Ronald and Major Mercer established in a well-furnished cellar right at the top of Cassel Hill, just below the Citadel. They told him that the Germans had launched a very big attack that morning, but that they thought their guns had disposed of 30 German tanks. One gun had knocked out three tanks in four shots.

Ronald and Major Mercer gave the Colonel an excellent lunch of bully beef, black cherries and champagne. Both were in excellent spirits, in fact the Colonel said afterwards he had never seen two people so cheerful. He left them at 3 o'clock and started back for Wormholt, but calling in on the way at his rear Headquarters he discovered, on sending a wireless message, that Wormholt had been captured. On reaching the Divisional Headquarters over crowded roads at 2 a.m. he was told that they had sent an armoured car to Cassel with a message to the Brigadier ordering him to retire that night.

In the meantime in Cassel Ronald kept bettering the position of his guns. On the morning that the attack started a troop was sent to meet the enemy two or three miles out of Cassel. All their guns and vehicles were eventually put out of action, although they knocked out several tanks first. Ronald put a gun in position on the St. Omer road. That day it knocked out three tanks, the next day five.

As the Germans began to advance on the town Ronald was working all the time, keeping up every one's spirits, helping to move a gun which had been put out of action, and finally taking a Bren gun himself, saying—"Leave this to me. I can manage it." He lay sighting it from underneath the shield of the anti-tank gun.

While the Colonel was at Divisional Headquarters he was told that the Cabinet had decided that the B.E.F. should be withdrawn, but he could get no details as to how it was to be done. He spent the next day collecting together the remnants of the Regiment, who had no anti-tank guns left except those at Cassel.

At Divisional Headquarters the Colonel was told to send the men he had gathered together on to the beach where it was hoped they would find a ship. The Colonel got them all off about 4 p.m. then waited until 9.30 p.m. for those from Cassel.

As there was no sign of them he went back to Divisional Headquarters to make inquiries and was told that the armoured car they had sent the night before had lost its way and never delivered the message. They were sending another one to tell Brigadier Somerset to withdraw that night at his discretion.

The Navy, the Merchant Service, and the little ships of England brought home the majority of the B.E.F.—men who had lost their equipment, men who had lost their weapons, but who returned with their heads held high, undaunted and undefeated. But of those numbers rescued despite the might of the German Army and the much-vaunted Luftwaffe—there was no one from Cassel.

June 6th, 1940.

"Mrs. Cartland Littlewood Nr. Malvern.
Regret to inform you that Major J. R. H. Cartland, M.P., R.A., is missing, further particulars will be forwarded as soon as received.
"Under Secretary of State for War."

"Mrs. Cartland Littlewood Nr. Malvern.
Regret to inform you that Captain J. A. H. Cartland, the Lincolnshire Regiment, is reported by his Unit as missing, further particulars will be forwarded as soon as received.
"Under Secretary of State for War."[1]

[1] It was not known until February, 1942, that Tony had been killed holding a rearguard trench in the retreat to Dunkirk. Survivors (prisoners of war) all spoke of his exceptional courage and bravery. Surrounded and greatly outnumbered, the German commander signalled to him to surrender but he replied that he would fight to " the last man and the last round." Although wounded, he fought on until finally he was killed by a shot from an automatic rifle.

January 4th, 1941.

Letter received from Lieut. Derek Woodward, 209 Battery Worcestershire Yeomanry. British Prisoner of War, OFLAG VII., Germany.

"All our guns were out of action and word had been given to make for the coast. On May 30th at about 8.30 a.m. we were about 20 miles from Cassel making our way about 2 miles east of Watou along a ditch bordering a lane, but we were not moving very fast as mist was rising and the country was getting open.

"Ronald called me forward. While with him we saw German tanks going into action against other troops half a mile ahead. We decided to conceal ourselves, but later three tanks converged on us and we had to get up. As Ronald rose he was hit in the head by a bullet and killed instantly. I was about five yards away with 50 men following. We were marched off immediately."

January 31st, 1941.

"BUCKINGHAM PALACE.

"The Queen and I offer you our heartfelt sympathy in your great sorrow.

"We pray that your country's gratitude for a life so nobly given in its service may bring you some measure of consolation.

"GEORGE R.I."

"*We die and are buried—the English people live on.*"

INDEX

Abercorn, Duchess of, 31
Acland, Sir Richard, 194, 224
Adams, Vyvyan, M.P., 184, 219, 220, 237
Amery, Rt. Hon. L. S., M.P., 7, 85, 125, 162, 177, 185, 198, 220, 221, 253
Anderson, Rt. Hon. Sir J., M.P., 171, 218
Arbuthnot, Gerald, 31
Astor, The Viscountess, M.P., 11, 112, 225
Astor, Hon. William, M.P., 84, 112
Atholl, Duchess of, M.P., 11, 194, 197
Atlee, Rt. Hon. Clement, M.P., 10, 194, 211, 230
Austin, Lord, 97, 111, 142, 237

Baldwin, Earl, 62, 130, 133, 151, 184, 211
Barnes, A., M.P., 132
Bartlett, Sir Basil, M.P., 112
Baxter, Beverley, M.P., 147, 216
Beane, Sir Frank, 192
Beauchamp, Earl, 12
Beaumont-Thomas, Major, M.P., 85
Beaverbrook, Lord, 41
Bent, E. L., 33–5
Bere, Rupert de la, M.P., 147
Bernays, Robert, M.P., 110, 125
Bevan, Aneurin, M.P., 118, 142, 145, 219
Birkenhead, Earl of, 180
Birkett, Norman, K.C., 67
Blunt, C., 73
Boothby, Robert, M.P., 133, 212, 220
Bousted, Edward & Co., 47–9, 52, 57
Bracken, Brendan, M.P., 10, 220, 224
Brett Young, Francis, 158
Brown, Rt. Hon. Ernest, M.P., 188–9
Buchan, John, M.P., 57
Burgin, Rt. Hon. Leslie, M.P., 206
Byng, Douglas, 111

Cadbury, family of, 107
Canterbury, Archbishop of, 184
Carlow, Viscount, 59, 64, 101, 140, 168, 227
Cartland, Miss Annie, 49, 107–8
Cartland, Captain Bertram, 25, 31–2, 36–8, 93
Cartland, Major Howard, 49–51, 62, 86, 168–9, 235, 251
Cartland, James, 26, 57, 86
Cartland, John, 86
Chamberlain, Sir Austen, M.P., 92, 114, 136, 145–6
Chamberlain, Rt. Hon. Neville, M.P., 15, 57–8, 109, 133, 151, 193, 201, 205–16, 225, 227, 229, 230, 232, 236, 250, 252
Chapman-Walker, Peter, 14
Chichester, Bishop of, 193
Christopher, Captain J., 180
Churchill, Rt. Hon. Winston, M.P., 10, 21, 113, 117, 121, 133, 172, 176, 181, 182, 185, 187, 198, 205, 207–10, 213–20, 225, 227, 236, 247, 253
Clarke, Colin, 130
Clarke, Fyfe, 151
Clifford, Lord de, 66
Cohen, Percy, 129
Colefax, Lady, 245
Combie, Miss Peggie, 140
Corvedale, The Viscount, 161
Coventry, The Earl of, 26

Coventry, Captain Dick, 47
Coward, Noel, 184
Cranborne, Viscount, M.P., 198
Crawshay, Captain Geoffrey, 123
Cripps, Hon. Sir Stafford, M.P., 107, 194
Crooke, Sir Smedley, M.P., 177
Crossley, Anthony, M.P., 198
Crossman, Richard, 161
Cunningham, Graham, 97

Daggar, G., M.P., 124
Davidson, Rt. Hon. J. C. C., M.P., 58, 224
Davies, Brigadier General Francis, 31, 38
Dawson, Christopher, 249
Dodgson, Miss A., 45
Donner, Patrick, M.P., 113, 114, 122
Duff Cooper, Rt. Hon. A., M.P., 157, 184–5, 198
Dunglass, Lord, M.P., 169
Dunn, Canon, 148
Dunne, Philip, M.P., 112

Eden, Rt. Hon. Anthony, M.P., 10, 167, 169, 170, 171–3, 185, 187, 189, 198, 202, 208, 211, 219, 230, 247, 254
Eden, Mrs., 169
Edward VIII, H.M., 139
Edwards, R. H., 87, 97, 167, 168, 216
Elizabeth, H.M. Queen Mother, 148, 204, 217
Emmott, Charles, M.P., 114, 122
Emrys-Evans, Paul, M.P., 8, 198, 201, 247

ffoulkes, Harold, 191, 204–5
Fleming, Mrs., 77
Fletcher, Frank, 40, 43, 48
Foot, Dingle, M.P., 224

Gallacher, W., M.P., 223
George V, H.M., 101, 112
George VI, H.M., 148–9
Gibbons, Major L. J., 13
Gill, Miss, 51
Gower, Sir Patrick, 61, 68
Graham, D., M.P., 117
Greenwood, Rt. Hon. Arthur, M.P., 202, 219, 230
Griffith, Kingsley, M.P., 119

Hacking, Rt. Hon. Sir Douglas, 168
Hand, Mr. and Mrs., 149
Halifax, Viscount, 208
Hall, George, M.P., 190
Hamilton, Dukes of, 28
Hannon, Sir Patrick, M.P., 51–3, 56, 86, 222, 224–5, 228, 237
Hardie, D., M.P., 134
Harold, King, 82
Hart, Liddell, 229
Hastings, Sir Patrick, K.C., 59, 67
Hastings, Lady, 59
Hastings, Patsy, Barbara, Nicky, Pip, 59
Herbert, Rt. Hon. Sir Denis, M.P., 191
Hills, Major, M.P., 172
Hoare, Rt. Hon. Sir S. G., M.P., 207
Hodge, M. F., 14, 93, 108
Holland, Robert, 66, 79
Horne, Rt. Hon. Sir Robert, M.P., 119
Horsbrugh, Miss Florence, M.P., 112
Howard, Peter, 121
Hulton, Edward, 66

Jardine, Mathieson & Co., 47
Johnson, Tom, M.P., 175

Keeling, E. H., M.P., 110
Kent, H.R.H. Duke of, 184
Kent, H.R.H. Duchess of, 184
Kerr, Smiley, Mrs., 139
Keynes, J. N., 58
Knebworth, The Viscount, M.P., 58, 60–2, 79
Knuthsen, Sir Louis, 77–9

Landau, Rom, 13, 64, 80, 121, 192–4

Lansbury, Rt. Hon. George, M.P., 107
Law, Richard, M.P., 8, 12, 198, 220, 250
Lawrence, T. E., 101
Lebrun, Monsieur & Madame, 205
Legh, Captain P. R., 9
Lennox-Boyd, Alan, M.P., 112–14, 122, 125, 133
Leonard, Miss Ruth, 153, 155, 168, 200, 214, 228, 239, 248
Lindsay, Noel Kerr, M.P., 147
Lloyd George, Rt. Hon. David, M.P., 64, 211, 244, 258
Lloyd George, Major G., M.P., 190
Lloyd George, Miss Megan, M.P., 137
Lloyd, Lord, 112
London, Bishop of, 158
Lush, A, 142, 161
Lyttleton, Hon. Charles, 13, 147, 180
Lytton, The Countess of, 79

McCorquodale, Alexander, 56, 67
McCorquodale, Hugh, 139, 152
McCorquodale, Raine, 67, 96
MacMillan, Harold, M.P., 119, 136, 198, 216, 223
Macnamara, Captain J. R., M.P., 136
Mander, Geoffrey, M.P., 121, 221, 222, 227
Margesson, Captain David, M.P., 86, 122, 136, 188
Marshall, A. P., 103
Mary, H.M. Queen, 101, 184
Mathew, Theobald, 139
Maxton, James, M.P., 136, 202
Medley, Colonel, 239, 245, 256
Mercer, Major H., 256, 257
Mitchison, G. R., 103, 107, 108
Mitchison, Naomi, 103, 108
Molesworth, Rev. Gilbert, 103, 156, 248
Monsell, Bolton Eyres, M.P., The Viscount, 25, 29, 56, 61, 72, 86, 111
Monsell, The Viscountess, 45, 56
Monsell, Hon. Diana, 72
Morgan, John, M.P., 224
Mount Temple, Lady, 76
Muirhead, Col. A., M.P., 180, 235–6
Munn, Miss Margaret, 41, 42

Nassau, ex-Bishop of, 234
Nicholson, Hon. Harold, M.P., 198, 214, 233
Nixon, Lawton, 234

Page Croft, Sir Henry, M.P., 51, 52, 56, 110, 125, 162
Pakenham, Mrs. F., 172
Palairet, family of, 28
Palairet, R. C. N., 48
Patrick, Mark, M.P., 198
Payton, E. L., 97
Plymouth, Earl of, 169
Plymouth, Countess of, 169
Portarlington, Countess of, 59, 61
Power, Sir John, M.P., 51
Pritchett, Geoffrey, 49, 51
Pritchett, Major T. B., 13, 87, 97, 108, 228
Profumo, J., M.P., 205

Radcliffe, Miss Cynthia, 72
Raikes, Victor, M.P., 220, 227
Reed, Douglas, 15, 213
Ridley, G., M.P., 134
Rothes, Countess of, 47
Rowlands, Joseph, 26

Salt, E. W., M.P., 175
Sandys, Duncan, M.P., 12, 110, 113–5, 121, 122, 133, 157, 212
Sassoon, Sir Philip, M.P., 140, 162, 233
Scobell, Colonel Sanford George, 26, 28, 29, 38
Scobell, Mrs., 38
Scobell, Major General John, 161
Scobehull, Thomas de, 28
Shields, Sir Douglas, 58
Shinwell, E., M.P., 210
Simmonds, O. E., M.P., 110

Simon, Rt. Hon. Sir John, M.P., 58
Simpson, Mrs. Wallis, 139
Sinclair, Rt. Hon. Sir Archibald, M.P., 211, 219, 230
Smith, Ellis, M.P., 16, 145, 174
Snagge, Sir Harold, 47, 52
Somerset, Brigadier Hon. N., 256
Spears, General, M.P., 172
Stanley, The Lady Maureen, 204
Stanley, Rt. Hon. Oliver, M.P., 110, 202
Stapleton-Martin, Marcus, 228
Stewart, Malcolm, 135
Stonehaven, Lord and Lady, 85
Storey, S., M.P., 136
Studley-Herbert, Derek, 59
Sweet, Clement, 16, 160, 176, 216
Sweet, Mrs., 168

Thomas, F. G., 160
Thomas, Rt. Hon. Jim., M.P., 111
Thomas, J. P. L., M.P., 11, 58, 59, 66, 94, 111, 164, 169
Thomas, Major W., 13
Thurtle, E., M.P., 62
Tinker, J. J., M.P., 125
Tiptaft, Norman, 161
Topping, Sir Robert, 168
Tree, Ronald, M.P., 12, 198
Troughton, Lt. C. H. W., 15

Unwin, Rev. R. E., 13

Waddilove, Lady, 161–2
Weir, General Sir George, 100–1
Williams, Miss Edith, 30
Williams, Sir Herbert, M.P., 219, 227
Williams, Colonel H. F., 52–5, 57–9
Wilson, J. R. N., 40, 43–4, 46–8
Wise, A. R., M.P., 113
Wolmer, Viscount, M.P., 11, 133, 134, 144, 198
Wood, Rt. Hon. Sir Kingsley, M.P., 175
Wright, Wing Comm., M.P., 175

Younghusband, Sir Francis, 192

THE AUTHOR

Barbara Cartland, the world's most famous romantic novelist, who is also an historian, playwright, lecturer, political speaker and television personality has now written over 280 books.

She has also had many historical works published and has written four autobiographies as well as the biographies of her mother and her brother.

She has also recently completed a very unusual book called *Barbara Cartland's Book of Useless Information,* with a foreword by the late Admiral of the Fleet the Earl Mountbatten of Burma. This is being sold for the United World Colleges of which he was President.

She has also sung an Album of Love Songs with the Royal Philharmonic Orchestra.

Barbara Cartland has, to date, sold 120 million books over the world. She has broken the world record four years running with twenty-one books in 1976, then twenty-four, twenty, and twenty-three. A special novel *Love at the Helm*, with which she was inspired and helped by Earl Mountbatten of Burma, is being sold for the Mountbatten Memorial Trust.

In private life Barbara Cartland, who is a Dame of the Order of St John of Jerusalem, Chairman of the St John Council in Hertfordshire and Deputy President of the St John Ambulance Brigade, has also fought for better conditions and salaries for Midwives and Nurses. As President of the Royal College of Midwives (Hertfordshire Branch) she has been invested with the first Badge of Office ever given in Great Britain, which was subscribed to by the Midwives themselves. She has also championed the cause for old people, had the law altered regarding gypsies and founded the first Romany Gypsy camp in the world.

Barbara Cartland is deeply interested in Vitamin Therapy and is President of the British National Association for Health. She has a Health and Happiness Club in England and has started one in America.

Also published by Sheldon Press

I Seek the Miraculous

Barbara Cartland

Barbara Cartland, the world's most famous romantic novelist, writes about the secrets that lie beneath the gaiety and the glory, the laughter and the tears in her exciting and fascinating life. She writes for the first time of her lifelong search for the Inner World and her experiences of the Supernatural. She says:

"This book is not an autobiography. I have set down the many incidents when I have been inspired, when I have had a glimpse of the World Behind the World. Also the times when I was disappointed and disillusioned. It has been a thrilling and absorbing search."

Barbara Cartland weaves together the threads of her varied experiences from the brights days of the twenties to her deep involvement with her brother's political career, her demanding family life and her crusades for social justice. Her story will hold the reader entranced to the very last page.

ISBN 0 85969 135 7

OTHER BOOKS BY BARBARA CARTLAND

Romantic Novels, over 250, the most recently published being:

The Drums of Love
Alone in Paris
The Prince and the Pekingese
A Serpent of Satan
Love in the Clouds
The Treasure is Love
Imperial Splendour
Light of the Moon
Prisoner of Love
Love in the Dark
The Duchess Disappeared
Love Climbs In
A Nightingale Sang
Terror in the Sun
Who can Deny Love
Bride to the King
Only Love
The Dawn of Love
Love has his Way
The Explosion of Love

Autobiographical and Biographical

The Isthmus Years 1919–1939
The Years of Opportunity 1939–1945
I Searched for Rainbows 1945–1976
We Danced All Night 1919–1929
Ronald Cartland (with a foreword by Sir Winston Churchill)
Polly, My Wonderful Mother
I Seek the Miraculous
Barbara Cartland's Celebrities

Historical

Bewitching Women
The Outrageous Queen (The Story of Queen Christina of Sweden)
The Scandalous Life of King Carol
The Private Life of King Charles II
The Private Life of Elizabeth, Empress of Austria
Josephine, Empress of France
Diane de Poitiers
Metternich – the Passionate Diplomat

Sociology

You in the Home
The Fascinating Forties
Marriage for Moderns
Be Vivid, Be Vital
Love, Life and Sex
Vitamins for Vitality
Husbands and Wives
Barbara Cartland's Book of Beauty and Health
Etiquette
The Many Facets of Love
Sex and the Teenager
The Book of Charm
Living Together
The Youth Secret
The Magic of Honey
Men are Wonderful

Cookery

Barbara Cartland's Health Food Cookery Book
Food for Love
Magic of Honey Cookbook
Recipes for Lovers

Editor of

The Common Problems by Ronald Cartland (with a preface by the Rt. Hon. the Earl of Selbourne, P.C.)
Barbara Cartland's Library of Love
Barbara Cartland's Library of Ancient Wisdom

Drama

Blood Money
French Dressing

Philosophy

Touch the Stars

Radio Operetta

The Rose and the Violet (Music by Mark Lubbock), performed in 1942

Radio Plays

The Caged Bird: An episode in the Life of Elizabeth, Empress of Austria. Performed in 1957.

General

Barbara Cartland's Book of Useless Information. (Foreword by the late Admiral of the Fleet the Earl Mountbatten of Burma)
Love and Lovers (Picture Book)
The Light of Love (Thoughts for Every Day)

Verse

Lines on Life and Love

Music

An Album of Love Songs sung with the Royal Philharmonic Orchestra

Special Publication

Love at the Helm, a novel inspired and helped by Admiral of the Fleet the Earl Mountbatten of Burma, and sold in aid of the Mountbatten Memorial Trust